1982–83

Britain by BritRail

HOW TO TOUR BRITAIN BY TRAIN

WRITTEN BY
George Wright Ferguson

EDITED BY
La Verne Palma

BURT FRANKLIN & COMPANY, INC.

Published by Burt Franklin & Co., Inc.
235 East Forty-fourth Street
New York, N. Y. 10017

Library of Congress Cataloging in Publication Data
Ferguson, George Wright.
Britain by BritRail.

(The Compleat traveler series)
Includes Index.
1. Great Britain—Description and travel—1971-
—Tours. 2. Railroad travel—Great Britain. I. Palma,
LaVerne. II. Title. III. Series: Compleat traveler
series.
DA650.F36 1981   914.1'04858   81-7848
AACR2
ISBN: 0-89102-230-9

Photographs on pages 16, 20, 38, 52, and 62
by courtesy of British Rail.

Manufactured in the United States of America

FOREWORD

This 1982–83 Edition of *Britain by BritRail* extends a hearty welcome aboard to all who have joined the ranks of its readers since its first year of publication (1980), and to those who have made use of its author's first rail-travel guidebook, *Europe by Eurail*. Adapting to British Rail's unique rail network throughout England, Scotland, and Wales, *Britain by BritRail* follows the format of its predecessor, *Europe by Eurail*, by adhering to the time-proven base city, day excursion format. Because of its adaptability, London has been selected as the base city for day excursions within England and Wales. The capital of Scotland, Edinburgh, with Glasgow as an alternate, serves as a base of operations for day excursions northward into the Highlands.

Readers are assured that everything written was learned through the personal research and experiences of *Britain by BritRail* staff members. Our pledge to constantly check, revise, and improve editorial matter in each edition continues.

Ferry crossings from Britain to Ireland and to the continent of Europe form a very important part of travel within the British Rail system. Consequently, several chapters describing the various ferry crossings are a permanent part of *Britain by BritRail*'s format.

Our determination not to include British Rail services within the pages of *Europe by Eurail* has paid off handsomely. Reader surveys and passenger interviews aboard Eurail and BritRail trains since 1978 have convinced us that readers appreciate the separate formats. We anticipate that *Britain by BritRail*, like its sister publication, will be appreciated and taken to Europe by readers who leave the bulky, worldwide tomes on the shelves of their local bookstores.

Train schedules, fares, and prices appearing in this edition are updated to press time. However, they are for planning purposes only. We cannot be held responsible for their accuracy. All photographs are by *Britain by BritRail* staff members, except as credited.

ABOUT THE AUTHOR

George Wright Ferguson was born in Philadelphia's Jefferson Hospital 20 minutes after his mother was taken from a Washington-New York express train. He grew up alongside the Baldwin Locomotive Works in Eddystone, Pa., on the "Pennsy" main line between New York and Washington. Trains have been part of his lifestyle since birth.

Graduating from Penn State in 1942, he served in Europe during World War II as a test pilot and engineering officer with the 8th Air Force. In 1943, he experienced his first British train ride between Glasgow and Bury St. Edmunds after disembarking from the *Queen Mary*. Amusingly enough, Ferguson's first continental European train ride was aboard a vintage 1918 "40-and-8" freight car between Munich and Antwerp returning home at the end of WWII, a trip lasting all of four days and four nights!

Following a stint as editor, and later publisher, of a farm equipment magazine in Philadelphia, Pa., Ferguson was recalled to military duty in the Air Force until his retirement in 1967 with over 5,000 flying hours logged. As a senior Air Force logistician, he was commended by the Secretary of Defense during Pentagon duty for his movement capabilities studies.

Mr. Ferguson's European experiences continued after his military career. Although his last European residence ended in 1974, he has returned annually to collect material for his travel publications and feature travel articles. Since 1969, he has used a total of 17 Eurailpasses to travel an estimated 84,000 miles on the Eurail system. Recently, he has returned to intensive travel on the British Rail system in preparation for *Britain by BritRail*. Supporting a pledge that everything he writes results from personal experience, he now spends several months each year in the British Isles as well as on the continent of Europe working on research for his publications. Ferguson's rail-travel guidebook *Europe by Eurail* has been published continuously since 1976.

Britain by BritRail is a culmination of many years' work and research by the author. He has several other train travel guidebooks "on the drawing board," including Canada, Eastern Europe, and Japan. A professional photographer/cinematographer and member of the National Press Photographers Association, he believes that using both words and pictures enhances his travel publications.

CONTENTS

As Edna St. Vincent Millay put it, "My heart is warm with the friends I make,/And better friends I'll not be knowing; /Yet there isn't a train I wouldn't take /No matter where it's going."

Britain By BritRail! You are about to embark on a unique and rewarding traveling experience. Like thousands of other discerning visitors, you are about to learn that the British Rail system offers a truly delightful way of vacationing throughout the length and breadth of Europe's only English-speaking nation —Britain.

London is a tourist magnet, but despite what other writers say, London is *not* Britain. Britain has some of the most beautiful countryside in the world. Its mountains are no match for the Alps; its seas are not azure blue like the Mediterranean. However, what it might lack in spectacular scenery is made up with a magical quality of green so peaceful and picturesque that in a mere glance the visitor becomes aware that what he sees is history. A visit to Britain that does not include at least a few days in the countryside is unthinkable.

The difference in traveling along Britain's congested highways and on British Rail's Inter-City trains must be experienced to be believed. By rail, it is a smooth, relaxing journey uninterrupted by traffic lights and traffic jams. Rent-a-car visitors are usually too involved with the transition to starboard steering and keeping a close watch on the car in front to appreciate much more about Britain than the fact that the road signs are in English.

Aboard a BritRail train, the driver (that's what the British call their train engineers) takes care of all these things while you sip on a beverage and enjoy an uninterrupted view of the countryside, stretched out in a comfortable seat. You can even respond to "nature's call" at your own option rather than sweating out making it to the closest petrol station, many of which are closed on weekends and holidays!

There are few places in Britain that cannot be reached by train. It is true that a number of branch and feeder lines have been shut down in the past decade or so. However, the main lines still connect all of the major cities and population centers throughout England, Scotland and Wales—the three countries served by BritRail, more formally known as British Rail. Northern Ireland, by the way, is a part of Great Britain, but its railways are operated by a separate company that does not accept the BritRail Pass.

Millions of Americans have either forgotten or have never had the opportunity to learn what travel by train can be like. You may rest assured that in Britain, as well as in the rest of Europe, the passenger train is alive and well today!

Britain By BritRail is a train travel guidebook which was written for the purpose of bringing train and train-related information to its readers in a direct, pragmatic manner. *Britain By BritRail* does not rate or recommend hotels. A quaint coaching inn or a hotel's convenient location to rail services may gain comment. However, the book's main purpose insofar as accommodations are concerned is to point out the most convenient tourist information center or hotel booking facility.

Restaurants are treated in the same manner. We appreciate good food, along with the service that complements it. But with few exceptions, the choice of what to eat and where to find it remains the option of the reader and the wealth of publications catering to this most worthy pursuit.

Britain By BritRail, like its sister publication, *Europe By Eurail,* is devoted to the visitor who comes to the country expecting that its train services will provide the necessary transportation for a holiday that is different. We have gone ahead of you, probed what can be done, and solved the problems of doing it long before you arrive. Every item has been personally experienced, and we are pledged to constantly recheck, revise, and expand subsequent editions.

Britain By BritRail

Britain By BritRail presents a new concept for comfortable, unharried travel by train in Britain by utilizing the economy of the BritRail Pass, along with the innovative, *fully* described base city-day excursion method of really seeing Britain at its best—by train.

Britain By BritRail is the perfect traveling companion for visitors using the BritRail Pass. The book helps to introduce and establish the reader in the base cities of London, Edinburgh, or Glasgow. Once comfortably ensconced in affordable accommodations and the sightseeing and shopping chores attended to, *Britain By BritRail* then introduces its recommended day excursions to interesting places based on train schedules that will assure your return each night to the same hotel room. With a BritRail Pass and a current copy of *Britain By BritRail*, you become your own tour guide and avoid the constant packing and unpacking that accompanies most bus tours attempting to cover the same territory. By BritRail, if it's Tuesday, it's London, unless you have made the decision to pack and move on to another base city. You are calling the shots, not the tour bus driver.

Britons and their Continental cousins have employed British Rail's services for "holiday-making" on the British Isles for decades. Train travel is too fast for any possible chance of boredom setting in, yet it is leisurely enough to fully enjoy the constantly changing scene of hills and hamlets, farms and forests, countryside and city—everything that makes up Britain's fascinating landscape.

Should you pause to ponder why, for example, an English gentleman would leave his motorcar at home when he's "off on holidays," your answer will be found very quickly when your train parallels a major highway or flashes across a bridge through the center of a British city. The superhighways right down to the ancient, narrow streets are packed with vehicles—all proceeding at a much slower pace than you and your train.

In the chapters describing the base cities and day excursions, *Britain by BritRail* meets the traveler upon arrival at the base city airport or train station and then *methodically* leads you—in a relative order of priorities—to those essential facilities such as currency exchange, hotel accommodations and tourist information sources. *Britain by BritRail* does not dwell on the sightseeing opportunities offered by the base city. It defers, instead, to the city's tourist information services for the current information available to visitors and the wealth of brochures, pamphlets, and books available for such purposes.

Britain by BritRail does concentrate on the day excursion opportunities made possible from the base city's geographic location and rail facilities. A résumé of the day excursions follows the book's introduction of the base city so that the visitor may begin sorting out those personally preferred. Whether you admit it or not, everyone has a problem budgeting vacation time. It's human nature to try to see as much as possible in as little time as necessary. This "sightseers' syndrome" (to paraphrase the smokers' warning) could be dangerous to your vacation. Avoid it by planning an itinerary that allows ample "free time." Also, vary the day excursions by going on a short one following a particular long outing away from the base city. Press too hard by trying to see and do too much on your vacation and you will return home as a living example of the old adage, "a person who looks like he needs a vacation usually has just returned from one."

To avoid reader frustration when searching for a single item of information or telephone number, *Britain by BritRail* groups much of this data in its appendix for ready reference. Along with addresses of information sources, useful telephone numbers are also compiled in the Appendix. Station plans, maps of the transportation facilities—even metric conversions—can be easily located beginning on page 315.

Travel Economy

Whether you have traveled in Europe recently or have been reading about it, no doubt you are aware that travel expenses can get out of hand rather quickly. Until recently, Britons faced the same economic woe common to their American cousins—a declining currency value. For a while, fortified by strengthening government and higher productivity, the British pound sterling had grown in stature on the world's money market and had regained much of its former value. More recently, this has been true of the American dollar. Inflation at home, combined with the varying strength of the dollar abroad, has kept the American tourist uncertain of his purchasing power.

Advance planning and purchasing vacation needs in advance (particularly transportation) in American dollars are probably the most effective ways to combat inflation. Basically, the program calls for buying as much of your vacation needs as you can before you go and planning to limit your out-of-pocket costs paid in foreign currency to a minimum. In this way, you are well protected against fluctuating currency values.

The opportunity of doing things in the 1980's that were previously thought impossible—like putting $40 worth of gas in a Volkswagen—emphasizes train travel in Europe as the best means of effectively conserving travel dollars. Prepayment plans, like the BritRail Pass, are ideal. Not only do you purchase the pass with American dollars prior to departure, but the BritRail Pass also provides the most inexpensive way to travel in Britain—the quickest, too!

American travel agents still have a penchant for wanting to sell a "fly-drive" program to any client who wants to vacation in Britain. In general, car rentals have one basic fault—"the price you see" is never "the price you pay"—it's *always* higher! As a rule of thumb, add another 20% for personal accident insurance, collision insurance, and taxes to the quoted price. After that, consider fuel costs. Then, insist that the agent provide you with an economical BritRail Pass.

Accommodations almost always account for the greater share of a traveler's budget. Low-cost air fares and transportation bargains like the BritRail Pass can get the traveler to the British Isles and provide the means for intra-Britain travel. However, the real bite out of the buck comes when the visitor opens his wallet to pay for a night's lodging.

Attractively priced accommodations packages are being offered by some American tour operators. But too few suit the needs of those preferring individual itineraries, as is the case for travelers on a BritRail vacation. However, with advance planning and advance payment, savings can be realized by those who are willing to put forth extra time and effort.

Well in advance of your intended departure date—preferably 2 months in advance, but no later than 6 weeks—write to one of the British Travel Authority (BTA) offices listed on page 290 of this edition and request information regarding lodging in the areas you intend to visit during your BritRail journey. You may make reservations, or "bookings" as the British call them, in various ways. Hotel accommodations may be arranged by mail with central booking offices in London and Edinburgh but generally not elsewhere. The best assurance that you will have a room waiting upon arrival is to make an advance deposit directly to the hotel, then take care of the balance with the hotel's cashier when checking out. By the way, always ask the hotel to confirm the room rate when you check in. This will avoid delays and possible financial embarrassment when leaving.

For the reader whose lifestyle absolutely precludes any preplanning, we suggest you use the British Transport Hotel (BTH) reservation system to assure reservations at least for your arrival date and the night prior to your departure back home. Information is contained in the Appendix on page 303. With lodging assured for these two important nights, you can then arrange for the balance of your housing needs at a more leisurely pace.

One final bit of advice on reducing the cost of accommodations in Britain—use your BritRail Pass! Too many of us overlook the fact that BritRail Pass actually can provide exceptional savings in housing costs by permitting you to stay outside the base city's center, where hotel rooms, pensions, and the like are far less expensive than their downtown counterparts.

London particularly lends itself to such an arrangement, for there are many areas outside the city's center that are readily accessible by rail. Anytime downtown accommodations become hard to find or too expensive for your budget, tell the housing people you have a Britrail Pass and can settle down in the suburbs equally well.

Staying in London's northern or western suburbs has other advantages, too. From many of the suburban stations, you can board a fast Inter-City train for a day excursion without ever going into a London terminus. You can return to the suburbs in the evening, too, without ever becoming involved in London's rush hours.

Watford Junction, 16 miles from London's Euston station, is one of the stations in London's suburbs which offers excellent Inter-City connections to such day excursion points as Birmingham, Chester, and Coventry. Most Inter-City departures from Euston Station on weekday mornings pick up at Watford Junction 16 minutes later. On weekday evenings, most Inter-City trains set down at Watford 20 minutes ahead of their arrival times in Euston Station.

Other rail points in London suburbs are Luton for direct rail connections to Nottingham and Sheffield; Stevenage lies along the main line to Edinburgh via York; and Slough or Reading have direct connections to Bath, as well as the Welsh cities of Cardiff and Swansea.

There are times when accommodations in the base cities are extremely limited. Edinburgh during its annual festival is an excellent example. Lodgings in the suburbs, a la BritRail Pass, can be more economical and just as convenient as those in the base cities.

Inter-City 125, the world's fastest diesel train, is British Rail's 'Journey Shrinker.' Along with speed, Inter-City 125 trains offer air conditioning, soundproofing, automatic interior doors, and food services including buffet, bar and restaurant with a wide choice of food and beverages.

Webster's Dictionary defines a plan as "a program of action." Plans vary in detail and complexity, according to the nature of the user. For example, one person may require a detailed hour-by-hour, appointment-by-appointment schedule for a day's activities; another may merely plan to get up in the morning and see what happens after that. This example categorizes the two general types of rail travelers we have observed down through the years—one adventurous, the other conservative. The former can get by with a plan that merely deals with the bare essentials; the latter requires a more detailed plan.

Time is the first consideration when planning any type of journey. "Do I have enough time to go shopping today, or should I plan to go tomorrow?" That is a basic question we frequently ask ourselves. "Do I have time enough to visit Britain this year, or should I plan to go next year?" Basically, the latter question is identical to the first, the only variance being the time frame—one day or one year. The second question has more impact than the first since the decision involves considerably more elapsed time than that involved in a routine shopping trip.

How long should your BritRail tour be? There are many factors bearing on such a determination, the most important being the individual. How much annual vacation time do you have? How do you take it—all at one time or in two or more segments? The folks issuing BritRail Passes are ready to accommodate just about anyone's personal needs, with passes ranging from 7, 14, and 21 days to 1 month.

Travel magazines and the travel section of the Sunday newspaper are usually loaded with one-week trips to almost anywhere—Europe and the British Isles included. From our own experience, we can categorically state that going to Europe for any period of less than 2 weeks is a waste of time and money.

In support of such a statement, we invite you to take a look at the logistics involved in such a journey. It takes an entire day to reach Europe by air from North America; an entire day to return. Although the flying time aboard a jet airplane ranges from 7 to 8 hours, airport to airport, it will be day 2 before you arrive in Europe. (Most eastbound transatlantic flights depart at night during day 1 and arrive the following morning.) During the flight, you will be exposed to a cocktail hour, a dinner hour, a break for an after dinner drink, followed by a full-length feature motion picture. In the morning, as the sun rises in the east over Europe, you'll be awakened an hour or so before landing to be served breakfast.

Add up the time consumed by all the scheduled events while enroute, and you'll quickly determine that your night spent in the sky over the Atlantic Ocean consisted of many things—except sleep. Even if you have managed to sleep during the entire trip, instead of eating, drinking, and waiting for Bo Derek to play *Bolero*, your body and all its functions will be arriving in Europe a few hours after midnight by North American time. You will crave adjustment to a phenomenon known as "jet lag," which will be trying its best to interrupt your plans for a carefree vacation.

When you discount the two full days involved in air travel, plus a minimum of one day to get your sleep-eat cycle performing properly again, the balance of time remaining in a one-week visit hardly seems worth making the trip.

Most of the economical excursion fares for transatlantic air travel evolve around day 14, meaning that your minimum time spent in Europe after departure from North America must be 14 days in order to qualify for the reduced fares. Consequently, in consideration of both time and money, we recommend your stay in Britain be a minimum of two full weeks.

Having determined the length of time you will have for your BritRail trip, the next phase of your trip planning should be developing a clear idea concerning where you want to go in Britain, what you want to see, and what you want to do. This process of developing objectives should be completed well before your date of departure. We disagree with those who feel that anticipation of travel is more rewarding than its realization. However, we do agree that the planning phase can form a very interesting part of your trip.

To get things started, write to the British Tourist Authority and BritRail International for information. You'll find the appropriate addresses listed on page 290 of this edition. *Be specific.* In your request, indicate *when* you will be going, *where* you wish to go within Britain, and *what* in particular you would like to see. If you have any special interests or hobbies, be sure to mention them in your request. The travel offices have a world of information at their fingertips, but they need to know specifically *what* you want them to send to you.

Don't overlook your local library as a valuable information source. For example, you will find an excellent condensation of British history in the *Encyclopedia Britannica.* Back issues of *National Geographic* magazine are excellent sources for first-person explorations of the British Isles. Seek out friends and neighbors who have been to Britain. No doubt, you'll find their experiences flavored with their own likes and dislikes. Nevertheless, any and all information you gather will eventually find its place in your memory bank and surprisingly enough, you'll find yourself recalling many of these bits and pieces during your own journey.

You are now ready for the decisive phase of your trip planning—the actual construction of an itinerary. The moment of truth is at hand! Your only limitation during this planning phase is the lack of more than 24 hours in a day and the fact that the week does not have any more than 7 days in its composition.

Train travel is conducive to facilitating new acquaintances or starting new friendships. When travelers (vacationers or business persons) are sitting next to you, they naturally will be inclined to strike up a conversation—if you are so inclined, too.

Draw out a blank calendar-style form covering a period from at least one week prior to your departure to a few days following your return. Have extra copies of the blank form made, for you are certain to need them. (Perfection is a long time coming in this project!) Now, begin to block your itinerary into the calendar form, being mindful that the itinerary can be changed but the number of days in a week remains fixed at all times. Possibly by the third time through the exercise, you'll begin to see the light at the end of the tunnel. It's human to try to cram too many activities into a 24-hour day. However, it is better to come upon this moment of truth before starting your trip rather than during the middle of it!

With your itinerary in calendar format, now you can determine your housing requirements, seat and sleeper reservations, and the other facets of your forthcoming trip. The days blocked out in advance of your departure can show your "countdown" items, such as stopping the newspaper, having mail held at the post office, etc. Make several copies of your completed itinerary and leave some behind with those folks who may have a need to stay in touch during your vacation. Above all, take copies of the itinerary with you. You'll find you will refer to it frequently.

One item that you can't leave home without is a passport. If you do not have a passport or if your passport has expired, write immediately to one of the U.S. passport offices listed on page 310 for information and applications. Allow an entire month for obtaining your passport. There are ways of expediting the process, but be safe by planning ahead and making this the first order of business when you've decided to make your trip abroad. U.S. citizens are admitted to Britain with only a passport. A visa is not required. Carry an extra certified copy of your birth certificate and extra passport photos with you. In case your passport is lost or stolen, go to the nearest U.S. Consulate.

What To Take?

Obviously, the practical answer to this question is, "as little as possible!" A tourist tends to pack everything he conceivably might use during a vacation, lug it everywhere, use it very little, and return home with longer arms than when he started. In these days of wash-and-wear fabrics (and deodorants), this is no longer necessary. A good rule of thumb is to take one medium-size suitcase and nothing else, except perhaps a shoulder bag. Hold to this rule and you will have a more comfortable, enjoyable trip.

For those seeking professional guidance in this matter, we heartily recommend Muriel Scudder's excellent publication, *Europe In A Suitcase*. This down-to-earth book is crammed with facts you won't find elsewhere. It discusses clothing to wear, how to pack, passport information, tipping, and much more. A highlight of *Europe In A Suitcase* is its "Get-Ready Schedule"—a countdown on every possible detail, such as newspaper delivery, mail forwarding, etc. First published in 1955, this durable and delightful guide is now in its 19th edition for $3.00 parcel post ($3.50 first class) directly from the author: Muriel Scudder, Box 72, Shelter Island Heights, New York 11965.

We also recommend Thomas Cook's *Continental Timetable* as a part of your BritRail trip planning. It is an invaluable aid to anyone planning a rail trip anywhere in Europe. It contains complete timetables covering every major rail route in Britain honoring the BritRail Pass. We suggest you purchase a copy prior to departing on your BritRail trip and that you take it with you. It may be a bit bulky, but you'll find yourself constantly delving between its covers for information.

In the United States and Canada, copies of the Thomas Cook *Continental Timetable* can be purchased from the Forsyth Travel Library, whose full services are described on pages 305 and 306.

How To Get There

Transatlantic air traffic is so frequent and varied today that no description of it—short of an entire book—could do it justice. Excursion fares are still available in a multitudinous variety. Charter flights are still available, and they are still money-savers in most cases. However, some excursion rates could mean further savings over charters, and there are always the "independents" such as Laker and Icelandair who keep coming up with variations on the theme. It's not uncommon on a regular scheduled airliner winging its way to Europe to find that every passenger in your row of seats paid a different fare for the same flight on the same schedule with the same service!

We refer readers to their travel agents for airline information. But, there has been a tremendous erosion of such information in travel agencies, brought about in general by the proliferation of air fares. The agencies face the almost impossible task of keeping tabs on the airline industry. Let's put it this way, if you've dealt with a reputable travel agency over the years, contact them the moment you've decided to BritRail through Britain and ask them to come up with some air excursion fare options. At your own leisure, contact the various airlines on their "800" telephone numbers and ask them for their suggestions and fare information. Don't be disturbed if you come up with a variety of responses. Sift them out until you find what you're looking for.

Long distance calls can be made without charge when calling businesses who have "800" service numbers. Getting the proper "800" number to call is simple: dial 1-800-555-1212 and tell the special operator the name of the airline information office with which you wish to speak. Playing no favorites, here's a partial listing of airlines to contact: Air Canada, British Airways, British Caledonian Airways, Icelandair, Laker, Pan Am, and TWA.

The BritRail Pass

BritRail Pass is a ticket for any train operated by the British Railways in England, Scotland and Wales. BritRail Pass also is accepted on the steamers of Lake Windermere and on the ships operated to and from the Isle of Wight. BritRail Pass holders do not have to obtain a separate ticket for each rail journey.

BritRail Pass may be purchased for first class travel or for economy (second class) travel. A first class Senior Citizen BritRail Pass (age 65 and over) and a Youth Economy BritRail Pass (age 14–25) are also available. Any of the four types of passes may be purchased for periods of 7, 14, and 21 days and 1 month validity. Information on the various kinds of passes can be found on page 311.

A SeaPass also may be purchased when you buy a BritRail Pass. The SeaPass provides passage between Britain and the Continent (SeaPass—Continental) and between Britain and Ireland (SeaPass—Ireland). The SeaPass includes the sea journey, plus connecting rail journeys between London and the ports of embarkation/disembarkation. Although you may only purchase a SeaPass at the time you purchase a BritRail Pass, the SeaPass does not have to be used during the validity period of the BritRail Pass. It must, however, be used within 6 months from the date of issue. The SeaPass is *not* good for train travel on the Continent, in Northern Ireland, nor in the Republic of Ireland. The Sea-Pass—Continental may be used on the Seaspeed Hovercraft services, as well as the regular Sealink ferries between England and France.

A BritRail Pass can be validated for the period issued (7, 14, 21 days or 1 month) at any time within 1 year from issue date. The validity period *begins* with your first trip and ends at midnight on the date of expiration. The BritRail Pass is *not* valid for use on Sealink or Seaspeed services without an accompanying Sea-Pass. The pass is not accepted for the Britainshrinkers programs (page 54) and supplements for sleeper accommodations and pullman services are not included.

Any visitors going to Britain should consider purchasing a BritRail Pass if they plan to do any travel by train during their stay there. To make your own decision on whether or not to purchase a BritRail Pass, we suggest you examine the selection of British Rail one-way fares on page 304 of this edition and then compare that cost with the BritRail Pass cost shown on page 311 for an intinerary of your own choice.

Keep in mind, when comparing the straight rail fares to the cost of the pass, that convenience in travel has a value, too. Standing in line ("queuing") to purchase train tickets is an inconvenience that can be avoided. With a BritRail Pass, you need do this only once—when you validate your pass. The rest of the time, you need only board the train and you are on your merry way.

A short-term visitor to London may want to consider the possibility of a dash to Scotland for a brief look around Edinburgh, Aberdeen and Glasgow before leaving to go back home. With the high speed Inter-City services between the cities mentioned, such a trip could be comfortably conducted in as little as 3 days. Adding up the fares for such a circuitous journey from the data given on page 304, travel by first class over the entire route would cost $269; for economy travel, the tab would be $181. For only $147, the traveler can purchase a first class, 7-day BritRail Pass and thus save a considerable amount of cash *and* gain an additional 4 days travel within the pass validity period! During those remaining 4 days of unlimited rail travel, the pass holder could continue to dash about the British Isles soaking up culture and scenery at a merry pace (see Chapter 7) or take a more leisurely trip and roam where the rails beckon.

Casual, short-term or business visitors to Britain may all benefit from a BritRail Pass tucked in their pocket before leaving home. Both the BritRail Pass and the BritRail SeaPass *must* be purchased in North America prior to departure. Expand your horizons—don't leave home without one!

Trip Tips

Here are some tips to help you enjoy your BritRail trip to the fullest: Don't carry more cash than you can afford to lose; carry travelers' checks. Whenever possible, cash your travelers' checks at the branch bank facilities located in or near the train stations and airports. The currency exchange services operated by Thomas Cook are also acceptable. The banks and the official currency exchange services are government supervised and are required to pay the official rates of exchange. Hotel and store cashiers seldom give you the full exchange value and often add a service charge.

Take a credit card with you. It usually proves to be an important adjunct to your enroute finances. American Express is by far the best card you can carry at the moment. The privilege of cashing personal checks at American Express offices is invaluable. Card members may now cash personal checks for up to $1000 ($200 in local currency and $800 in travelers' checks). Mastercard and Visa are gaining popularity in Europe and can be used in a number of places, mostly stores and restaurants. Diner's Club and Carte Blanche are also accepted by most hotels and restaurants.

Picking pockets is an art which is practiced throughout Europe. Gentlemen's breast pockets are the main targets. Foil the thief by sewing two medium-size buttons, one above and one below the pocket opening. Loop a piece of shoestring or other strong string around the buttons when carrying valuables. Avoid carrying anything more valuable than a handkerchief in hip pockets. Ladies' pocketbooks should be the shoulder-type and carried that way at all times. Don't let the thought of pickpocketing alarm you. Just be aware of it and protect yourself against it. It is mild, considering what might happen to you on Main Street in your own home town after dark!

Don't leave your cash, cameras and other valuables in the hotel room or lock them up in a suitcase. Take them with you or leave them in the hotel safe.

With all the luxuries of flight that modern aircraft offer, there is still something about flying as a passenger that makes it a bit more demanding on your system than a similar amount of time spent at home or in the office. A transatlantic trip with a minimum of incidents and inconveniences is what we're after. Here are some suggestions that we have found helpful on our flights; perhaps they may help on yours.

Cash, Cards, and Credentials

You'll need some cash on your flight to pay for tips, snacks, refreshments, and taxi fares at your arrival point. Don't carry it all in one big roll—distribute it around in pockets, a briefcase, or a money clip. A money belt is an ideal way to carry the larger notes. List the number of each credit card you plan to take. Leave a copy at home and pack one in your suitcase or carry-on bag. List passport numbers, too. When anything is lost or stolen, the police are primarily interested in its serial number. A certified copy of your birth certificate and a few passport photos will save you days of delay if you lose your passport.

Luggage

One suitcase, one shoulder bag. Check the suitcase and carry the shoulder bag. Be sure the carry-on bag has a small supply of toilet articles, stockings and underwear—just in case your matched luggage takes a while getting back together again.

In-Flight Comfort

If you plan to catch some shut-eye enroute, ask for a seat alongside a bulkhead. Bulkheads don't mind being leaned on, but passengers do. Passengers in the forward section of the airplane generally experience less vibration. Wear loose clothing. Unfasten your shoes, but don't take them off. Your feet will swell following several hours of immobility. Best remedy is to walk the length of the aisle in the airplane every hour or so. Try deep knee bends. Flying dehydrates your body. Drink lots of water and watch what you mix with it—alcohol dehydrates, too! Special meals for special diets are no problem with the airlines, but requests should be made at the same time as reservations.

Cameras, Film

If you plan to take a foreign-made camera with you, save yourself a lot of headaches by visiting the U.S. Customs Office before leaving the country and have your equipment registered. Carry a copy of the registration form with your passport and a spare copy tucked away in the camera case or shoulder bag. Despite what airport officials tell you, their electronic luggage checking devices can fog your film. The best way to avoid it is to report for check-in early and ask that your cameras and film be inspected by hand. Special lead-lined bags are available at most camera stores. Color film in Britain includes processing and is usually more expensive than that which you can buy at home. Solution? Take the film you'll need with you.

Tax-Free Purchases

Every international airport now has a "tax-free" shopping service. The routine is universally the same. You select your purchases, pay for them and add them to your carry-on luggage, find safe storage for it, and then haul it off the airplane. In JFK New York, you select the items from a sample or catalog. The items are then delivered "for your convenience" to your departure gate for pick-up. The hazards of this system are many. If the delivery boy gets things mixed up and fails to make the right gate at the right time, you'll be off into the wild blue yonder sans purchases. Or, if you are late passing the pick-up point, sometimes an unknown "benefactor" tries to help by taking your purchases on board the plane ahead of you. Finding the so-called "benefactor" can prove to be difficult, too. Solution? Buy your "booty" aboard the airplane while enroute. "Tax-free," by the way, is a misused term. Most items, with exception of alcohol and tobacco, normally can be purchased cheaper in the arrival city.

Before Arriving

Fill out all the customs forms your flight attendant gives to you and keep them with your passport and airline ticket. Keep this packet handy, but secure, until the credentials are asked for.

Jet Lag and What to Do About It

Earlier, we mentioned jet lag. It can seriously affect your transatlantic trip unless you understand it and know how to deal with it. The following explanation of what jet lag is and some means to combat it should prove helpful to any traveler undergoing 4 or more hours of time change.

The human body has numerous rhythms. Sleep, for example, is one of them. Even without sunlight, as in a cave, the body will still maintain a 24-hour awake/sleep cycle. The heart rate is another cycle which falls to a very low ebb in the early hours of the morning when you are usually asleep. Body temperature, which affects the mental processes, also drops during this time. Consequently, if an air traveler were transported rapidly to another location where the time zone difference is 5 or 6 hours, even though it may be 8 or 9 o'clock in the morning at the arrival point in local time, the traveler's body functions are at a low ebb. As a result, the traveler feels subpar and this feeling can persist for as long as 2 or 3 days unless something is done to correct it. This is jet lag.

To lessen the effects of jet lag, avoid excessive drinking and eating enroute. Following your arrival, exercise the first day by taking a vigorous walk, followed by a long nap. Set your watch to local time at your destination as you depart on your flight. By doing this, you will subconsciously accelerate your adjustment to the new time zone. For example, how many times have you looked at your watch and *then* realized you were hungry? Get plenty of rest on the day of your arrival and begin doing everything you normally do back home on the new local time. Respect jet lag by taking these precautions and you'll enjoy your vacation.

Prestwick Airport is Scotland's international air terminal. Positioned 29 miles southwest of Glasgow, the airport serves scheduled transatlantic air carriers as well as charter flights. Rail connections to Glasgow and Edinburgh are available from the train station in the nearby town of Prestwick.

That big moment is about to happen. Years of dreaming, months of planning and weeks of anticipation are about to become a reality. The "No Smoking" and "Fasten Seat Belts" signs have been illuminated and the cabin attendants advise that the aircraft will be landing in a few minutes. If this is your initial visit to Britain, you'll be straining to get your first glimpse of the land from your window; if you have been to Britain many times before, you'll be straining to get a glimpse of the land right along with the other passengers! There is always an unexplainable thrill about arriving in a foreign country. Enjoy this emotion, for it is part of the reason for your journey—to experience the adventure of travel, to probe beyond the normal confines of our environment, to meet other people, to enjoy a bit more of the world than you did before the "Fasten Seat Belts" sign came on.

The Airports

Within Britain, there are seven airports managed by the British Airports Authority—Heathrow, Gatwick, and Stansted in the London area; Glasgow, Edinburgh, Prestwick and Aberdeen in Scotland. Your destination airport will be according to the routing you selected and the air carrier taking you there. If your destination is London, your arrival airport could be either Heathrow or Gatwick. Check with the air carrier to be certain.

The British Airports Authority publishes an 84-page handbook entitled *Airport Information* containing all you need to know about traveling through any of its seven airports. Each chapter contains a map of the airport and five sections of information covering telephone numbers, travel to and from the airport, airport services, information services, and local hotel listings. Copies of this informative book are available free of charge from British Airports Publications, Brochure Department, Wellington Rd., Cheriton, Folkestone, Kent England.

Transportation between London and the Heathrow and Gatwick Airports is described on page 69. Similar information for Prestwick Airport in Scotland may be found on page 223.

Clearing Customs

The customs information cards given to you by the cabin attendants before landing will expedite your clearance through arrival formalities. Actually, you will go through two processes—customs and immigration—although they appear to be integrated. Immigration officials will want to examine your passport. This is usually conducted at a barrier gate enroute to the baggage claim area in the airport. After collecting the checked baggage, you should proceed to the customs inspection area, where you will find two color-coded lanes—green for "Nothing to Declare" and red for "To Declare." Everyone has some apprehension about passing through customs. For the most part, the apprehension is based on the question, "Am I doing it properly?" Doing it properly in Britain consists of going straight through the "Nothing to Declare" channel, unless you are asked to stop by an officer, and moving through into the airport's general assembly area. If the customs officials want to examine your luggage, they'll indicate that as you approach them. Don't go through the "To Declare" lane unless you have brought amounts of tobacco or liquor with you that exceed the duty-free limits or have purchased a gift that you will be leaving with someone in Britain with a value exceeding £28.

The type and amount of duty-free goods that you may bring into Britain vary with where you are arriving from—a European Common Market country or otherwise. For transatlantic passengers, the limit is 400 cigarettes and a liter bottle of liquor or two bottles of sparkling wine and two bottles of still wine. You will have plenty of advance advice on duty-free imports posted in your departing airport and you can check with the cabin attendants on the airplane as well. Know before you go, and the clearing procedures in Britain will present no problem.

The phrase "know before your go" also applies to your return to North America. The Treasury Department, the folks who operate the U.S. Customs services, publishes a very informative booklet containing customs hints for returning U.S. residents. A card or letter request to the Department of the Treasury, Washington, D.C. 20229, will get you the "Know Before You Go" booklet. For U.S. Customs information while in London, telephone 499-1212 for the Treasury Department representative at the American Embassy.

When clearing through foreign customs, keep in mind that the average customs inspector is more interested in the luggage of a returning national than in yours. Always carry your customs declaration along with your passport and in full view as you pass the customs inspector.

British Currency

Say a silent prayer of thanks for the new British decimal currency system. Prior to the seventies, Britons added their money in three columns—pounds, shillings, and pence. One pound sterling consisted of 20 shillings: a shilling equaled 12 pence. The new British currency is still based on the pound sterling, but it's divided into 100 pence to the pound—a decided improvement.

British bank notes (as in most of the rest of the world) vary in size according to denomination. The notes are issued in values of £1, £5, £10, and £20. A variety of British paper money can bring havoc to the orderliness of a North American's wallet. Certain bills, £20 and £10 notes in particular, require folding before they will fit in a standard wallet. However, before criticizing the system, answer the query we were once asked as we displayed our "same-size, all denomination" currency to a thoughtful Irish matron, "How do your blind people tell the difference?" The British decimal coins are 50 pence (7-sided and similar to the U.S. Susan B. Anthony dollar—except in popularity), 10 pence, 5 pence, and the bronze 2, 1, and ½ pence coins. For example, £2.20 means 2 pounds, 20 pence.

British Telephones

Old-timers who toured the British Isles under the auspices of General Eisenhower and their local draft boards will welcome the news that the dreaded "A" and "B" buttons have been removed from most British telephones. Many people thought that when the British removed all their road signs to confuse possible invaders during World War II, they added "A" and "B" buttons to the telephones to confuse—possibly even eliminate—telephone communications by invaders and visitors alike. We've even heard it whispered by off-duty State Department personnel that Britain was denied participation in the Marshall Plan due to huge amounts of money Americans had "hung up" in British pay phones somewhere between the "A" and "B" buttons.

All that is legend. The new public coin-box telephones now in operation throughout Britain are simple—with a bit of explanation, that is. Basic differences between British phones and ours still exist—particularly in the signals they make. A ringing signal is two short rings, followed by a pause. The busy signal sounds the same—only busier! An all-circuits-busy signal is a rapid series of high-low tones, but when you have reached a telephone number not in use, a high-pitched continuous tone quite reminiscent of a WWII air raid siren will be heard.

To master the modern British pay phone, arm yourself with an ample supply of decimal coins. Lift the receiver, listen for the dial tone (a purring sound), then dial the number you want. The ringing signal will be heard until you are connected with your party. A series of rapid pips will signal you to drop a coin into the appropriate slot. If the rapid pips return during your conversation, you need more coins.

Don't despair if you can't master the system. Merely lift the receiver and dial 100 for the operator. Do not insert money until the operator tells you. To summon emergency services (fire, police or ambulance), dial 999. Do not insert money.

British Traditions

Some visitors entering Britain for the first time will find some of the British traditions, customs, and way of life a bit difficult to understand. Perhaps what follows may assist in the transition.

If a Scot from Edinburgh, a Welshman from Cardiff and an Englishman from London were traveling together in North America, they would describe themselves as being "British." But, among themselves, they would be Scot, Welsh and English. These three nationalities, joined by the Ulstermen of Northern Ireland, make up what we refer to as the United Kingdom. Since the BritRail Pass is not accepted for rail travel in Northern Ireland (as previously mentioned), references in this book are to *Britain* rather than the *United Kingdom*, and the term "British" refers to the peoples of England, Scotland, and Wales.

The British character will wear well on you after a few days. If you are taken by the strangeness of their manners, remember that they are a well disciplined people. If anything is at fault, more than likely it is the visitor, not the host. You might spill your tea the first time a waitress calls you "Dearie," but you'll learn very quickly that these figures of speech are actually a kind of politeness. You'll also learn very quickly that the British queue is the quintessence of "first-come, first-served."

On the surface, Britons may appear to lack a sense of humor. However, once their facade is penetrated, you will find them capable of the highest mark of humor—they can laugh at themselves. This becomes most evident in their observations regarding their weather. "The way to ensure summer in England," snapped Horace Walpole, "is to have it framed and glazed in a comfortable room." Byron's observation was perhaps more terse, "The English winter—ending in July to recommence in August." Britain does have a tendency to be moist at times. You won't regret taking a small folding umbrella with you.

The Language Barrier

By now, you'll notice that there is one! It has often been said that the two great countries of America and Britain are divided only by a common language—English. Terminology, more so than pronunciation, appears to be the problem whenever an American and a Briton cannot communicate effectively with each other. Several of our readers report that *British Self-taught, with Comments in American* by Norman W. Schur, published by the Macmillan Company, of New York, in 1973, can be most helpful during an initial visit to Britain.

Reading the daily newspapers and listening to the British Broadcasting Corporation (BBC) or watching the telly (television) are quick remedial methods for learning the language. These media communicate through a more or less middle-of-the-road lexicon. Regional and local dialects can be extremely difficult to comprehend on occasion. It has been said that if an Oxford graduate and a Cambridge graduate were locked up together in the same room, neither would be able to converse with the other—even after being properly introduced!

One of the first things a visitor from "the Colonies" will notice is the manner in which directions are given. Americans geographically locate a point within a city by referring to the number of "blocks" distant from the point of inquiry, for example, "two blocks down the street." Britain's early road builders, however, never thought too much about a grid system and permitted their streets to wander along the easiest gradient. Consequently, directions given by a constable or a man on the street will usually be in terms of linear directions, i.e., "straight ahead for 100 yards," "a quarter-mile," "a mile or two," etc. Visual objects often are employed in direction giving, i.e., "straight away to the pub," "keep walking 'til you come to the third traffic light," etc. Cabbies (taxi drivers) are particularly good sources for directional information and advice. Every cabbie carries a street map in his taxi.

Nuances in the American/British vocabulary can sometimes lead to trouble. In a public place, such as a train station, those in search of toilet facilities will do well to employ the term "lavatory" in their quest. The "WC" (water closet) seems to be losing its effectiveness in Britain, although it still brings direct results when used in continental Europe. However, if you want to be up on slang expressions, you might ask for the "loo"— that's where the "in crowd" goes to "spend a penny." Requesting directions for the "bathroom," particularly in a train station, might lead you to the public showers. So, take our advice and stay with "lavatory."

Terminology in a train station should not present much difficulty. The baggage room is "left luggage," "lost property" translates easily into lost and found. Elevators are labeled "lifts," but "subway" means a pedestrian underground street crossing. The "underground," or "tube," is the British version of our subway.

A "carriage" is a (rail) coach and a "coach" is a long-distance bus. Should you hear the term "goods wagon" or "goods train," when converted to American terminology, that translates to a freight car or a freight train. Aboard a train, the conductor usually is referred to as the "guard"; the engineer becomes the train "driver."

The British measure their body weight in stones—a stone being a unit of 14 pounds. A person weighing 14 stone 6 pounds would gross out at 202 pounds avoirdupois. A popular measurement of elapsed time is "a fortnight," meaning 14 days or 2 weeks. Britain's conversion to a decimal currency system has not changed the slang for the pound sterling—it's still a "quid." You may hear a price quoted in "guineas," a holdover from the old days meaning one pound and one shilling—now, £1.05.

For those who plan to nip into a pub or two during their visit to Britain, the announcement, "time, gentlemen, time," will become very familiar. It signals that closing time has arrived and it is time to drink up.

Food on the move includes a variety of service and menus. Inter-City trains (above) feature three types of menus: Gold Star, Main Line, and Grill. Buffet service (below) offers a wide range of snacks and drinks. Food service cars (carriages) are identified by an exterior red band above the windows.

Over the last decade, the services on the British Rail passenger network have come a long way—with yet a long way to go. There is still a discernible difference between the operating speeds and the passenger comforts experienced on the railroads of Continental Europe and those of the British, the latter being the lesser, but the gap is narrowing.

The front runner of British Rail's stable is its new High-Speed Train (HST), the Inter-City 125. Nicknamed the "Journey Shrinker," the world's fastest diesel train is now shrinking journeys on many of the main routes out of London. From King's Cross Station, for example, the *Flying Scotsman*, an Inter-City 125, covers the 379 miles between London and Edinburgh in 4 hours and 37 minutes—an average of 82 miles per hour, including a station stop at Newcastle in England before crossing the Scottish border! Hourly service by 125's now links the two capitals. Inter-City 125 service has now been extended out of London to Plymouth and Penzance. Leading the 125 fleet over this rail route to England's west is the *Golden Hind*, appropriately named after Sir Francis Drake's famous sailing vessel.

Inter-City 125 trains offer comfort as well as speed. They have a whole range of luxury features, including air conditioning, soundproofing, automatic interior doors, and a wide choice of meals, snacks, and drinks. The trains are powered by two 2,250-horsepower diesel electric engines—one at each end of the train. The 125 coaches are identified by letter (A, B, C, etc.), and the stations they serve have their platform positions marked accordingly.

Already off the drawing board and operating as a prototype on selected test runs, the Advanced Passenger Train (APT) is being readied in the 1980's by British Rail to operate at 155 miles per hour. The light at the end of BritRail's tunnel draws closer and closer! By Inter-City 125 service, you can now reach Wales in less than 2 hours and York in exactly 2 hours from London.

Aside from the Inter-City 125's and the equally fast and comfortable all-electric passenger trains operated by British Rail on its major routes (the London-Glasgow line is completely electrified), there is a paucity of modern commuter-type trains on many of its intermediate lines. For example, although train service south of London is completely electrified, for the most part it is served by "four-car units," some of which have already passed their 30th "birthdays." These trains have seen yeoman duty over the years and show more than a fair amount of wear and tear.

Along with Beatlemania, graffiti arrived in Britain, accompanied by modern packaging, which produces litter in abundance. The older trains were designed in the days when cleaning labor was abundant and cheap. Washing as many as 80 separate windows on a single coach wasn't a problem then, but it is now! Air conditioning is nonexistent in the older trains, although that's no great problem since summers in the British Isles are generally milder than those of North America. However, heating can be a problem. Not many years ago, train passengers set out on their journeys wrapped in heavy overcoats and shod with thick-soled shoes. Full heat in the coach brought complaints of stuffiness. Today's grumbles from thinly clad travelers are very much the opposite.

The "old units" are gradually being replaced by new suburban-type trains and some of the vintage units are being refurbished with more comfortable seats, better lighting, heating, and soundproofing. Nevertheless, it will be a while before the "generation gap" in British Rail's rolling stock is overcome.

Possibly on a day excursion off the main lines, you may ride in a locomotive-hauled coach with an exit door for each compartment. We've counted as many as 9 doors to a side on some coaches. These cars are relics from the days when station porters opened and closed the doors for passengers. Consequently, you won't find any door handles inside the compartment. Don't panic! To get out, lower the window and open the door from the outside.

Sleeping, restaurant, buffet and Pullman cars are operated by British Rail, along with the standard passenger carriages (coaches). British Pullman cars differ from the Pullmans of North America in that they do not convert at night to provide sleeping accommodations. Instead, British Rail Pullmans are the elite of the line, the best in daytime comfort, and exclusively first class. Even travelers holding first class BritRail Passes are required to pay a supplemental fare (U.S. $4.00/£1.50) for occupancy, and seat reservations are obligatory. This luxury service operates on the London-to-Manchester/Liverpool route. Basically, it is designed to offer the businessman morning and afternoon services between England's capital and its leading commercial center. It is worth the experience, but we suggest that you dress appropriately for the occasion if you want to engage in tycoon-to-tycoon conversations with other passengers. In London, the Pullman trains depart from Euston Station. When accommodations are still available, last-minute reservations and the supplementary payment can be arranged with the train conductor.

First class sleeping cars have single-berth compartments; second class sleepers have two-berth compartments. Sleeping car charges in Britain are most economical—$21 for first class; $17 per person in second class. Sleeping car passengers are served with morning tea or coffee and biscuits free of charge and they generally can remain in the sleeping cars at destination until 0730. The charges are standard for all destinations regardless of the distance.

With such attractive prices, an overnight trip aboard a sleeper may outweigh the alternative of seeking a night's lodging in a city and an early morning departure in order to make your destination on time. We suggest you consider the sleeping cars for excursions to Plymouth, Penzance, and Inverness.

Sleeper services operate between London and the main centers in Scotland, the north of England, south Wales and the west of England. "Nightcap" service is available, too, in case you're interested.

Most Inter-City trains haul restaurant cars. If not, there usually is a buffet car from which you can obtain snacks and beverages. Aboard the Inter-City fleet, restaurant cars offer a wide range of freshly prepared traditional dishes. Gold Star restaurant service is available on many 125's and on selected "business" trains—the Manchester/Liverpool Pullman, for example. Passengers holding first class tickets who wish to take meals can reserve seats in the restaurant car or in adjacent coaches. Breakfast aboard British Rail trains has always been a great attraction—about one million are now served annually. They're hearty and generally very good.

Some buffet cars offer "grill" meals which you may enjoy in the buffet car, or you may bring them back to your seat. Seating in the buffet cars is unassignable, thereby providing a reasonable opportunity to be seated while you select from the bill of fare. One innovation found aboard many British Rail food service cars is beer and lager on draught. This, according to many railroad buffs, is an outstanding stride forward in the annals of railroad engineering!

Admittedly, dining aboard a speeding train is an unusual gastronomic experience, but it can be on the expensive side. Although British Rail's food catering aboard is far more economical than similar services on the trains of the Continent, those seeking less expensive food may want to utilize the Travellers-Fare facilities found at most rail stations in Britain. They range in service from complete restaurants serving a variety of hot and cold dishes to a snack bar-type operation. Some have off-license provisions where you may purchase alcoholic beverages for consumption elsewhere, but all bars operated by Travellers-Fare, unlike the trains, must observe the local licensing hours for serving drinks.

The most economical food you may enjoy on a train in Britain is, of course, that which you bring aboard yourself. Many of the Travellers-Fare restaurants will prepare box lunches for you to take on your trip. Ask for the "buffet-pack" service.

First Class, Second Class?

On most British Rail trains you have a choice of first or second (economy) class travel. BritRail Passes are sold for both classes. First class seats are wider and more spacious. If that is the sort of accommodation you want, then it is worth paying the extra price. However, second class on British Rail is an excellent standard. All the facilities aboard the trains, such as restaurant and buffet services, are available for both first and second class travelers.

The average citizen of Britain travels by second class carriage (coach). In fact, it is so much the custom that should you desire to purchase a first class ticket, you must specifically state "first class;" otherwise, you will automatically get an economy class ticket. This does not mean that you will find the second class carriages crowded while the first class sections remain all but vacant. First class offers extra comfort and is less crowded. First class accommodations for weekend and holiday travel are particularly desirable. However, seats may be reserved in both classes, which is a wise move if your particular journey is a "must" and the distance is great. "Riding the cases" (sitting on your suitcase in an aisle or passageway for lack of a seat) is not the most comfortable way to travel!

Seat reservations may be made in any major train terminal throughout Britain, or you may obtain advance reservations prior to arriving in Britain through the international offices representing the British Rail system. The U.S. charge is $1.50 per seat.

Travelers holding first class BritRail Passes may travel in either first or economy class carriages—which is a nice option when the good-looking "bird" you've been yearning to chat with boards the second class section. It's a disaster, however, if she moves to the first class section with you holding a second class ducat!

You will find some single-class trains operating on branch lines. This means that first class accommodations are not available aboard that particular train. It is a nice, polite British way of avoiding the somewhat unrefined term, "second class only."

Similar to the Continent, the first class British Rail cars are distinctively identified by a yellow band running the length of each car above its doors and windows. On other than mainline service, where both first and second class accommodations may be provided in the same car, a yellow band will be shown for only the first class portion of the car. Restaurant cars, buffets and cars containing other forms of food-catering facilities are identified by a red band above their doors and windows.

Unlike the Continent, except for the Inter-City 125's (page 39), it is difficult to determine exactly where the first class coaches will halt in an enroute station stop. The non-English-speaking nations of Europe generally provide a diagram of each train's composition and where it will stop in the station. Not so in Britain. According to the equipment in use, the first class section of a British train can be at the head, the rear, or in the middle of the train. Station porters (there are a few left) generally speculate on where the yellow-striped cars will stop. But few are definitive—even if they are handling your luggage. Through experience, we have devised a system that is relatively effective. Position yourself midway on the platform and scan for the yellow band as the train enters the station. Should it pass you, take off to the head of the train; if it doesn't, head in the other direction. Should the yellow-striped car stop directly in front of you, fate has been kind to you this day, but you can bet it won't happen again for at least a fortnight!

An increase in the nonsmoking accommodations aboard British trains is becoming apparent. Originally, about 50% of the accommodations on mainline trains and about 60% on suburbans were allocated to nonsmoking areas, but the overall percentage of nonsmoking seats presently is about 75%, reflecting the noticeable change in the public attitude towards smoking. The fine for violating the rule is £50. So, if you are a smoker, keep your eyes alert for the red nonsmoking signs and smoke only in the areas so designated.

44

Train Schedules

British timetables generally are divided into sections according to the pattern of services provided. A typical two-part division is "Mondays to Saturdays" and "Sundays." However, you may run across a mix, including "Mondays to Fridays," "Mondays to Saturdays," or "Saturdays and Sundays." All days stated are inclusive. In other words, "Mondays to Saturdays" includes all six days. (The schedules appearing in *Britain by BritRail* are stated as "Mondays *through* Saturdays" to conform more to North American terminology.)

Always be certain that you look at the correct part of the schedule for the particular day of the week on which you wish to travel. Another caution: services may be modified on days preceding and immediately following bank holidays. Best bet for a "must" trip, a late night return, or an early morning departure is to check your plans with the British Rail personnel in the station Travel Centers. Extensive engineering work is often conducted on the British Rail system on weekends, which frequently affects passengers' schedules. Telephones may also be employed for inquiries. Useful telephone numbers are given on the *Britain by BritRail* schedules for this purpose. You will also find the innovative "Talking Timetables" invaluable whenever a printed timetable is not available.

You should experience little difficulty in verifying the departure time of your selected train or locating the platform from which it departs once you've made it to the station—providing in London that you've gone to the proper station! Airport-style digital displays are the usual source of such information in most British stations. You will find them in the main station hall and also on the train platforms in many stations. However, even the old fashioned train bulletin boards (page 288) can still provide the needed information. Augmenting displayed train departure information are the usual voice announcements in the station halls and on the platforms. For the most part, they vary from those made by Amtrak in that you can understand them! Perhaps it's the accent that makes it possible!

Weekend/holiday travel need not be avoided on British Rail services as long as you accept the fact that trains will be crowded. Seat reservations in advance will help. Aids to passenger control, such as this queue marker, do much to expedite travelers boarding trains to holiday destinations.

"What affects men sharply about a foreign nation," wrote G.K. Chesterton, "is not so much finding or not finding familiar things, it is rather not finding them in the familiar place."

For many of us coming to Britain for the first time, we find a confusion of terminology and learn too late that what we sought was really available throughout our visit. Our problem was merely not knowing the proper place to look, or not knowing the proper name to ask for. Perhaps some things might be set in better order for the pleasure of your BritRail adventures with the following train travel tips, explanations, and illustrations to guide you.

One extremely important tip to mention first is that British Rail is leading the world in providing facilities in its stations and aboard its trains for the disabled and the handicapped. Through such efforts, rail travel is becoming more and more a chosen method of transportation and recreation for disabled persons. Many aids for the handicapped have been incorporated into British Rail's code for station design. Trains are being designed with wider doors for wheelchair access, some even have a removable seat to make room for a wheelchair. Ramped access to toilets, buffets, and other facilities is being provided. Folding wheelchairs are also available at main stations so that occupants may be transferred to a regular seat once aboard the train. British Rail is most anxious to provide as comfortable a journey as possible for the disabled passenger. To do this, prior advice of the intended travel plans would be most helpful to the traveler and to the authorities.

For those readers who want to learn more about this innovative approach to travel for the disabled and the handicapped, we suggest writing to the Royal Association for Disability and Rehabilitation, 25 Mortimer Street, London, W1N 8AB, England, for details. The association has published *A Guide to British Rail for the Physically Handicapped* (second edition, 1979) and has many other similar publications available.

Many otherwise able train visitors to Britain impose a severe handicap upon themselves by arriving with more luggage than three men and a small boy could possibly carry. Train porters are an endangered species and their demise is being expedited by the luggage trolley—Britain's version of our baggage cart—an elusive device that haunts the extreme opposite end of the train platform from your position. Our number 1 tip (repeated from Chapter 2) to all train travelers is to "go lightly." At most, take one medium-sized suitcase, augmented by a modest shoulder bag. Even then, there will be times when you will wish you could completely unburden yourself by discarding your suitcase!

Rather than relying upon the trolleys in the train stations, you might consider investing in your own personal model to take with you. You will see more and more train travelers proceeding through rail stations in Europe rolling their bags behind them. For our money, there is only one baggage cart worth buying—the Cart-A-Bag. It's collapsible and holds up to 150 pounds of luggage. It folds small and packs into its own vinyl case. When not on the road, we even use it around the office to cart books and things to the post office. TWA's Flight Shop sells them, and most of the better luggage shops do, too. Cheaper carts are on the market, but not for long. Within days of their purchase, you'll find parts of their wheels scattered about in some airport or train station and the rest of the device in a dustbin (that's British for "trash can")!

Another tip regarding loading your cart or British Rail's trolley is to keep the load as narrow as possible. You must pass through ticket barriers going to and coming from the trains. The barriers are rather narrow. A Samsonite suitcase will just clear, but a full-figured lady with a wardrobe case is in trouble every time! The trolleys provided by the station should not be taken aboard the train, although we've seen it tried. When taking your own cart with you, fold it before boarding. If you don't you may spend an embarrassing 10 minutes extracting a hapless fellow traveler from it.

The greatest problem in using the train station's luggage trolleys (or your own baggage cart) is traversing the station hall to the platform area, since practically every station has stairs. You can overcome this problem by using the station's lift (elevator). This polite announcement is found posted in most British Rail stations: "Lifts are available for passengers who have difficulty in using the stairs. Please contact station staff if assistance is required." In searching for a lift, don't keep looking for a modern, automatic-door elevator brightly lit with soft music playing in the background. What you will find instead is the old fashioned double-door, manually operated freight elevator, large enough to hold a Mack truck and usually illuminated with a single bare lightbulb—but it works! As the sign says, station staff will assist you. However, if you use the lifts frequently, you will develop the knack of handling them all by yourself. One word of caution: the lift will not operate until *both* barriers (usually a door and a gate) have been closed securely. Furthermore, the lift will be left inoperative if you fail to close the doors after you have used it. Be considerate of other passengers, as well as the station staff, by making certain that the lift is left operable for the next user.

Porter service is on the wane but still available in many train stations throughout Britain, particularly in the larger ones. The best way to locate a porter is to inquire at the "Left Luggage" (baggage storage) area or at the station's incoming-taxi stand. If your luggage has been checked in at the station, there will be a handling charge, but the tip remains a personal item between you and the porter. We suggest 25 pence per parcel (50 pence minimum) as a reasonable gratuity. Most porters will take your bags to the train and place them aboard in the luggage racks over your seats. Porters are rather scarce on arrival platforms. If you must have assistance, inform the stationmaster's office or the train conductor prior to departure with the request that a porter be asked to meet your train upon arrival at your destination.

Readers who have traveled on the trains of Continental Europe will note a few basic differences between Eurail and BritRail operations.

The cars (carriages, if you please) are identified by the standard "smoking" or "nonsmoking" pictographs. First class conveyances are appropriately identified with the yellow band, but unlike their Continental cousins, British Rail cars do not display the destination panel on their sides. (Eurail cars are marked with the name of the city from which they originated, the final destination, and the major in-between stops.) Nevertheless, British Rail trains do "split." Dual-destination trains in Britain will be identified in the departing station by dividing boards—first at the ticket barrier where a bulletin board will state the train's composition. (For example: "First 4 cars—Dover. Remaining Cars—Ramsgate.") At the head of the first four cars, you wil find a platform sign advising "Ramsgate Ahead. Turn Back for Dover."

The best solution we have found in a situation like this is to *ask the train conductor before boarding and again aboard the train when you present your BritRail Pass or ticket*.

Another thing missing on the BritRail scene that we rather enjoyed when traveling by Eurail are the vendors, trackside as well as aboard the train. The construction of the "4-car unit" makes access impossible to the other units making up the train. So, the vendor and his "goodies" cart moving through the train while enroute is automatically ruled out. On BritRail's long-distance trains, the restaurant and buffet cars further preclude the vendor's presence.

Most of all, we missed the trackside vendors who can provide all the essentials of life—food and beverage alike—through an open train window during a 2-minute station stop! BritRail's counter to the trackside vendor is the snack bar kiosks located on the train platforms. Leaving the train to make a purchase at one of the kiosks is a bit risky—particularly if wife, kids, and *your* suitcase depart without you!

50

A few more train travel tips to make your trip more enjoyable.

"Mind the doors!" British Rail cars of the vintage class appear to provide a door for each passenger. There is a great din of door slamming prior to departure and an equal amount of confusion each time the train makes a station stop. If you are waiting at an enroute station for a train, stand well back from the platform edge. Passengers impatient to alight from the train are prone to open the doors before the train comes to a complete stop. In so doing, they're actually extending a bludgeon that could kill you, maim you for life, bruise you, or scare the daylights out of you—the last being much preferred over any of the others.

British Rail has posters positioned in all of its stations where these multi-door cars are in service asking folks to "please don't open the carriage door until the train has stopped" and "please don't stand close to the platform edge." Most of the posters are illustrated by a picture showing a person being struck by a door. Be certain that you are neither the hapless victim nor the unmeaning culprit by observing the rules. The final caption on the poster sums it up succinctly: "A moment's impatience, a lifetime of remorse."

The British are without doubt the most polite people in the world. Match their politeness and you are in for a most enjoyable visit. On the other hand, flaunt your "rights" as a free spirit and citizen of another country, and you'll soon find out what British authorities are capable of. They are particularly harsh with drug-use offenders.

Show your BritRail Pass, or ticket, upon request, and in the case of the pass, have your passport handy should the conductor like to see it. Don't place your feet on the seats of the train unless you have removed your shoes or have provided a protective covering for the seat. Place your luggage in the overhead racks provided for that purpose—not on the seats so that other passengers won't be able to "crowd" you. Observe the smoking/non-smoking areas and rules.

Hovercraft skim across the English Channel between England and France in 35 minutes! They depart from the British ports of Dover and Ramsgate, and the French terminals are Calais and Boulogne. Once separate operations, British Rail's Seaspeed hovercraft have been combined with Hoverlloyd services as *Hoverspeed* for all "flights" connecting the British Isles with the Continent.

In addition to the day excursions offered in this edition of *Britain by BritRail*, there are some special itineraries which are possible through the unique features of British Rail services and its facilities. Two of them, the "Continental Quickie" and the "BritRail by Night" excursions, are our own concoctions. Britainshrinkers, however, have been offered by British Rail continuously since their introduction in 1973. All three itineraries have a tinge of adventure to them.

Continental Quickie

If you have never been to Continental Europe before, British Rail's Hoverspeed hovercraft services make a day excursion to either Boulogne or Calais in France possible. Train connections are made out of London's Charing Cross Station (page 59) to Dover's Priory Station, where a transfer to the hoverport on Dover's Western Docks is accomplished by a special bus. The Hovercraft skims across from Dover to Boulogne in 39–45 minutes.

Boulogne is the largest fishing port in France. It was from Boulogne that Caesar set out to conquer England. Boulogne is really two towns—the Basse Ville that lies along the waterfront is very modern, and the Haute Ville poised on the hillside behind the new city is much older and has a fine medieval wall surrounding it. Calais was occupied by the English during the Hundred Years' War and has been an important shipping port for the English trade for centuries. Calais is almost as familiar to British travelers as Dover.

Holders of the round-trip SeaPass—Continental have their train and Hoverspeed journeys already paid for a "quickie" on the Continent. The $50 supplement to the BritRail Pass for the SeaPass is a real bargain when you consider that the hovercraft round-trip fare alone is $49; add second-class round-trip rail fare out of London to either Boulogne or Calais, and the total becomes $77.40 ($91.60 for first-class train accommodations). Check with the British Rail Travel Center in Charing Cross Station for details.

Britainshrinkers

This sounds like it could be the title of a James Bond thriller—and well it may be. British Rail's brochure describing this program states: "A fast, comfortable train takes you to your destination where a motor coach is waiting. A young, attractive, intelligent and carefully trained guide escorts you all the way from London back to London." Sound interesting? Read on.

Britainshrinkers is a program of fully escorted tours leaving London after breakfast and returning in time for dinner. Lunch in a genuine pub is included, as are the entrance fees to places of interest which you will visit. The Britainshrinkers also offer two-day tours called "overnighters." These enable you to visit places more distant from London and include accommodations for one night, along with dinner and breakfast.

The Britainshrinkers and overnighter programs differ from *Britain by BritRail's* day excursions and out-and-back excursions only in that the Britainshrinkers are fully escorted. *The BritRail Pass is not accepted as supplemental payment for the rail portion of the Britainshrinker tours.* As British Rail officials point out, the Britainshrinkers program was devised to serve the needs of London visitors who were unable to take more than a day or two visiting the British countryside. The program now lists 11 day excursions and 5 overnighter tours. Nearly 150,000 people have participated in the program since its inception.

Rather than attempt to cram a few of the Britainshrinker details into this chapter, we suggest that readers who are interested in the program write for the full brochure which is revised and updated annually. Write to **The Travel Guide Company, Box 20334, Columbus, Ohio 43220** or contact any of the BritRail Travel International offices listed in the Appendix of this edition on page 290.

A word of caution. BritRail believes that a tour with their Britainshrinkers might spoil you for sightseeing for the rest of your life! They may well be right, too.

BritRail by Night

Here's something that you can do with your eyes closed! As a rule, we do not advocate using sleeper cars when traveling by train in Europe. However, in the case of the excellent sleeper car services offered by British Rail—and their modest cost—we are making an exception to our rule.

British Rail operates its sleeper services between London and the main centers in Scotland, the north of England, south Wales, and the west of England. First class sleepers accommodate one person; connecting bedrooms are available. Economy (second) class sleepers offer double accommodations—the two berths are stacked one over the other like bunk beds. Both services provide wall-to-wall carpeting, hot and cold running water, soap and towel, a comfortable mattress—and that all important call button that will bring you a nightcap or your wake-up coffee.

The cost of such accommodations based on single occupancy is $21 for first class; $17 for second class. Usually, you can take occupancy 30 minutes before train departure time and generally stay aboard until 0730, even though the train arrives at your destination several hours earlier.

The major sleeping car routes to points described in this edition are: Paddington Station to Penzance and Plymouth and to Cardiff in Wales; Euston Station to Glasgow and Inverness; King's Cross Station to Edinburgh and Aberdeen. Sleeper service also is available from either Edinburgh or Glasgow to Inverness.

Overnight sleeper service opens up a new door to the adventurous train traveler. The sleeper charge compares favorably to the most economical hotel rates in Britain. You can make the sleeper your "hotel on the move." By booking sleeper accommodations for successive nights, an itinerary could be planned for a night on the train, a day at the destination, a night on the train returning to London and then sightseeing, shopping or a short day excursion out of London, followed by a night to another destination.

Sealink ferries provide vehicle and passenger service between Great Britain and Continental seaports as well as to Ireland and the channel islands. Sealink services out of Folkestone include the Belgian port of Oostende (4½-hour voyage) and the French ports of Dunkerque (2½ hours), Calais (1¾ hours) and Boulogne (1¾ hours).

There was a time when it was fashionable to cross the English Channel on the *Night Ferry*, a train in many respects equal in prestige to the *Orient Express* and *Le Train Blue*. Against a backdrop fit for a Sherlock Holmes mystery, passengers gathered in Victoria Station in the late evening with trunks and valises piled high on porters' carts to await the loading of the *Night Ferry*. Once aboard, the travelers would settle comfortably in their compartments or Pullman accommodations as the train sped south toward Dover. There, with the exception of the engine, the entire train was loaded aboard a waiting ferry, which, in turn, plied through the darkness toward the French coast.

In the faint light of dawn, the ferry unloaded its cargo onto the quay at Dunkerque. A French locomotive then hauled the train across the French countryside through Lille and Amiens before coming to a halt at the Gare du Nord (North Station) in Paris.

At the same time as the *Night Ferry* left Victoria Station in London, an identical unit moved north out of Paris. The two trains would pass each other in the English Channel, as ships do, in the night.

The presence of adventure and romance aboard the *Night Ferry* was undeniable. But the English Channel would, on occasion, seemingly go out of its way to make the crossing other than tranquil. To prevent the trains' coaches from bashing about during the voyage, they were secured to the deck of the ship by chains, an operation that produced more than an ample amount of noise on embarking and again on debarking. It was virtually impossible for anyone except a very deep sleeper to doze comfortably during the crossing.

After decades of service, the *Night Ferry* ceased operations in 1980. Its passing was mourned by many. The train is but a memory today, a victim of the advance of transportation technology.

The most convenient and economical way of crossing the English Channel between Britain and the

Continent is by Sealink or Hoverspeed. Sealink is the conventional ferry service; Hoverspeed service utilizes the hovercraft. For either service, you will be required to leave the train to board the water-borne conveyance. Unlike those of the *Night Ferry*, the rail coaches are not transferred aboard the ferries or hovercraft.

Sealink

Sealink services on the English Channel are one class only. However, both first and second class accommodations are available on the boat trains between London and Dover or Folkestone. Seat reservations are obligatory throughout the year for the boat trains departing from London's Victoria Station. It should be mentioned at this point that the term "boat train" applies to those trains departing from Victoria Station for direct connection at either Dover's Western Docks or Folkestone's harbor terminal with Sealink ferries crossing to Calais, Boulogne, or Dunkerque in France or Oostende in Belgium. These boat trains go directly to the pier. Boat trains going to the port of Folkestone do not call at Folkestone's Central Station. Regular train service is available to Dover, terminating at Dover Priory (Dover's main station) and to Folkestone, where trains call at Folkestone Central but not at Folkestone Harbor. For an expanded overview of these various services, the following Thomas Cook Timetable should be consulted. *Boat Train Services* departing Victoria Station for direct, scheduled connections with Sealink at Dover Western Docks or Folkestone Harbor for Sealink connections to France or Belgium: *Cook Tables 50 and 52*. *Regular Train Services* departing London from either Victoria or the Charing Cross Station to Dover and Folkestone: *Cook Table 512*.

Readers are encouraged to check with the Sealink Travel Center adjacent to platform 2 in the Victoria Station for additional information, reservations, and current schedules.

Hoverspeed

Without doubt, the hovercraft is the most spectacular form of transportation ever devised by man. Watching it in operation, it's hard to determine if the hovercraft's origins are from *Star Wars* or *Close Encounters of the Third Kind*. Nevertheless, it is an ideal means of crossing the English Channel, which it can do between Dover and Calais in 34 minutes from pier to pier!

The name, "Hoverspeed," is the trademark of British Rail Hovercraft, Ltd. Rail passengers have the option of either Sealink or Hoverspeed passage to and from the Continent with no difference in fares. Both offer "one class" accommodations.

Hoverspeed hovercraft depart on their "flight" from the hoverport on Dover's Western Docks. However, travelers intending to use Hoverspeed rather than Sealink should be aware that *the boat train does not terminate at the hoverport* when it arrives at Dover's Western Docks. Hoverspeed hovercraft passengers should leave the train at Dover Priory (Central) where a bus connection is available for transfer to the hoverport. The bus service is free of charge to those holding Sealink/Hoverspeed cross-channel tickets. The bus stand is well marked alongside the entrance to Dover Priory Station. The train for direct connections with the Hoverspeed hovercraft service departs from London's Charing Cross Station rather than Victoria. Although you may take the Sealink boat train from Victoria to Dover and de-train at Dover Priory for the hovercraft transfer, we suggest you depart from Charing Cross for better schedule coordination. We recommend that readers check in with a BritRail Travel Center for full details, reservations, and current schedules prior to departure for their Hoverspeed crossing. For planning purposes, consult Table 49 of Thomas Cook's *Continental Timetable*.

Another source of information for Hoverspeed services is the previously mentioned Sealink Travel Center located adjacent to platform 2 in London's Victoria Station.

SeaPass—Continental

BritRail Pass holders may wish to consider purchasing a SeaPass—Continental if planning to visit the Continent during their stay in Britain. This pass is an extension of the BritRail Pass and works in the following manner.

The SeaPass provides one or two single journeys by Sealink or Hoverspeed hovercraft services between the Continent and Britain. The connecting rail journeys between London and the ports of embarkation/disembarkation to and from the Continent are included in the price of the SeaPass. The SeaPass does not have to be used during the validity of your BritRail Pass, but it must be used within 6 months of date of issue.

For example, the SeaPass—Continental enables holders to stay in London after the expiration of their BritRail Passes and then travel to the Continent by rail and Sealink/Hoverspeed connections at a later date— as long as it is within the 6-month period from date of issue. The reverse, from the Continent via Sealink or Seaspeed and then train to London is also possible. In this case, you can stay in London and sightsee until you are ready to use your BritRail Pass. The SeaPass does not cover train travel on the Continent and the SeaPass issued for travel to and from the Continent cannot be used for similar services to Ireland. A separate SeaPass Ireland is sold for this purpose. Current prices are given on page 311 of this edition.

Hoverlloyd

Hoverlloyd and Seaspeed merged their hovercraft operations under the aegis of *Hoverspeed* in 1981, but Hoverlloyd continues to offer express coach services from Calais to Amsterdam, Brussels, and Paris. The fares are quite reasonable, but no discounts are granted to BritRail or Eurailpass holders. Hoverlloyd's separate services are described in an advertisement in Cook's *Continental Timetable*. Check the Timetable's "List of Advertisers" for the proper page, although it usually appears with Cook's Table 49, which describes the Hoverspeed services.

Other Sealink/SeaPass Routes

In addition to those previously mentioned Sealink routes, there are two more crossings to the Continent that accept the SeaPass—Continental.

Newhaven-Dieppe: If you are looking for an alternate route between Britain and France, Sealink services are available from the English port of Newhaven, east of Brighton, to the maritime terminal of Dieppe in France. The sea route is 71 miles, as compared to the 25-mile span between Dover and Calais. Consequently, the crossing takes 5 hours between Newhaven and Dieppe as compared to the Dover-Calais time enroute of only 1¾ hours.

If the English Channel isn't in a huffy mood, this can be a very pleasant crossing. The French National Railroads' express train service between Dieppe and Paris takes slightly over 2 hours. Thomas Cook's Table 51 carries all the details of this route, including the connecting British and French train schedules. The London terminal is Victoria Station; St. Lazare is the Paris terminal.

Harwich-Hook of Holland: This is an excellent routing for travelers ranging between Britain and The Netherlands. It is the most direct sea link between London and Amsterdam. Convenient connections may also be made from the Hook of Holland (Hoek Van Holland) to Brussels, Belgium.

Both day and night crossings are available on this North Sea route. Sleeping accommodations aboard begin at very modest prices. Reservations for the night crossings are obligatory and should be made well in advance of your journey. Departure out of London is from the Liverpool Street Station. The Thomas Cook *Continental Timetable* carries full information on this routing in Table 66.

Please note again that BritRail Passes alone are not accepted for Sealink or Seaspeed services. Furthermore, SeaPass—Continental does not cover train travel on the Continent or Sealink services to Ireland. A separate pass, SeaPass Ireland, is for that purpose.

Sealink vessels, a combined fleet of British, French, Belgian and The Netherlands registries, composes one of the world's largest passenger-carrying fleets. They link London to Amsterdam, Brussels, Dublin and Paris.

Many of the ferry crossings on the Continent of Europe involve loading the passengers' rail cars aboard the ferry. When this occurs, the passengers need not disembark. But at all ferry ports in Britain, passengers are required to leave the train and board the ferry. Then they board another train after landing. You will find that this change of transportation mode is no great hardship. In fact, it can be a very enjoyable experience by including drinks and dinner aboard the ferry, followed by a chat with fellow passengers. There's no finer place than the salon of a ferry for meeting people. Everyone has a common interest in travel, and everyone is going to the same destination. What better conditions would you want for starting a conversation?

Crossing the Irish Sea is very much like crossing the English Channel, except you cannot forward your luggage on to the Republic of Ireland. What you take is what you carry. So, again, adhere to our admonition to "go lightly" when it comes to luggage.

Visiting Ireland, keep in mind that the Republic of Ireland and Northern Ireland are two separate political states. Northern Ireland is a part of Britain, while the Republic is independent. There are no customs to contend with when arriving in Northern Ireland from England, Scotland or Wales. On the other hand, customs formalities entering the Republic of Ireland should present no problem for the bona fide traveler. The efficient "declare" or "nothing-to-declare" system is used by Irish Customs.

British Rail provides Sealink services to Northern Ireland through Stranraer in Scotland to Larne, with train connections from there to Belfast. From Holyhead in England, Sealink ferries cross to Dun Laoghaire, a suburban port of Dublin; from Fishguard in England, Sealink connects with Rosslare, 100 miles south of Dublin for direct train connections to southern points.

SeaPass Ireland

Similar in nature to the SeaPass issued by British Rail for cross-channel services to the Continent, SeaPass Ireland is an extension of the BritRail Pass offering one or two sea journeys by Sealink shipping services, with connecting rail journeys between London and the ports of embarkation to Ireland. The journeys may be made at any time within the 6-month period from date of issue of the SeaPass. It does not have to be used within the validity period of the holder's BritRail Pass. The SeaPass offers several unusual opportunities. A traveler could journey from Ireland to London, validate the BritRail Pass issued with the SeaPass when convenient, return to London at the expiration of the BritRail Pass, and then—at any time within the 6-month period of validity—use the SeaPass to return to Ireland. Another option offers the traveler the opportunity of an extended visit to Ireland before or after using the BritRail Pass.

By the way, the SeaPass for either the Continent or Ireland is sold only in conjunction with the BritRail Pass. Furthermore, the SeaPass Ireland cannot be used for channel services to the Continent and vice versa. Neither the SeaPass nor the BritRail Pass can be used for train travel in Northern Ireland or the Republic of Ireland to the south.

Current SeaPass prices are given on page 311 in the Appendix of this edition. SeaPass cannot be purchased separately and must be purchased as an extension of the purchaser's regular BritRail Pass.

Sealink service between the ports of Fishguard in England and Rosslare in southern Ireland is by one-class ship. Otherwise, the Sealink ferries crossing from Holyhead, England, to Dun Laoghaire in the Republic of Ireland and the Sealink crossing between Stranraer in Scotland to Northern Ireland via the port of Larne offer both first and second class accommodations. Paying a small supplement will enable you to occupy first class sections if you are holding a second class BritRail Pass/SeaPass combination.

Sea Links to Ireland

Stranraer—Larne. A short crossing of 2 hours, 15 minutes port to port. Larne to Belfast takes another 45 minutes on the train. The BritRail Pass is not accepted on trains in Northern Ireland. Food and beverage services are available aboard. No customs formalities for entering Northern Ireland from Scotland. No tax-free shops aboard. Train connections from London through Euston Station with overnight sleeper service available between London and Stranraer. First and second class accommodations. Direct train service from the Glasgow Central Station, 2½ hours.

Holyhead—Dun Laoghaire. Crossing from Holyhead in Wales to Dun Laoghaire (a suburb of Dublin). The elapsed time from port to port averages 3 hours, 30 minutes. Connections from the port into Dublin can be made by train, city bus, or taxi. All three transportation modes are right at the pier. The BritRail Pass or its extension, SeaPass Ireland, cannot be used for transportation in the Republic of Ireland. The Eurailpass is accepted on the railroads. However, it would not be economical to have your Eurailpass validated for the short ride into Dublin if you plan several days sightseeing there before traveling to other parts of the country by train. Food and beverage services are available aboard the ferries and tax-free shops are open during the crossing. Customs formalities are observed upon disembarkation. Train connections from London's Euston Station to Holyhead provide through-coach and sleeper accommodations. First and second class accommodations aboard the ferries.

Fishguard—Rosslare. This ferry crossing is recommended for train travelers bound for Cork, Killarney and the Shannon Airport. Crossing takes 3 hours, 45 minutes port to port. Food, beverages, and tax-free shops available during the voyage. One-class service. Customs formalities observed at disembarkation. Daytime train service only from Paddington Station in London. Train time between London and Fishguard is 6 hours.

Big Ben, London's most famous landmark, stands in the clock tower of the Houses of Parliament (officially known as the Palace of Westminster). Actually, it's the bell, not the clock, which is called Big Ben. The 13½-ton bell's name is in honor of Sir Ben Hall, Commissioner of Works in 1858.

"When a man is tired of London," wrote Samuel Johnson, "he is tired of life; for there is in London all that life can afford." London is a wonderful mixture of ancient elegance and modern technology, of outdated traditions and contemporary inconveniences. While plumed guardsmen mount jet-black horses in Whitehall, bankers examine computer print-outs on Lombard Street.

London sits astride the Thames River about 40 miles inland from its estuary on the North Sea. One of the largest cities in the world, London, like a typically modern megalopolis, has failed to come to terms with the present century, yet has managed to preserve many of the virtues of those past.

It is difficult to get the first-time visitor to Britain interested in anything other than London until he has seen the great city. Despite the fact that London is Europe's largest city, most of its historic sights are clustered around a rather compact area. A reasonable stroll will take you past the Houses of Parliament and its clock tower housing Big Ben, Westminster Abbey, Whitehall, No. 10 Downing Street, Buckingham Palace, and Trafalgar Square. If strolling is not your thing, then you can take the advice that Prime Minister Gladstone once gave a group of American tourists, "See London from the top of a bus." London Transport makes this very convenient by running buses around a 20-mile circular tour in about 2 hours' time, during which they pass most of London's major landmarks.

After you have seen London, follow on by seeing more of this wonderful country of Britain where, among many of its advantages, everyone speaks your language—well, almost everyone! You cannot get to know the country without experiencing the attractive charms of its other cities and seeing firsthand the loveliness of the rural areas that separate them. There is no better way to do this than to view the passing scene and to converse with the British themselves—aboard a train!

DAY EXCURSIONS

Like the road builders of Rome, Britain's rail builders laid their tracks leading to London—or, more properly, out of London. Picture, if you will, London as the center of a somewhat lopsided spider web with its radials running east and south to the sea on the short side of the web and the longer extensions running west to Wales and north into Scotland. Thirty-two day excursions await your pleasure out of London. They have been selected for a variety of reasons—varied reader interest being the main consideration—but any "mix" should certainly provide the desired cross-section of this green and pleasant land.

Like a knight of old, perhaps you would prefer to sally forth on a short sortie before departing on a crusade. In that case, you will find the Greenwich, Windsor, and St. Albans day excursions to your liking. Ranging southeast out of London, Kent beckons with its towns of Canterbury, Dover, Folkestone and Ramsgate. Southward, rail trails lead along the English Channel and the port/resort towns of Hastings, Brighton, Portsmouth, Southampton, and the Isle of Wight.

West from London, excursions to Salisbury and Stonehenge, Bath, Gloucester, and Cardiff (Wales) await the train travelers. Ready to crusade? Go further west to the pilgrims' Plymouth or the pirates' Penzance. (You may want to make these "out-and-back" visits.) In the heart of England you will find excursions awaiting you to Birmingham, Stratford-upon-Avon, Coventry, Nottingham, Sheffield, Lincoln and York, and more westerly, to Chester.

Northeast of London in East Anglia, historic King's Lynn, Bury St. Edmunds and Ipswich wait to greet you. For the academic flavor of the country, you may want to visit Cambridge or Oxford (or both) for the cap-and-gown atmosphere. School-tie types will appreciate Eton, a stone's throw away from Windsor.

Select your day excursions carefully. Don't rush—take time to enjoy the flowers!

ARRIVING AND DEPARTING

By Air: London has two international airports, Gatwick and Heathrow. The latter handles nearly 24 million passengers a year through its three terminals. Gatwick, second largest in Britain, has more than 7 million passengers using its facilities annually.

Heathrow is connected to London's Underground (subway). The time enroute from the Heathrow Central Underground Station to Piccadilly Circus is 47 minutes. The fare is £1.55; BritRail passes are *not* accepted. Trains run every 4 minutes at peak times and every 8 to 10 minutes during off-peak hours and Sundays. The airport's terminals connect with the Underground station by moving walkways, where you will find a Travel Information Center operating daily from 0800-2130 (summer), 0800-1930 (winter). Services include tourist information, BritRail Pass validation, hotel bookings, plus a currency exchange. *Only British currency is accepted on the Underground.* British Rail operates express motor coaches connecting Heathrow with its train services. There is a rail service counter in each of the airport's terminals where you can validate your BritRail Pass for use on the system.

A word of caution: If you cannot carry all of your luggage, travel to London on one of the motor coaches operated by the major airlines, or take a taxi. The average taxi fare from Heathrow to central London (15 miles) is £9.00 plus tip.

Gatwick Airport has its own rail station within the airport complex. Victoria Station in London is less than 40 minutes away from Gatwick by fast train. The fare is £2.10; BritRail Passes *are* accepted. Trains depart every 15 minutes between 0600 and 2400 and hourly throughout the night. There is no regular airline bus service to Gatwick, although some charter flights provide motor coach connections. London taxicabs are not available. There are a British Rail information desk in the international arrivals hall and currency exchanges in both departure and arrival halls.

London taxi stands briefly in front of Eros Fountain in the center of London's most celebrated traffic circle, Piccadilly Circus. The steps of the fountain were at one time the "marketplace" of London's flower sellers. Officially, the fountain is a memorial to the philanthropist Lord Shaftesbury.

By Train: Even though you arrive in London by air, you most probably will utilize some form of rail transportation to reach the center of the city in order to check in with the facilities of the London Tourist Board. If you go to London by Underground and do not utilize the Heathrow Information Center, transfer from the Piccadilly Line to the Victoria Line at Green Park, one stop before Piccadilly Circus, and ride one stop south to Victoria Station for information services.

From Gatwick Airport, trains terminate in Victoria Station. The London Tourist Board's information and accommodations center is adjacent to platform 15 in the station. At the opposite side of the hall, under a "Hotels" sign, a free reservations service for London's hotels is available. Two currency exchange facilities, the National Westminster Bank and Thomas Cook, are also in the station complex. For other than accommodations, the London Tourist Board also operates an office in Grosvenor Gardens, 200 yards from the station—just follow the "i" signs. Should you choose to use the British Rail motor coach-train services from Heathrow via the Feltham rail station, you will arrive in London's Waterloo Station. Since there are two Underground routes connecting Waterloo and Victoria Stations, we suggest you make inquiry at the Underground ticket barrier in Waterloo before proceeding.

Coming from the channel ports of Dover or Folkestone, you will arrive in Victoria Station. Such is not the case should you arrive in London after crossing from Northern Ireland through Stranraer or the Republic of Ireland through Holyhead. In this case, your arrival station will be Euston Station, where you can easily connect with the Victoria Underground Line. Passengers traveling from Ireland through Fishguard will terminate in London's Paddington Station. The Circle Line of the London Underground connects Paddington Station with Victoria. All major Underground stations in London have travel information centers.

LONDON'S TRAIN STATIONS

If the major cities of the world were to enter a train station contest, London would win! Perhaps a glance at the London Station Plan on page 296 of this edition would be helpful at this point as we try to put things into order verbally. You will note a total of 15 stations listed in the plan, which looks very much like a quarter-back's option play for the Pittsburgh Steelers! For the sake of brevity, we will reduce the number of station descriptions to the manageable number of 8—those stations of major arrivals, departures, and *Britain by BritRail* day excursions out of London.

By the way, you can take heart! All of the major train terminals of London are linked by the London Underground, principally by the Circle Line. For a quick reference, check the Inter-Terminal Plan on page 297 of this edition.

Victoria Station handles all Sealink services to the Continent via the channel ports of Dover and Folkestone. A special Sealink Travel Center is located on platform 2 to cater to the more than 2 million passengers who pass through Victoria Station every year on their way to and from the Continent. Victoria Station is the gateway to Gatwick Airport. A "Next Train to Gatwick Airport" indicator is located between platforms 9 and 15 to assist air/rail travelers. Train departures for connections to the Continent are also displayed in this area. Most important to *Britain By BritRail* readers is the location of the London Tourist Board's information center adjacent to platform 15. Victoria is the only train station in the London area with these facilities. It is also one of the few London stations providing currency exchange facilities within the station. "Operation Victoria," an immense program to modernize the station and its track system, has been in progress since 1977. Planned for completion in 1984, Victoria Station is staying in step with the times. Inconveniences during this modernization are being held to a minimum.

Euston Station is closely grouped with St. Pancras and King's Cross Stations for rail services to England's Midlands, northern England, and Scotland. Euston Station is one of the most modern facilities in the British Rail system. It is the Sealink terminal for services to Belfast via Stranraer and to Dublin via Holyhead. It is also the London departure point for the all-electric hauled Inter-City trains to Glasgow. As you face the train departure/arrival announcement board in the Euston Station, the Travel Center will be on your left. The train information windows are 12 and 13; hotel bookings (for Dun & Bradstreet rated hotels only) may be obtained at windows 16 and 17. Other windows, according to their signs, provide sleeper and seat reservations, air tickets, special events reservations—even a special information window for travel to Ireland. In general (although some functions operate at different hours), the Travel Center in Euston Station is open year-round from Monday–Saturday, 0700–2330; Sunday, 0800–2330. Waiting rooms, restaurants, and other conveniences are located on the far side of the station hall from the Travel Center. A Barclays Bank operates Monday–Friday, 0930–1530, on a pedestrian esplanade beyond the restaurants.

St. Pancras Station is undergoing major repairs which are scheduled for completion by 1982 to coincide with the introduction of all-electric services between London and Bedford. Every facility within the station has a "temporary" look about it. However, services are being maintained at a minimum of inconvenience. Directional signs for the Euston and King's Cross Stations, plus the London Underground, are strategically placed throughout the station area. After exiting the St. Pancras Station, a stairway to the left leads to a Thomas Cook office which operates Monday through Friday between 0900–1700 and on Saturday between 1000–1200. Immediately across from the Thomas Cook office, you will also find a Midland Bank and a Barclay Bank for currency exchange and other banking needs.

London's Tower Bridge has remained in constant service since its construction between 1886 and 1894. The huge bascule sections of the drawbridge remain in operation although the footbridge at the top has been closed for some time. Lying at anchor (right foreground) for exhibition is the cruiser *HMS Belfast*, a ship of the line in the D-Day invasion of Normandy.

Charing Cross Station is under extensive renovation. Direct train service to Folkestone is provided, plus connections at Dover (Priory) for the Hoverspeed hovercraft services from Dover to Boulogne and Calais on the Continent.

King's Cross Station is the London terminal for Inter-City 125 train service to Aberdeen and Edinburgh. The station's Travel Center provides its major services from 0700-2300 daily, with its hotel bookings section closing at 1900. Full information, reservations, and advance ticketing services are available. Outside the station, to the left, a Bureau de Change is open daily from 0800 to 2000.

Paddington Station serves the west with its Inter-City 125 service through Plymouth to Penzance. It is also the London terminal for Sealink services to Ireland via the ports of Fishguard and Rosslare. All facilities operated within the station are exceptionally well marked with overhead signs and directional signals. Paddington's Travel Center to the left of platform 1 is in operation from 0800 to 2130 Mondays through Saturdays, and 0900 to 2000 on Sundays. Three banks (Barclay, Midland, and Westminster) are close to the station on Craven Road.

Liverpool Street Station is a cavernous structure with its various facilities scattered about in a profusion of locations. The best means of orientation we have found are the station's porters who obligingly will point out or escort you to anything you're looking for. (For this, a tip is welcomed, but not mandatory.) The Travel Center has the same hours of operation as Paddington. Train service from Liverpool Street Station serves England's eastern counties.

Waterloo Station is primarily for trains to the south of England, including the Isle of Wight. Its Travel Center is located at the end of tracks 15 and 16, opposite the Underground entrance. The center operates 0800-2200, seven days a week. A Westminster Bank facility is situated between tracks 18 and 19. A station map is positioned at track 13.

LONDON'S VISITOR SERVICES

"Everything should be made as simple as possible," wrote Albert Einstein, "but not simpler." It would appear that this is the organizational pattern of London's Tourist Board. Its personnel are trained to professionally respond to the basic questions asked them by visitors: "Where can we stay tonight?" "How do we get there?" "What's going on in London?" "Where are the sights?"

These are the primary points of contact with the London Tourist Board and their hours of operation:

Victoria Station, adjacent to platform 15. Summer hours, 0745–2215 daily; winter hours, 0900–2030 daily. Services available: visitor information, accommodations, free and salable publications, tourist tickets for bus and Underground.

Heathrow Central Station. Summer hours, 0800–2100; winter hours, 0800–1930. Services available: same as Victoria Station, except tourist ticket sales.

Selfridges, Oxford Street, ground floor. Open during normal store hours. Services available: visitor information, free and salable publications, tourist tickets for bus and Underground, sightseeing/tour tickets.

Harrods, Knightsbridge, 4th floor. Open during normal store hours. Services available: same as Selfridges. (Macy's *does* tell Gimbels!)

Telephone Information Service. Call 01-730-0791 Monday–Friday, 0900–1730, or TELETOURIST 01-246-8041 (24-hour service). Services available: selection of attractions and special events.

Tourist Information Center and Bookshop, 26 Grosvenor Gardens (5 minutes' walk from Victoria Station). Summer hours, 0900–1830 daily; winter hours, Monday–Friday, 0900–1700. Services available: visitors' information on London and other parts of England, theater and sightseeing tickets, free and salable literature, tourist tickets for bus and Underground. (For accommodations, go to Victoria Station.)

LONDON'S VISITOR INFORMATION

Hotel Accommodations may be obtained in advance by writing to the London Tourist Board, Tourist Information Center, 26 Grosvenor Gardens, SW1, London, England, at least 6 weeks before your planned arrival date. Reservations upon arrival are handled at the information centers at Victoria Station and Heathrow Central. A £4.00 deposit must be paid with the reservation, which is deductible from your hotel bill.

Accommodations may be booked on the day needed at the London Tourist Board's tourist information centers at Victoria Station and Heathrow Airport. A deposit of £4.00, deductible from the hotel bill, is required at the time of the booking. Additionally, a booking-fee service charge of £1.00 will be made. Hotel and guest-house bookings start at £4.50 per person.

Licensing Hours in central London are between 1130–1500 and 1730–2300 Monday through Saturday. If you are staying in a licensed hotel, you may order alcoholic beverages at any time. In a licensed restaurant, you may order alcoholic beverages with your meals outside of normal licensing hours.

Banking Hours are normally from 0930 to 1530, Monday through Friday. Other exchange facilities at railway stations and airports are open longer hours.

British Rail Travel Centers are located at Lower Regent Street, SW1; Oxford Street, W1; The Strand, WC2; and Victoria Street, SW1. Hours of operation are 0900–1700 Monday through Friday. No telephone service. Domestic British Rail tickets and British Transport Hotel (BTH) bookings available. Tickets for Seaspeed, Sealink and Continental Europe available only from Lower Regent Street Travel Center.

London Taxis may be hailed if the yellow "For Hire" sign is lit up. Fares and supplemental charges are displayed inside the cab. For radio taxi service, telephone 01-286-4848, 01-272-3030, or 01-286-6010. (Disregard the "01" part of the telephone number when dialing from within London.)

Royal Guardsmen, hallmark of Britain's allegiance to her sovereign, stand duty at royal buildings and residences. The regimental identification of the guards, who traditionally wear the bearskin, scarlet tunic and dark blue trousers, is distinguished by badges, buttons and various insignia.

LONDON–EDINBURGH TRAIN SERVICE

(First & second class accommodations for all services listed.)

DEPART FROM KING'S CROSS STATION*	ARRIVE IN EDINBURGH			
	Weekdays	Saturdays	Sundays	NOTES
0100	0923	Same	N/S	(2)
0800	1302	Same	N/S	(1)
0900	1412	Same	N/S	(1)
1000	1443	Same	1540	(1)
1100	1558	Same	1638	(1)
1200	1648	Same	1735	(1)
1300	1803	Same	1830	(1)
1400	1849	Same	1927	(1)
1500	2003	Same	2023	(1)
1600	2049	Same	N/S	(1)
1700	2207	Same	2157	(1)
1800	2307	2316	2259	(1)
2215	N/S	0717	N/S	(3)
2230	0557	0832	N/S	
2355	0657	0945	0700	(3)

Distance: 393 miles/632 km

References: British Rail Table 26
Thomas Cook Table 575

*See Appendix, page 296, for London station plan

N/S—No Service

(1) High-speed train, food service available
(2) Sleeping cars to Newcastle, regular coaches Newcastle-Edinburgh
(3) Sleeping cars only
(4) Sleeping cars and regular coaches

USEFUL PHONE NUMBERS

Edinburgh Tourist Information Office
All Scotland: 031-332-2433
Local Information: 031-226-6591
Accommodations: 031-1225-8821
Train Information
London Information: 01-278-2477
London Talking Timetable: 01-278-8201
Edinburgh Information: 031-556-2451

GETTING AROUND IN LONDON

London has been described as "a whole world wrapped up in a unique city." For sightseeing in London during your visit, London Transport has many convenient, time-saving ways for you to see the city. The fastest, get-acquainted mode of seeing London's highlights is the "Round London Sightseeing Tour" by bus. In about 2 hours, it passes most of London's major landmarks. There is no guide, but a free illustrated map points out what to look for. After your tour, you can then go back to those places of particular interest for a closer look.

You may start your "Round London Sightseeing Tour" from any one of three points: Piccadilly Circus, the Speakers' Corner at Marble Arch, or Grosvenor Gardens. Look for signs reading "Starting Point of the Round London Sightseeing Tour." The tour covers a 20-mile circular course (fare for adults, £2.00; children under 15, £1.30). Pay as you board the bus; tickets are not sold in advance. Buses run daily (except on Christmas Day) at least every hour as follows: summer (April–September), 0900–2000; winter (October–March), 1000–1600. The tour is included when you purchase a "Go-As-You-Please" ticket.

The "Go-As-You-Please" ticket will make your London visit smoother, faster, and more enjoyable. It gives you 3, 4, 7, or 14 days of unlimited travel on all London red buses and the Underground.

A helpful adjunct to the "Go-As-You-Please" ticket is the "Open-To-View" ticket, which admits purchasers to hundreds of Britain's major historic sights for 1 month. Both tickets may be purchased at any of the London Transport Travel Information Centers in the city. They are open daily from 0830–2130. You may telephone for information on 01-222-1234 any time day or night. You may also purchase vouchers for both tickets from any BritRail Travel International office in the United States or Canada prior to your trip. (See page 311 of this edition.)

LONDON-GLASGOW TRAIN SERVICE
(First & second class accommodations for all services listed.)

DEPART FROM EUSTON STATION*	ARRIVE IN GLASGOW CENTRAL			
	Weekdays	Saturdays	Sundays	NOTES
0735	1249	N/S	N/S	(1) (4)
0805	1341	Same	N/S	(1)
0940	1511	Same	N/S	(1)
1045	1611	N/S	1833	(1)
1245	1807	Same	N/S	(1)
1400	1954	Same	N/S	(1)
1445	2013	Same	N/S	(1)
1645	2208	Same	N/S	(1)
1745	2201	Same	N/S	(1)
2300	0708	0811	0708	(1)
2330	0608	0825	0608	(2) (3)

Distance: 402 miles/647 km
References: British Rail Table 65
            Thomas Cook Table 565

*See Appendix, page 296, for London station plan
N/S—No Service

(1) Food service available
(2) Sleeping cars only
(3) Passengers may remain aboard until 0730
(4) Reservations obligatory

USEFUL PHONE NUMBERS
Glasgow Tourist Information Office
All Scotland: 031-332-2433
Local Information: 041-221-7371/2 and
221-6136/7

Train Information
London Information: 01-387-7070
Talking Timetable: 01-388-7984
Glasgow Information: 041-221-3223

British Transport Hotels
Central Reservations Service (London): 01-278-4211
Scotland (Glasgow): 041-221-3945

The Great Roman Bath attracted visitors from all parts of the Roman Empire between the first and fifth centuries. It was constructed around a natural hot spring which rises from the ground at 124°F (51°C). The abbey church tower of Bath looms in the background.

From London ...

A DAY EXCURSION TO BATH

DISTANCE BY TRAIN: 107 miles (172 km)
AVERAGE TRAIN TIME: 1 hour, 20 min.

Bath has been in the limelight of social attention during two eras of recorded history—once during the Roman occupation of Britain and again in the 18th century when Bath became the "in place" for royalty and other well-to-do's. Development of the only hot spring in Britain is attributed to the Romans soon after Emperor Claudius invaded the land in 43A.D. The second revitalization of the city, a cultural one, began in 1705 with the arrival of 31-year-old Richard Nash. Like the Romans, he too conquered, but not by force. Nash was Bath's first public relations expert. When he died at the age of 88, he had created a kingdom of taste and etiquette over which he reigned as Beau Nash, King of Bath.

To the Romans, the city's name was *Aquae Sulis*—literally translated, "sulfur springs." By the end of the first century, a great bathing facility had been established. The magnificent hot baths made *Aquae Sulis* famous throughout the Empire. Its fame lasted 400 years until the rising sea level and the fall of the Roman Empire brought the city's prosperity to an end. By the end of the 17th century, the city was described as "a ghostly ruin with crumbled masonry fallen into dark pools, overgrown and bird haunted, but still a wondrous sight." The Roman ruins remained buried, even during the times of Beau Nash, although the gilded bronze head of Minerva was uncovered by workmen while digging a sewer in 1727.

The restoration of Bath's Roman past and the combining of the city's two eras of fame finally began in 1878 when the city engineer, while investigating a water leak, came upon the Roman reservoir and the huge complex of baths which it fed. In other words, someone finally called a plumber!

A Day Excursion From London

DEPART FROM PADDINGTON STATION*	ARRIVE IN BATH SPA STATION†	NOTES
0720	0842	(1) (2) (3)
0820	0930	(1) (2) (3)
0920	1028	(1) (2) (3)
0945	1112	(1) (2) (3)
0945	1129	(3) (4)

(Plus other frequent service)

DEPART FROM BATH SPA STATION	ARRIVE IN PADDINGTON STATION	
1622	1747	(1) (2) (3)
1722	1841	(1) (2) (3)
1942	2116	(1) (3)
2022	2152	(1) (2) (3)

(Plus other frequent service)

Distance: 107 miles/172 km
References: British Rail Table 127
Thomas Cook Table 535

* See Appendix, page 296, for London station plan
† Travellers-Fare catering facility

(1) Daily, except Sundays and holidays
(2) Food service available
(3) High-speed train
(4) Sundays and holidays only

Train Information
Bath Train Station: 0225-63075
Inter-City Services: 01-262-6767

Talking Timetable
London-Bath: 01-402-1171

Bath abounds in sightseeing opportunities. Proceed to Bath's tourist information center after arrival and let them assist you in your visit. During summer, their hours of operation are Monday-Saturday, 1000-2000; Sunday, 1400-2000. Winter hours are 1000-1700 Monday-Saturday. The center books local accommodation too, should you succumb to Bath's charms and decide to stay awhile.

To reach the tourist information center, proceed up Manvers Street, directly in front of the Bath train station, until you cross North Parade Street. From here, the Bath abbey looms into view on your left, and you'll find the information center by passing to the rear of the abbey via its right side.

The tourist information center has a wealth of information. We suggest you consider purchasing at least two of the publications on sale there. First is the beautifully illustrated *Official Guidebook*. You'll want to show it to the folks back home. The other is a 4-page pamphlet, "Walks Around Bath." This informative paper details two different walks around the city. The *Official Guidebook* also devotes a part of its pages to "Wandering Through Bath," for a third alternate walking tour.

While on the subject of walking tours, check to see if you may avail yourself of the Mayor's Corps of Honorary Guides. They conduct tours at various times throughout the summer season at no charge. The tours, which depart from the abbey churchyard, are approximately 1½ hours. If you're on a tight schedule, the best sights in Bath are in the same area as the information center. The Roman baths and the abbey practically adjoin each other. Upstairs from the baths, the Pump Room is the place to sample the waters from the hot spring—if you dare. If you miss the Pump Room, there is a fountain dispensing the same water in Stall Street just outside. During your visit to the Roman baths, take time to touch the worn paving and run your hand along the lead lining of the pools. In that moment, you can recall the glory that was Rome.

Stately statue of Britain's Queen Victoria overlooks the plaza fronting Birmingham's Council House. One of the world's great industrial cities, Birmingham has made spectacular strides in developing itself as a beautiful residential city and is no longer England's "ugly duckling."

A DAY EXCURSION TO BIRMINGHAM

DISTANCE BY TRAIN: 119 miles (191 km)
AVERAGE TRAIN TIME: 1 hour, 35 min.

Birmingham has more canals than Venice. This is rather unusual because Birmingham claims to be Britain's "city at the center." Although it is in the approximate geographic center of the British Isles, it was once the center of England's waterways which carried most of the nations' industrial traffic. With the development of other forms of transportation, particularly rail, canal transportation dissipated. Many have been developed into recreation areas with walks, pubs, and restored buildings along their right-of-ways.

For decades, Birmingham has been internationally recognized as one of the world's great industrial cities. Along with the recognition came the image of a smoke-filled, grimy, Victorian sprawl of a city. Since WWII, Birmingham has made spectacular progress in developing a beautiful residential city. The center of the city has been completely rebuilt. One of the newest landmarks marking the city center is the Rotunda, a 250-foot tower. Beneath the tower is the "bull ring," the most spectacular shopping center in Europe. The multilevel, temperature-controlled bull ring shopping center is completely traffic-free and linked by subways with major shopping streets of the city. It connects directly with the New Street train station where you will arrive from London on your day excursion. If you experience difficulty in gaining your bearings in the vast New Street Station, consult the Travel Center (train information) in the station's main hall on the extreme far right as you exit from the train platforms.

To reach the Birmingham tourist information center at 110 Colmore Row, make your way to Victoria Square from the station. The office is open Monday-Friday, 0845–1715; closed Saturday and Sunday.

BIRMINGHAM—*HEART OF ENGLAND*

A Day Excursion From London

DEPART FROM EUSTON STATION*	ARRIVE IN BIRMINGHAM NEW STREET STATION†	NOTES
0835	1013	(1) (2)
0935	1114	(1) (2)
0940	1144	(2) (3)
1040	1222	(1) (2)

(Plus other frequent service)

DEPART FROM BIRMINGHAM NEW STREET STATION	ARRIVE IN EUSTON STATION	
1548	1736	(1) (2)
1718	1901	(1) (2)
1748	1933	(2) (3)
1929	2111	(1) (2)

(Plus other frequent service)

Distance: 119 miles/191 km
References: British Rail Table 66
Thomas Cook Table 552

* See Appendix, page 296, for London station plan
† Travellers-Fare catering facility

(1) Daily, except Sundays and holidays
(2) Food service available
(3) Sundays and holidays only

Train Information
New Street Station: 021-643-2711
Inter-City Services: 01-387-7070

Talking Timetable
London-Birmingham: 01-388-4064

Something unusual in the development of a modern city is Birmingham's National Exhibition Center. For years the exhibition centers in continental Europe lured the larger trade fairs. Now Britain has its own showcase at Bickenhill, only 1 hour and 20 minutes from London by Inter-City Trains. This modern exhibition and conference center is on a 310-acre site readily accessible by rail. Rail connections to the exhibition center may be made through the New Street Station on any train departing in the direction of London. The stop, Birmingham International, is a short 17-20-minute ride. Obtain full details from the tourist information center. The exhibition site has five halls grouped around a central plaza. A sixth hall that is separate from the main complex has been designed for small exhibitions. Restaurants and bars are located throughout the complex and two new hotels rest in a lakeside setting on the southeast side. There is an information bureau in the exhibition center for out-of-town visitors going directly to the exhibition site.

Check with the city tourist information center concerning a walking tour. In spite of a massive redevelopment program to reconstruct after WWII, the best of the old has been carefully preserved. The city has an interesting skyline. Historic buildings appear unexpectedly among the new in a way that emphasizes the quality of both. Worthy of a visit for their classic elegance are the Town Hall and the Council House. Other historic buildings close to the city center are the Sarehole Mill at Hall Green, an 18th century water mill restored to working order, and Blakesley Hall, a 17th century timber-framed yeoman's house furnished in period style and with an interesting garden. For rail buffs, a visit to the science museum is a must. It houses the earliest English locomotive actually built (1734).

Birmingham has undergone many structural changes in recent years and undoubtedly, it is becoming one of Europe's outstanding cities.

Brighton's Royal Pavilion, onion-domed creation and seaside home of England's King George IV, still contains most of its original furnishings. Each summer, the Banqueting Room is set out with period glass and gold plates in the festive style of an era past.

From London ...

A DAY EXCURSION TO BRIGHTON

DISTANCE BY TRAIN: 51 miles (82 km)
AVERAGE TRAIN TIME: 55 minutes

The British have mixed emotions regarding their country's best-known seaside resort. For some, Brighton is everything that is wrong with England's southern coast. Other British avoid it for its "tackiness," and in some circles of society, it is known as a "tourist purgatory." With all this, it's a small wonder that anyone goes to Brighton at all—but they do and in droves!

Perhaps Brighton would have remained a tiny, humble fishing village originally known as Brighteimstone if it were not for the efforts of Dr. Richard Russell and the Prince Regent (who later became King George IV). In 1750 Dr. Russell, a Brighton resident, published a book extolling the magical effects of sea air and salt water. This started a fashionable trend that brought royalty and commoner alike to Brighton. The gifted and wayward prince first visited Brighton in 1783. Enamored by it all (and well-heeled with royal funds), he ordered his Royal Pavilion constructed there. Completed in 1822, it has been termed the most bizarre and exotic palace in all Europe. The pavilion's ostentatious onion-domed exterior, looking very much like a series of hot air balloons about to ascend, is only surpassed by its even more amazing interior. It is fully furnished in its original style and open to the public daily. Queen Victoria, not at all amused by the pavilion's architecture, calculatedly was permitting it to fall to ruin when Brighton's citizenry saved it from demolition in 1850.

The city maintains "the lanes," where you take a step backwards into the old fishing village days. The buildings in these narrow, twisting passages were fishermen's cottages in the 17th century. Now, they are quaint shops selling antiques and curios.

BRIGHTON—*COLORFUL SEASIDE RESORT*

A Day Excursion From London

DEPART FROM VICTORIA STATION*	ARRIVE IN BRIGHTON†	NOTES
0818	0942	(1) (3)
0936	1048	(1)
1008	1106	(1)
1208	1306	(1) (2)

(Plus other frequent service)

DEPART FROM BRIGHTON	ARRIVE IN VICTORIA STATION	
1634	1736	(1) (2)
1734	1833	(1) (2)
1934	2033	(1) (3)
2138	2301	(1) (3)

(Plus other frequent service)

Distance: 51 miles/82 km
References: British Rail Table 186
                   Thomas Cook Table 518

* See Appendix, page 296, for London station plan
† Travellers-Fare catering facility

(1) Daily, including holidays
(2) Food service available
(3) Food service available Monday through Friday.

Train Information
Brighton Train Station: 0273-25476
Inter-City Services: 01-928-5100

The architecture of Brighton's train terminal reflects the town's 19th century motif. There is a manually operated dispatch board of wood construction at the head of the train platforms. Quaint, original, and still operational, it bears inspecting. The station's rail information center is located at the head of platform 6. As you exit the station, you'll find the taxi queue ahead and on the left. The city bus information kiosk is on the right. A bus departs for the main tourist information center every 30 minutes, or you can begin walking down Queen Street to the sea. A leisurely pace will bring you to the tourist information kiosk at the sea wall within 10 minutes. The kiosk is open from Easter through September from 1000-1800 daily.

The main tourist information center is located at Marlboro House, 54 Old Steine Road. Old Steine Road begins at the gate to the Palace Pier, which is east of the kiosk along Grand Junction Road. The center is open Monday-Friday, 0900-1700; Saturday, 0900-1230; and closed Sunday. The Royal Pavilion lies a short distance away on the left-hand side of Old Steine Road.

If you'd like to participate in a guided walking tour of Brighton's "Old Town," obtain details from the information center. From June through mid-September, the tours start at Marlboro House. Or, you can pick up the Brighton "Mini Guide" at the main information center. The "Mini Guide" features a town plan showing where to go and what to see.

Brighton's shopping center, including the new Churchill Square Pedestrian Precinct, is one of the largest in southern England. The kids will love the aquarium, dolphinarium and Peter Pan's playground. Young and old alike should take a ride along the sea front on the Volks Railway, Britain's first public electric railway.

If you get caught up in Brighton's festive mood, you can check with the tourist kiosk for accommodations and catch a morning train back to London.

"Fowl play" did not this tower tumble! In 1327 the Abbey of St. Edmunds was destroyed by townspeople protesting monastic control. Earlier, in 1214, English barons swore before the Abbey's high altar to force King John to ratify the Magna Charta—which he did the following year.

94

From London ...

A DAY EXCURSION TO BURY ST. EDMUNDS

DISTANCE BY TRAIN: 74 miles (119 km)
AVERAGE TRAIN TIME: 2 hours

In his *Pickwick Papers*, Charles Dickens described Bury St. Edmunds as " ... a handsome little town of thriving and cleanly apearance." So it remains today. A monastery was built on the present site of Bury St. Edmunds in 633 A.D. The town gained its name in 903, when 33 years after being killed by the Danes at Hoxne, the body of King Edmund of East Anglia was brought to the town by Bishop Theodred. The first abbey church was built soon afterwards to honor the memory of the King. For many, Bury St. Edmunds is regarded as one of the most famous towns in all England. In 1214, barons gathered at the high altar of the abbey to take a solemn oath to force King John to grant a charter of liberties. This was regarded as one of the events leading to the granting of the Magna Charta in 1215.

The town center is most notable for its pleasant Georgian atmosphere, recalling the days when the town was a leading social center within East Anglia. The great abbey was one of the largest churches in Europe at one time. In 1327 it was sacked by the townspeople protesting against monastic control and again in 1381 during the Peasants' Revolt. In 1465 a severe fire damaged the church, which had to be extensively repaired. It was subsequently robbed of much of its stone for use in building materials in the town. A placard on the abbey gate indicates that the gate was destroyed along with the abbey by the townspeople in 1327, but was rebuilt in 1347. It is apparently the only structure that was rebuilt out of the entire enclosure compound.

Across from the abbey gate is the Angel Hotel, more than 500 years old, known for its association with Charles Dickens. His room, No. 15, is preserved exactly as it was more than a century ago.

BURY ST. EDMUNDS—*MAGNA CHARTA*

A Day Excursion From London

DEPART FROM LIVERPOOL STREET STATION*	ARRIVE IN BURY ST. EDMUNDS†	NOTES
0836	1030	(1)
0936	1130	(2)
1036	1334	(3)

DEPART FROM BURY ST. EDMUNDS	ARRIVE IN LIVERPOOL STREET STATION	
1529	1805	(1)
1646	1935	(4)
1756	2311	(2)

Distance: 74 miles/119 km
References: British Rail Table 15
              Thomas Cook Tables 585, 589

* See Appendix, page 296, for London station plan
† Via Cambridge, service thru Ipswich also available. See British Rail Table 15 or make inquiries with train information personnel.

(1) Daily, including holidays
(2) Sundays and holidays only
(3) Monday through Friday only, except holidays
(4) Daily, except Sundays and holidays

Bury St. Edmunds Tourist Information Office (N)
Summer: 0284-64667
Winter: 0284-63233

During WWII, Bury St. Edmunds was ringed with American air bases. Today, the Third Air Force of the U.S. Air Force European Command operates RAF Mildenhall, west of Bury St. Edmunds. Visitors are welcome at the base but are advised to contact the base information office or its community relations advisor before proceeding there. The tourist information center can provide complete details.

The tourist information center stands immediately inside the abbey gate entrance to the ruins of St. Edmunds Abbey, a short distance from the train station. Station personnel will gladly provide directions. The information center, which is still housed in a temporary structure, is open during the summer months only. Hours are Monday, 1000–1600; Tuesday-Friday, 1000–1730; Saturday, 1000–1600; closed Sundays.

Sightseeing in Bury St. Edmunds is, of course, highlighted by the abbey ruins and gardens. St. Mary's Church which borders the southern boundary of the abbey grounds is also a popular visiting spot. The Burrow Museum is an interesting building, constructed in the latter part of the 12th century as Moyses Hall. It is a fine example of Norman domestic architecture. Before becoming a museum, the hall was used for many purposes, including a house of correction and a police station.

There are two distinct parts to the town. As was customary in most medieval towns with a monastic foundation, there was a physical division between the monastery and the townspeople. This division resulted in the business section and public buildings standing on a hill to the west of the abbey ruins today.

Bypassed by time, Bury St. Edmunds is essentially a country town that was spared the industrial expansion of the Victorian Age. One of the local products is its ale. We suggest you take a pint in the Nut Shell, the smallest pub in England. Its single bar measures 12 feet by 7 feet!

King's College Chapel in Cambridge, universally known as one of the world's finest architectural structures, took 70 years to build.

The "backs," that portion of the River Cam passing the college buildings and gardens, is ideal for a placid boat tour of Cambridge.

From London ...

A DAY EXCURSION TO CAMBRIDGE

DISTANCE BY TRAIN: 56 miles (90 km)
AVERAGE TRAIN TIME: 1 hour, 10 min.

Oxford graduates often refer to Cambridge as "that other university." Both universities hold one thing in common—they are organized along the classic federal structure of the university in which are grouped a number of largely autonomous colleges. Comparisons stop here. Cambridge is Britain's "university city." It is said that if you visit only one other English city besides London, it should be Cambridge.

Cambridge is situated on the River Cam around the original bridge through which all trade and communications passed between central England and East Anglia and then on to continental Europe 1000 years ago. It was a natural spot for travelers to pause to exchange news and opinions, thereby preparing the ground for a center of learning.

During the summer from Easter to October, there are daily tours of the colleges with qualified guides who can tell you about the university and its colleges. Tickets for the tours are sold at the tourist information center. A note of academic etiquette, please: College members are happy to welcome you to the grounds and their historic buildings, but they ask you to respect their need for quiet and privacy.

Arriving by rail from London, take the bus located immediately in front of the train station to Market Square, which lies between the two main streets of Cambridge, one of which is devoted to commerce and shopping, and the other is the academic "main drag." Cambridge is a complex blend of market town, regional center, university, and tourist attraction and defies neat analysis. Consequently, after dismounting the bus in Market Square, ask for directions to the tourist information center on Wheeler Street a few short blocks from the market.

CAMBRIDGE— *UNIVERSITY CITY*

A Day Excursion From London

DEPART FROM LIVERPOOL STREET STATION*	ARRIVE IN CAMBRIDGE†	NOTES
0736	0859	(1) (2)
0836	0940	(1) (2)
0936	1044	(2) (3)
1036	1139	(2) (3)

(Plus other frequent service)

DEPART FROM CAMBRIDGE	ARRIVE IN LIVERPOOL STREET STATION	
1700	1805	(2) (4)
1720	1842	(5)
1832	1935	(2) (4)
2142	2311	(4)

Distance: 56 miles/90 km
References: British Rail Table 22
              Thomas Cook Table 589

* See Appendix, page 296, for London station plan
† Travellers-Fare catering facility
(1) Monday thru Friday only, except holidays
(2) Food service available
(3) Daily, arrives later Sundays
(4) Daily, except Sundays and holidays
(5) Sundays and holidays only

Train Information
Cambridge Train Station: 0223-59711
Inter-City Services: 01-278-2477

Talking Timetable
Cambridge-London: 0223-59602

The tourist information center is open Monday-Friday, 0900-1800; Saturday, 0900-1700; and on Sunday, 1030-1530. Ask for the pamphlet "Cambridge, A Brief Guide for Visitors." It provides basic information about the colleges and museums and includes a street plan of the city. The *Official Guide* is available (at a nominal charge) for those wanting to know more about the history of Cambridge and places of interest outside the city.

If you plan to see Cambridge on your own, planning an itinerary may be difficult since there is so much to see. King's College Chapel is universally regarded as one of Cambridge's finest architectural structures. It took nearly 70 years to build and was completed in 1515. Trinity College's great court is the largest quadrangle in England. It's so large that much of its detail goes unnoticed. Taking advantage of this situation, Byron used to bathe in the nude in the fountain and shared his room with a pet bear which he claimed he kept for the purpose of taking the Fellowship examinations. Sir Isaac Newton first measured the speed of sound in the great court by stamping his foot in the cloister along the north side of the court.

The Cam River, the source of Cambridge's being and a delightful area throughout every season, deserves a portion of your visit. A tour of the city by boat along the "backs," as the placid stretch of the river is called, is undoubtedly an experience not to be missed. You can hire a punt, rowboat, or canoe to boat along the backs.

Visitors have a wide choice of museums covering a wide range of interest. Allow yourself time to wander in at least one of them. The Fitzwilliam Museum on Trumpington Street features medieval and renaissance objects of art, arms, and armor. The Folk Museum on Castle Street contains a vast array of domestic articles. Another point of interest is Kettles Yard Art Gallery at Castle Street on Northampton with its fine collection of modern paintings and sculpture.

The Old Weaver's House in Canterbury owes its name to Flemish and Huguenot weavers who came to the city in the 16th century and set up looms in private houses along the River Stour. Now a small and unimpressive stream , the river played an important role in Canterbury's earlier times.

A DAY EXCURSION TO CANTERBURY

DISTANCE BY TRAIN: 62 miles (99 km)
AVERAGE TRAIN TIME: 1 hour, 25 min.

Canterbury was originally a huddle of huts that the Romans captured as they penetrated inland from the Kentish coast. They fortified the area, built their roads to London and beyond, and along these roads came the Roman legions of occupation. Although the Romans' domination of England ended in the 5th century, the road between London and Canterbury remains heavily traveled even today.

In early times, the River Stour meandered through the valleys creating a large boggy area. At Canterbury there was a ford for crossing the watery barrier. The selection of the Canterbury site for settlement probably was dependent on its natural advantage as a ford and on the consequent communications which spread out from it.

Canterbury has had a hectic history. In the year 1011, it was sacked by the Danes. It was again invaded by the Normans, who founded the modern city of Canterbury as we know it today. The victory of William the Conqueror began an era during which the city developed in an orderly manner until the Reformation. In England, the Reformation lasted several decades, during which time there were martyrs in Canterbury on both sides of the dispute.

Thomas à Becket was made Archbishop of Canterbury in 1162. He was murdered in his own cathedral in 1170 and immediately declared a saint. Becket's murder induced vast pilgrimages to Canterbury, enriching both the cathedral and the city's development during the Middle Ages.

During World War II, Canterbury was the victim of air raids, and bombs destroyed about one-quarter of the city. Only the West Gate, of the city's seven medieval gates, managed to survive the blitz.

CANTERBURY—*AND THE CATHEDRAL*

A Day Excursion From London

DEPART FROM VICTORIA STATION*	ARRIVE IN CANTERBURY EAST STATION†	NOTES
0739	0901	(1) (3)
0809	0934	(1) (3)
0909	1034	(1) (3)
0939	1058	(1) (3)
0906	0738	(2)

Additional trains depart at 10 and 40 minutes
past the hour through 2240

CAUTION: Train splits at Faversham—one stop from Canterbury East Station. Ride in coaches marked "Dover Marine" (not "Margate-Ramsgate").

DEPART FROM CANTERBURY EAST STATION	ARRIVE IN VICTORIA STATION	
1439	1606	(1)
1508	1636	(1)
1539	1706	(1)

Additional trains depart at 08 and 39 minutes
past the hour until 2208

Distance: 62 miles/99 km
References: British Rail Table 212
Thomas Cook Table 514

* See Appendix, page 296, for London station plan
† Travellers-Fare catering facility
(1) Monday through Friday only, except holidays
(2) Saturdays and Sundays
(3) Food service available Monday thru Friday

Train Information
Canterbury East Station: 0227-65151

Canterbury has two train stations—the West Station and the East Station. Trains departing London's Charing Cross and Waterloo Stations arrive at Canterbury West. Those departing London's Victoria Station arrive at Canterbury East. For simplicity, day excursion schedules are given for Victoria and Canterbury East Stations only.

Arriving in Canterbury East Station, use the pedestrian tunnel to reach the main station to the city. There's a taxi queue just outside the station entrance, or you can walk to the city center and the cathedral in about 15 minutes. From the station entrance, you'll see a sign across the street which says "Bus Station Cathedral." A blue sign showing a person walking indicates where to cross the highway. Proceed along the city's old Roman walls which enclose Dane John Park. Climb the mound in the park for a view of the town and the cathedral. Further along, you'll come to the city bus station. Descend from the wall at this point onto St. George's Street. Turn left and walk until the cathedral is in view through the Christ Church Gate. Passing through the gate will bring you onto the cathedral grounds. A cathedral information office is located just inside the Christ Church Gate on the left.

Just outside the Christ Church Gate is the Longmarket, a paved pedestrian area beginning at the intersection of Rose Lane and Longmarket. Daily guided tours of the city depart from the kiosk in Longmarket on weekdays at 1415.

The tourist information center is located at 22 St. Peter's Street, which is actually an extension of St. George's Street. St. George's Street first changes into High Street before finally becoming St. Peter's. The information center is open Monday-Saturday, 0930–1730; closed Sunday. Before arriving at the center, you'll pass over a narrow bridge crossing the River Stour. On the far right of the bridge you will see the Old Weaver's House, built in 1500. It is an interesting sight and a great place to browse and shop in.

Castle Clock Tower, an outstanding feature of Cardiff, was designed by Victorian architect William Burges. Commissioned by the Marquis of Bute in 1865 to restore Cardiff Castle, Burges replaced a turret of the castle with this magnificent clock tower as part of the restoration.

From London ...

A DAY EXCURSION TO CARDIFF

DISTANCE BY TRAIN: 145 miles (233 km)
AVERAGE TRAIN TIME: 2 hours

A triple treat lies in store for those who take this delightful day excursion to the Welsh capital of Cardiff. The first is the opportunity to travel on one of British Rail's "journey shrinkers"—the fabulous Inter-City 125 trains. As an example, the 0915 Inter-City out of London's Paddington Station will set you down in Cardiff Central Station exactly 101 minutes later, averaging an amazing speed of 86 miles per hour over the 145 miles separating the two capital cities. As an added bonus, you can savor a delicious English breakfast while watching the western English countryside slide by.

Arriving in Cardiff, your second treat is sampling the scenery of a historic city of the Empire which has cast off its grim mantle of industrialism to reveal a sparkling center of shopping arcades, a glistening white array of impressive civic buildings, a most memorable museum (well worth the trip), and a genuine 1,900-year-old castle smack in the middle of town!

If you recover in time, you'll be off on a short 15-minute train ride from the city's Queen Street Station for the third treat to nearby Caerphilly Castle, second in size only to Windsor Castle. It's crammed with interesting things including a tower that even Oliver Cromwell's gunpowder couldn't topple—at least not completely!

Cardiff was first developed by the Romans, followed by the Normans. Both left their mark in the form of formidable fortifications. However, the city as we see it today was largely a creation of the 19th century. Cardiff is accustomed to welcoming visitors and does it well. Go and sample a little bit of Welsh hospitality. We're sure you will find yourself returning there again and again.

CARDIFF—*CAPITAL OF WALES*

A Day Excursion From London

DEPART FROM PADDINGTON STATION*	ARRIVE IN CARDIFF CENTRAL STATION†	NOTES
0700	0903	(1) (2) (3)
0915	1056	(1) (2) (3)
1015	1203	(2) (3) (4)
1115	1256	(1) (2) (3)

DEPART FROM CARDIFF CENTRAL STATION	ARRIVE IN PADDINGTON STATION	
1638	1831	(1) (2) (3)
1738	1937	(1) (2) (3)
1838	2039	(2) (3) (4)
1938	2137	(1) (2) (3)

Only HST (high speed train) schedules shown
above. Additional services available.

Distance: 145 miles/233 km
References: British Rail Table 127
Thomas Cook Table 540

* See Appendix, page 296, for London station plan
† Travellers-Fare catering facility
(1) Daily, except Sundays and holidays
(2) Food service available
(3) High-speed train
(4) Daily, arrival time varies slightly on Sundays

Train Information
Cardiff Central Station: 0222-28000
Inter-City Services: 01-262-6767

Talking Timetable
London-Cardiff: 01-402-2161
Cardiff-London: 0222-371371

We suggest that you first visit the Cardiff information center on Castle Street to get your bearings, pick up some brochures (including a map of the city), and then begin your sightseeing. If you are not certain of directions, check in with British Rail's Travel Information Center in Cardiff's Central Station. It's on your far right as you exit from the ticket checker's booth. You'll find a free direct-access telephone in the office which connects with the tourist information center on Castle Street.

One block to the right of the station is St. Mary's Street. Turn left onto it and walk about 10 minutes. During your walk, St. Mary's Street becomes High Street which intersects with Castle Street. A left turn onto Castle Street brings you immediately to the information center. It's open Monday-Friday, 0900-1700; Saturday, 1000-1500; closed Sundays. Sunday, by the way, is not the best time to visit Cardiff—the train service slows down and many of the city's attractions are closed.

Lofty Cardiff Castle looms in front of the information center. It is like Bo Derek—you can't overlook it! The shopping arcades are back down High Street or on Queen Street. Many are pedestrian precincts—Cardiff claims to have had them long before the phrase was invented! The city map will help you in your orientation. We specifically recommend the *Cardiff Guide* booklet with the Cardiff Castle clock tower on its cover.

Cardiff's civic center lies beyond the castle, as does the National Museum of Wales. Here, among other art treasures, you may now view four recently discovered tapestry cartoons by Rubens. Trains depart Cardiff's Queen Street Station for Caerphilly hourly at 23 minutes past the hour. Trains returning to Cardiff depart Caerphilly hourly at 6 minutes past. Returning to Cardiff, ride through to the Central Station for connections with Inter-City 125 trains back to London. Central Station is 3 minutes beyond the Queen Street Station stop.

World-famous Rows, a double tier of shops with walkways at ground and first-floor levels, is Chester's most distinctive architectural feature. The Rows line streets originally laid down by Roman engineers almost 2000 years ago. Extensive rebuilding followed the disastrous fire of 1278.

A DAY EXCURSION TO CHESTER

DISTANCE BY TRAIN: 178 miles (287 km)
AVERAGE TRAIN TIME: 2 hours, 40 min.

"All's well" in Chester, but don't take our word for it—check personally with Chester's town crier. He appears twice daily in the center of the city to announce that fact—first at noon and again at 1500. Chester is one of the few cities in England with its encircling walls completely intact. It is a splendid example of a fortified medieval town.

The center of Chester, known as the "Cross," takes its name from the stone "High Cross" standing in front of St. Peters Church. From this point you may view Chester's distinctive landmarks, the Rows—two tiers of shops (one at ground level, the other immediately above), each with its own walkway. The Rows are unique and justly world famous. The upper levels are great for people watchers who like to linger undisturbed while observing the stream of passers-by in the streets below. The true origin of the Rows has never been satisfactorily explained, but they far exceed any modern day shopping center in utility and beauty.

The Romans gave Chester its street plan. Walk today along the four main streets within the city's walls and you will follow the lines laid down by Roman engineers almost 2000 years ago! Part of the Roman wall survives and is incorporated in the massive 10th century fortifications enclosing the city. A walk on the walls provides an opportunity to enjoy the vista of the surrounding countryside. Restoration has thrived on a large scale in Chester. Entire blocks have been renovated in massive programs. The city's famous "black and white" Tudor buildings survived the ravages of time but did not escape alterations to their facades by Victorian achitects. In all, however, Chester has managed to preserve its pleasant medieval appearance.

CHESTER—*MODERN "MEDIEVAL" CITY*

A Day Excursion From London

DEPART FROM EUSTON STATION*	ARRIVE IN CHESTER†	NOTES
0650	0945	(1)
0805‡	1041	(1)
0855	1223	(2)
0855‡	1141	(1)

DEPART FROM CHESTER	ARRIVE IN EUSTON STATION	
1438	1804	(1)
1617	1911	(1) (3)
1759	2037	(2)
1935	2217	(1)

Distance: 178 miles/287 km
References: British Rail Table 83
              Thomas Cook Table 557

* See Appendix, page 296, for London station plan
† Travellers-Fare catering facility
‡ Change at Crewe required; direct inquiries to train information staff
(1) Daily, except Sundays and holidays
(2) Sundays and holidays only
(3) Food service available

Train Information
Chester Train Station: 0244-40170
Inter-City Services: 01-262-6767

Talking Timetable
Chester-London: 0244-46661

The train station in Chester is about a 20-minute walk from the city's center. City Road at the front of the station will get you off in the right direction. Change at the pedestrian underpass onto Foregate Street, which turns into Eastgate Street. Or, you can board a bus at the side of the Queen Hotel just across the street from the station and the town hall. You will arrive at the town hall in approximately 5 minutes for a nominal charge of 6 pence. Taxi meters click off between 50 and 60 pence over the same route.

Chester's street plan and directions to its tourist information center are graphically displayed under the Queen Hotel's sign. Operating hours for the information center are also posted there: from May through September, 0900-1900 on weekdays and Sundays from 1200-1600. For the balance of the year, it's open only on weekdays from 0930-1230 and 1330-1630.

The official guidebook of the city is on sale at the information center for 50 pence. On summer weekdays, tours of the city depart from this point at 1045 and 1430. On Sunday, there is only one guided tour, which begins at 1045. The information center is located within the town hall on the west side of Northgate Street. Opposite the town hall is Abbey Square, an island of quiet in the center of the city. Enter it through the massive 14th century gateway. Within the square you will find various buildings ranging in origin from the 16th century to the 19th.

Chester boasts a cathedral which is within sight of the town hall. It also has a castle that had its origins soon after the Norman Conquest. It is a short walk back down Bridge Street to Castle Street to view it. At this point, a walk to the city's walls would be in order since you are only a short distance from one of the entry points, Eastgate. For an unusually good audiovisual story of Chester and a view of a typical 19th century city street, seek out the British Heritage Exhibition on Vicar's Lane. There you will find the town crier's room. We hope you will find that "all's well" there, too!

Stark ruins of Coventry's Cathedral of St. Michael stands alongside the city's fine new cathedral. Totally destroyed in a 1940 air raid, an altar of broken stones surmounted by a charred cross stands at the eastern end of the ruins, backed by the words "Father, forgive."

From London ...

A DAY EXCURSION TO COVENTRY

DISTANCE BY TRAIN: 100 miles (161 km)
AVERAGE TRAIN TIME: 1 hour, 5 min

Explore the legend of Lady Godiva! Did she actually put everything on a horse—or has this tale, retold through the ages, changed with the telling? Was there a "Peeping Tom?" Was he late for the show? Coventry holds the answers!

Coventry is best described as a modern city with ancient roots. Among tall office buildings, new streets and attractive shops, there is a scattering of old homes and churches, Coventry's remnants of its far-reaching past. The city was devastated in 1940 by Nazi bombers, but after careful and patient rebuilding, a bright new city emerged.

Coventry's new cathedral stands as visible proof that today's craftsmen can, in fact, create memorable works of supreme beauty as did their medieval counterparts. Alongside the new, stands the old Cathedral of St. Michael, reduced to ruins by one dreadful air raid in November, 1940. An altar of broken stones surmounted by a charred cross stands at the eastern end of the ruins, backed by the words "Father, forgive." A visit to both cathedrals should not be missed.

Coventry's rail station lies outside its "ringway," a circular super highway surrounding the city. The bus station joins the rail terminal. At the bus stop, you'll find a city map and information regarding Coventry's information center. Buses marked "Cathedral" (No. 25) will take you to the center of town for only 7p over a route that requires 20-25 minutes to walk. Dismount at the shopping square by the Leofric Hotel. Lady Godiva's statue stands in a park immediately opposite the hotel, silhouetted against the spires of the cathedrals. Catch the return bus at a shelter directly in front of the Holy Trinity Church, opposite the hotel.

COVENTRY—*LADY GODIVA LAND*

A Day Excursion From London

DEPART FROM EUSTON STATION*	ARRIVE IN COVENTRY†	NOTES
0802	0958	(1)
0935	1046	(1) (2)
0940	1115	(3)
1110	1221	(1) (2)

(Plus other frequent service)

DEPART FROM COVENTRY	ARRIVE IN EUSTON STATION	
1610	1736	(1) (2)
1740	1901	(1)
1807	1933	(2) (3)
1953	2111	(1) (2)

(Plus other frequent service)

Distance: 100 miles/161 km
References: British Rail Table 66
           Thomas Cook Table 552
* See Appendix, page 296, for London station plan
† Travellers-Fare catering facility
(1) Daily, except Sundays and holidays
(2) Food service available
(3) Sundays and holidays only

Train Information
Coventry Train Station: 0203-28201
Inter-City Services: 01-387-7070

Talking Timetable
London-Coventry: 01-388-4064

The bus stop at the Leofric Hotel is Broadgate. The tourist information center is located at 36 Broadgate and found via well-placed direction signs. The center operates Monday-Friday, 0830-1900; Saturday, 0830-1600; closed on Sundays, but remains open on bank holidays (except Christmas) from 0900-1700. Among many informative publications, be sure to acquire the blue and white "City of Coventry" brochure. It contains a plan of the city's central area, along with a listing of restaurants and places of interest. Also described is "An Hour's Walk Around the City Center," which will lead you from Broadgate to a number of interesting places, including the two cathedrals.

Lady Godiva was the wife of Leofric, the "grim" Lord of Coventry. Evidently, she took to bugging him about the heavy tax burdens he had levied on the townspeople. Legend says Leofric, weary of her persistence, agreed to decrease the tax rate if Her Ladyship would increase the town's morale by riding naked through its streets. Modern historians seriously doubt that Godiva made her gallop without benefit of even a riding crop. They believe her husband challenged her to ride *stripped of her finery and her jewels* and to ride humbly as one of his people—and in full sight of them. Stripped of her rank—or just plain stripped—Her Ladyship *did* make the ride and *taxes were lowered,* but she commanded the people to remain indoors with windows barred. Legend says that one town resident called "Tom" unbarred his window to peep as she rode by. Before he could satisfy his gaze, he was struck blind, poor man! Oddly enough, the Godiva story was told for some 500 years before the "Peeping Tom" version was added. In any case, a stunning bronze statue worthy of a *Playboy* centerfold perpetuates Her Ladyship's memory in Broadgate Park as Tom peeps out at her on the hour from the Broadgate clock. We can't help but wonder what effect Lady Godiva's ride might have had on our modern day Internal Revenue Service!

Famous white cliffs, probably Dover's best known landmark, attract thousands of sightseers. Dover Castle, standing guard atop the cliffs, boasts a fine keep, a lighthouse of Roman origin, and a church dating back to Saxon times. Dover's importance as a port began during the Roman invasion of England. Today, Dover is still the principal British maritime port for passenger traffic to and from Europe.

From London ...

A DAY EXCURSION TO DOVER

DISTANCE BY TRAIN: 77 miles (124 km)
AVERAGE TRAIN TIME: 1 hour, 30 min.

For centuries Dover has been one of Britain's major channel ports. In theory, this is where England ends and the Continent begins. Here is where countless Englishmen have been parted from or united with their homeland. Here stand the white cliffs of Dover. Below, on the beaches, the legions of the Roman Empire stormed ashore. Atop the cliffs broods Dover Castle. Initially constructed in the 1180's by Henry II to repel invaders, it has been reinforced frequently at every threat to England's shores, including Hitler's in 1940.

You cannot escape it—Dover is dramatic. A brooding of peril hangs over it on a rainy, windswept day; a dimension of grandeur surrounds it on a clear one when, for example, Boulogne in distant France becomes discernible. The deafening ramjets of the WWII German V-2 "buzz bombs" have been replaced by the humming vacuums of the hovercraft. But the screams of the gulls and the relentless crashing of the sea continue on unchanged by aeons of time. If you are one to "stand in history," Dover becomes a must visit during your stay in Great Britain. Few other places on earth swell the imagination as do the "white cliffs of Dover."

Train service from London to Dover follows two routes. Departures from Victoria Station split destinations at Faversham—part of the train proceeds to Dover, the other part to Margate and Ramsgate. As a precaution against "splitting," our schedule is based on direct train service to Dover from London's Charing Cross Station. However, readers can avail themselves of either rail route. As a suggestion, depart Charing Cross and return via Faversham to Victoria Station. This way, you will be "joined" by the Ramsgate train instead of being "split" by it.

DOVER—*ON THE "WHITE CLIFFS"*

A Day Excursion From London

DEPART FROM CHARING CROSS*	ARRIVE IN DOVER PRIORY†	NOTES
0800	0931	(1) (2)
0820	1004	(1) (2)
0900	1031	(3)
1000	1131	(3)

(Plus other frequent service)

DEPART FROM DOVER PRIORY	ARRIVE IN CHARING CROSS	
1610	1743	(3)
1726	1917	(1)
1826	2017	(1)
2126	2317	(1)

(Plus other frequent service)

Distance: 77 miles/124 km
References: British Rail Table 207
                     Thomas Cook Table 512

* See Appendix, page 296, for London station plan
† Dover Priory is the last stop before the train arrives at the train ferry docks for transport to Continental Europe. Hovercraft passengers also should leave the train at Dover Priory, connecting with bus service to the hoverport. See page 302 for Dover station plan. Travellers-Fare catering facility.

(1) Daily, including holidays
(2) Food service available Monday thru Friday
(3) Daily, except Sundays and holidays

Train Information
Dover Priory Train Station: 0304-201753
Inter-City Services: 01-928-5100

Leave the train at Dover Priory Station. If you remain on the train, you could find yourself being loaded aboard a Sealink ferry for France, for the next (and last) station on the line is Dover Marine where that sort of thing takes place. There's a bus service from Dover Priory to Townwall Street where you will find the tourist information center next door to the Holiday Inn—America's contribution to historic landmarks! It's all downhill from the station and in the direction of the sea, so you may elect to walk and arrive at the center in 10-12 minutes.

The information center is extensive, since Dover is a major debarkation point for visitors from the Continent. Due to its national status, the center can provide information regarding all of Great Britain, as well as the local Dover area. The center operates daily from 0800 to 2400, including Sundays and holidays. Ask the center for full information on Dover Castle and how to reach it. No doubt you will be interested in visiting the Roman-painted house in Dover. It was discovered by an archaeological unit in 1971! Roman legions took over the structure about 300 A.D. for shore defense purposes. It gains its name from the brilliantly painted plaster of its walls. The house is now a permanent museum, open every day except Monday from March through November.

Have you ever been to France? If not, now's your chance! You can whisk across the English Channel to Boulogne in about 35 Hovercraft minutes. Day trips out of Dover to the Continent are very popular. Stock up on wine and cheese, plus a yard or so of crusty French bread during your visit and load up with duty-free tobacco and booze on the journey back. Plan ahead by asking any train-information office for information on Sealink or Hovercraft service. There are many excursions available. Free bus service runs between Dover Priory and the Hoverport at Dover's western docks.

Small boat harbor provides protected haven for Folkestone's fleet of fishing and recreational craft. As a cross-channel port, Folkestone stands second only to Dover in passenger traffic aboard Sealink vessels calling at the city's harbor train station pier and the Continent.

From London ...

A DAY EXCURSION TO FOLKESTONE

DISTANCE BY TRAIN: 70 miles (113 km)
AVERAGE TRAIN TIME: 1 hour, 20 min.

Folkestone is a "triple treat" seaside resort. You may stay within its confines for a delightful day of sightseeing and seafood, or ply between Folkestone and Boulogne or Calais in France aboard Sealink, or elect to survey the 8½ miles of right-of-way on the world's smallest public railway—the Romney, Hythe and Dymchurch Light Railroad. Each of the three options should take a full day to enjoy, so perhaps you had better plan on making several trips out of London to Folkestone during your visit—or even stay over in Folkestone for a day or two!

With so many possibilities, we strongly suggest you make your way to Folkestone's tourist information center immediately following your arrival. This may be accomplished by either of two bus services, Courtesy or City, from the Folkestone Central Station. Sealink operates a free shuttle bus between the Central Station and Harbor Station. For the shuttle bus, "queue up" at the "Sealink Bus to Folkestone Harbor" sign. You will find it on the left of the Central Station entrance. A schedule is posted nearby explaining the shuttle bus service, which operates from 1000-2310 daily. Alternately, you can ride the city bus to the harbor for 10p. The city bus shelter is on Kingsnorth Street.

The city bus stops a short distance from the information center situated at the head of Harbor Street. The shuttle bus passes the information center but cannot stop until it reaches the Harbor Station. One merely walks back along the side of the harbor, a scant 5 minutes to retrace his steps to the center. Considering that the walk back to the center is along the seawall of Folkestone's outer harbor, the scenery should be interesting, to say the least—and you have saved yourself the tidy sum of 10p as well!

FOLKESTONE—*BEAUTIFUL KENT SEAPORT*

A Day Excursion From London

DEPART FROM CHARING CROSS*	ARRIVE IN FOLKESTONE CENTRAL†	NOTES
0800	0920	(3) (4)
0830	0959	(2)
0900	1018	(1)
1000	1118	(1)

(Plus other frequent service)

DEPART FROM FOLKESTONE CENTRAL	ARRIVE IN CHARING CROSS	
1623	1743	(1)
1743	1917	(4)
1843	2017	(4)
2143	2317	(4)

(Plus other frequent service)

Distance: 70 miles/113 km
References: British Rail Table 207
                      Thomas Cook Table 512

* See Appendix, page 296, for London station plan
† See page 302 for Folkestone station plan. Travellers-Fare catering facility.
(1) Daily, except Sundays and holidays
(2) Saturdays and Sundays
(3) Food service available Monday thru Friday
(4) Daily, including holidays

Train Information
Folkestone Central Station: 0303-55134
Inter-City Services: 01-928-5100

Folkestone has a dual distinction. As a cross-channel port, it is second only to Dover in total passenger traffic. For beauty of location, it probably stands second to none. The Leas, Folkestone's famous cliff-top promenade, surveys the town's beach from a vantage point more than 200 feet above it. From there, one can view the landscape from Dover to Dungeness. Below the Leas, at Harbor level, lie the city's marine gardens and the busy harbor pier where the Sealink vessels can be watched arriving and departing from atop the raised promenade that runs the full length of the pier. Admission to the promenade is 20p. Those interested in the opportunity of making a day trip to Boulogne or Calais on the French coast can be ticketed at the pier office. BritRail Pass holders with the Seapass option included may use their pass for such a voyage.

Trains meeting the Sealink vessels at the Harbor Station proceed to London via Dover *and do not call at Folkestone Central.* This, of course, makes a circuitous train trip back to London possible. However, it could also lead to a bit of embarrassment if you boarded a London-bound train at the Folkestone Harbor Station with friends or family waiting to join you at the Folkestone Central Station!

A bus from the city bus station will take you to the town of Hythe to the west of Folkestone in about 22 minutes' running time. There, the young—and those not so young—may board the fascinating Romney, Hythe and Dymchurch Light Railroad for a delightful run by steam traction to New Romney, with stops in Dymchurch and St. Mary's Bay. Service is generally every hour, so you can stop enroute at Dymchurch, England's "children's paradise" or at St. Mary's Bay where boating and fishing are two highlights of that holiday center. The RH&D Railroad terminates its services in New Romney, except during high season service when it steams on to Dungeness, another 5½ miles down the RH&D "road." At Dungeness you'll find great contrast between its fishermen's shacks and its atomic plant!

Gloucester Cathedral, originally of Norman design (1089-1260), was remodeled during 1331-1370 to house the tomb of English King Edward II. The east window of the cathedral, the largest in England, was erected as a memorial to those who fought for England at Crécy in 1346.

A DAY EXCURSION TO GLOUCESTER

DISTANCE BY TRAIN: 114 miles (184 km)
AVERAGE TRAIN TIME: 2 hours, 7 min.

Gloucester is steeped in history. First to arrive were the Romans, following their invasion of the British Isles. A legion fort was erected at the site of the present city center, and by 96-98 A.D., the Roman city of Glevum (now Gloucester) was established and flourishing. Little remains of the Roman presence in modern Gloucester. None of the Roman wall is now visible above ground, but its line is still followed by the principal streets of the city.

Gloucester's showplace is its cathedral. It consists of a Norman nucleus (1089-1260) with additions in every known style of Gothic architecture. Topped by a towering 15th century pinnacle that rises 225 feet above ground level, Gloucester's cathedral is judged to be one of the six most beautiful buildings in Europe. If you have a limited amount of time to spend sightseeing in Gloucester, you will make the best use of it by concentrating on the cathedral and the 12-acre college green that surrounds it.

The city's tourist information center is located at 6 College Street, virtually in the shadow of the cathedral. Its hours of operation are Monday through Saturday, 1000-1830; Sundays, 1300-1700. City bus transportation from Gloucester's Central Station to the information center requires a transfer and the taxi fare varies widely, according to the route which the driver selects due to the city's complex of one-way streets. Walking toward the cathedral from the Central Station until you intercept Northgate Street is the shortest route to take on foot. At Northgate Street, turn left to where it intersects Westgate Street at the "Cross" (center of the city). A right turn onto Westgate will bring you to College Street with the information center on the right-hand side of the street.

GLOUCESTER—*ON THE RIVER SEVERN*

A Day Excursion From London

DEPART FROM PADDINGTON STATION*	ARRIVE IN GLOUCESTER†	NOTES
0745	0955	(1)
0815	1055	(2)
0945	1153	(1)
1145	1345	(1)
(Plus other frequent service)		

DEPART FROM GLOUCESTER	ARRIVE IN PADDINGTON STATION	
1550	1747	(1)
1732	1937	(1)
1735	1933	(2)
1843	2039	(1)

Distance: 114 miles/184 km
References: British Rail Table 127
                    Thomas Cook Table 537
*   See Appendix, page 296, for London station plan
†   Travellers-Fare catering facility
(1) Monday thru Friday only, except holidays
(2) Sundays and holidays only

Train Information
Gloucester Train Station: 0452-29501
Inter-City Services: 01-262-6767

Sightseeing in Gloucester has been made easy by the "Via Sacra," a walkway around the city center that follows the line of the original city wall. It is described in several publications which are available in the information center. It can be recognized by the pattern of dark paving placed in the sidewalk to keep visitors from going too far astray. The "Via Sacra" information sheet, the "Gloucester 1712" folder, and the "City of Gloucester" brochure all describe this suggested walk in good detail.

At the beginning of the walking tour, you can observe a considerable variety of early English architecture, ranging from 15th century timber-frame structures to the Tudor facades of the present county offices. You will pass Blackfriars, the best preserved medieval Dominican friary in Britain. Although it's under restoration, a portion is open to the public. Greyfriars is also on the route. Unlike Blackfriars, however, most of it stands in ruins.

Stopping in the city museum and art gallery affords the opportunity to examine many archaeological items, including a part of the original Roman city wall. The museum is open Monday-Saturday from 1000-1700. It is closed on Sundays. The tour passes not only the old points of interest in Gloucester, but many of its new ones as well. Just beyond the city museum, for example, you will see the Eastgate Shopping Center which provides traffic-free areas at ground level and rooftop car parking. The tour ends at the cathedral, St. Lucy's Garden, forming the approach to the previously mentioned college green.

Gloucester abounds with interesting eating establishments ranging from Wimpy's (Britain's answer to McDonald's) to such ancient eateries as the New Inn. Don't let the name fool you. The New Inn was built by St. Peter's Abbey to accommodate pilgrims in 1450! It is said to be the finest medieval open-galleried inn in England, and the food matches the excellence of its interesting decor.

Cutty Sark, built for the China tea trade, rests in dry dock at Greenwich. One of the fastest of sailing ships, she once logged 363 nautical miles in 24 hours! Launched at Dumbarton, Scotland, November, 1869, the dry-docked ship was opened to public view by Her Majesty Queen Elizabeth in 1957 following refit.

130

From London …

A DAY EXCURSION TO GREENWICH

DISTANCE BY TRAIN: 7 miles (11 km)
AVERAGE TRAIN TIME: 12 minutes

Greenwich is the cradle of Britain's maritime history and the home of time. Henry II and Elizabeth I were born in the Royal Palace of Greenwich. It was here that Elizabeth greeted Sir Francis Drake upon his return from sailing around the world in 1580. Queen Elizabeth II knighted Sir Francis Chichester for his solo circumnavigation of the world at a public ceremony at the Royal Naval College which now stands on the site of the Royal Palace. The clipper *Cutty Sark*, one of the fastest of sailing ships, lies in dry dock at Greenwich. The world's largest maritime museum, the National Maritime Museum of Greenwich, has in its fascinating collection the paddle tug *Reliant*, often described as "the world's largest ship in a bottle." At the Old Royal Observatory, visitors can stand astride the brass strip marking the Prime Meridian for Greenwich Mean Time (GMT), with one foot in an east longitude and the other one in west longitude. If time permits, you can walk *under* the Thames River to the Isle of Dogs and treat yourself to a panoramic view of Greenwich from that vantage point. Greenwich has much to offer.

Upon arrival in the Greenwich train station, use the pedestrian subway (underpass) to the main station and the street. Turn left and walk down the hill into the town. Follow the signs guiding you to the National Maritime Museum and the *Cutty Sark*. Where they split, continue to follow the *Cutty Sark* signs until the ship's masts come into view. The local Greenwich information booth is immediately beyond the bow of the *Cutty Sark*. The booth is open daily from 1000-1800 and Sundays from 1330-1800—summer service only. Of all the various publications available at the information booth, we recommend the bilingual booklet *Greenwich* with the map on its back cover.

GREENWICH—*ON THE PRIME MERIDIAN*

A Day Excursion From London

DEPART FROM CANNON STREET STATION*	ARRIVE IN GREENWICH	NOTES
0939	0951	(1)
1019	1031	(1)

Additional trains depart at 19 and 39 minutes past the hour through 1939

Saturday and Sunday service departs from London Bridge Station. Consult British Rail Table 204 or make inquiries with train information personnel.

DEPART FROM GREENWICH	ARRIVE IN CANNON STREET STATION	
1517	1531	(1)
1537	1550	(1)

Plus frequent service serving Charing Cross, London Bridge, Waterloo (East), as well as Cannon Street station. Consult British Rail Table 204 or make inquiries with train information personnel for Saturday and Sunday service.

Distance: 7 miles/11 km
References: British Rail Table 204
* See Appendix, page 296, for London station plan
(1) Monday thru Friday only, except holidays

Train Information
Greenwich Train Station: 01-858-3488

The *Cutty Sark* was launched in 1869 and served in the China tea trade, as well as the Australian wool trade. Her curious name, which means "short chemise," originated in "Tam o'Shanter," a poem by Robert Burns. The wearer, witch Nanny, is depicted by the ship's figurehead. A short distance away stands the 53-foot ketch, *Gypsy Moth*, that Sir Francis Chichester sailed solo around the world during 1966-67. Immediately behind the tourist information booth is the domed entrance of the Greenwich foot tunnel under the Thames River.

A few yards beyond the *Cutty Sark*'s stern is the entrance to the Royal Naval College. Visitors are admitted to its Painted Hall and the Chapel. The Painted Hall is now used as the officers' mess of the college. The interior decorating, by Sir James Thornhill, took 19 years to complete. (You'll find out why when you see it!) Benjamin West's painting of the shipwrecked *St. Paul* in the college chapel is one of the highlights of that beautiful structure.

There is an admission charge (adults, 50 pence; children, 25 pence) for the *Cutty Sark*, but admission is free to the Royal Naval College and the National Maritime Museum. To reach the museum, turn left on King William walk, leaving the naval college. Walk past the Seamen's Hospital to Romney Road. Cross over and turn left. The museum entrance is a few yards beyond. The National Maritime Museum tour leads you through its west wing where you can view the *Reliant* and the state barges once used on the River Thames. The central building houses an amazing display of old ship models, and the east wing features naval history of the 19th and 20th centuries.

In Greenwich Park, next to the museum, you may enter the Old Royal Observatory, an integral part of the museum. Admission is free. The Prime Meridian marking the line of 0° longitude on which GMT is calculated is located in the courtyard of the observatory's meridian building.

Hastings Castle beckons to visitors from atop the city's west hill where it was built by William the Conqueror in 1067 following the Battle of Hastings the previous year. Below the fortress in the old city's narrow streets are many 18th century houses.

From London...

A DAY EXCURSION TO HASTINGS

DISTANCE BY TRAIN: 63 miles (101 km)
AVERAGE TRAIN TIME: 1 hour, 45 min.

Undoubtedly, 1066 is one of the most well-known dates in history. As dusk fell at the field of Senlac near Hastings on October 14, 1066, William the Conqueror, Duke of Normandy, had defeated the Saxon army of slain King Harold and had become the new king of England. Hastings holds the lore of the Battle of Hastings plus the lure of its ancient fishing village and Norman castle.

In addition to its rich historical heritage, Hastings has been an attractive seaside resort since the mid-18th century when London physicians began prescribing sea air and salt water as a panacea for all their patients' ills. Three miles of promenades line its beaches, much of which is two-tiered with sun-trapped shelters overlooking the English Channel. Sun is more sought after in Hastings than surf, since the water is very cold. Examine any photo of an English seaside resort and you'll see that the majority of the bathers are found on the beach rather than in the sea!

There are four railway stations within the Borough of Hastings. Use the Hastings Central Station as a focal point. The tourist information center is located at 4 Robertson Terrace. Leaving the Central Station, walk downhill to the seaside and orient yourself on Carlisle Parade. The Queens Hotel is plainly visible from here on the eastern edge of the Robertson Terrace ellipse. The information center is on the west end. During summer, the office operates Monday–Friday, 0900–1730; Saturday, 0900–1300 and 1430–1730; Sunday, 1030–1300 and 1400–1700. The sign on the center entrance reads "Tourism and Recreation Centre." During winter, the center is closed on Sundays, but it's open Monday–Friday, 0900–1300 and 1400–1700; Saturday, 0900–1300 and 1430–1700.

HASTINGS—*FAMOUS BATTLE SITE*

A Day Excursion From London

DEPART FROM CHARING CROSS*	ARRIVE IN HASTINGS‡	NOTES
0745†	0932	(1)
0845†	1030	(2)
0945	1130	(2)
1045	1230	(2)

DEPART FROM HASTINGS	ARRIVE IN CHARING CROSS	
1532	1712	(3)
1640	1832	(2) (5)
1744	1932	(2) (5)
1940	2132	(2) (4) (5)

Distance: 63 miles/101 km
References: British Rail Table 206
Thomas Cook Table 515

* See Appendix, page 296, for London station plan
† Departs 3 minutes earlier Monday thru Friday
‡ Travellers-Fare catering facility
(1) Daily, except Sundays and holidays
(2) Daily, including holidays
(3) Monday thru Friday only, except holidays
(4) Food service available
(5) Departs Hastings 4 minutes later on Saturdays and Sundays

Train Information
Hastings Train Station: 0424-429325

Contrary to popular belief, the Battle of Hastings was not fought in Hastings, nor was the Norman castle in Hastings involved! After landing, the Norman army marched northward about 6 miles where they engaged the Saxons on the field of Senlac. The castle in Hastings, formerly a timber fort, was converted to stone in 1067, a year *after* the battle.

Harold's troops were not pushovers. Nineteen days prior to the Battle of Hastings, his men had put a Norse army to rout at Stamford Bridge near York. In the initial onslaught at Senlac, the Normans retreated with the Saxons in hot pursuit. In so doing, the Saxons had to break the tight formation of their Saxon wall of shields, and the Norman cavalry quickly took advantage of the hole opening up in the line and inflicted heavy losses upon the Saxons. This tactic was twice repeated and the conflict ended. Today's Super Bowl tactics may have first developed in Hastings!

For sightseeing at the battleground, board local bus 5, 252, 485, or 486 for "Battle Abbey." Get complete details at the information center. The center has an excellent information sheet entitled "The Old Town Walk." With it in hand, you can easily visit the Norman castle via the west hill lift. After drinking in the panoramic sights from atop the hill you can drift back toward the sea and Hastings's "Old Town." On Hill Street, observe the two cannonballs on either side of St. Clemens church belfry. The right one was shot into the tower by the French; the one on the left was added by the locals to balance things off.

You'll pass many interesting points on your walk. Stop for a closer examination of the Old Town Hall; the "Shovells," reputedly the oldest house in town; and the "piece of cheese," no doubt the funniest house in town. Don't miss the 243-foot embroidery in the new Town Hall. It depicts 81 of the greatest events of British history since 1066, including the Battle of Hastings, the Boston Tea Party, and the first television broadcast.

Station Hotel is a relatively new addition to the city of Ipswich, which was chartered in A.D. 1200. It stands opposite the town's rail station, and its memorabilia of railroading provide a pleasant decor for luncheon, dinner or a pint of ale while waiting for your train.

From London...

A DAY EXCURSION TO IPSWICH

DISTANCE BY TRAIN: 63 miles (101 km)
AVERAGE TRAIN TIME: 1 hour, 15 min.

Ipswich reflects its history in its architecture. It was bypassed by the Romans, therefore, it is void of any former grandeur of Rome. A seafaring community long before King John granted the city's first charter in 1200, Ipswich has always been engaged in commerce and has risen or declined along with the fortunes of its enterprises. The lack of Georgian buildings in Ipswich is evidence of the town's decline during that period caused by the loss of its famous Suffolk cloth trade. A revitalization of its harbor by mid-19th century brought new prosperity to Ipswich and accounts for the number of splendid public buildings erected then, as well as the Victorian type of architecture of its homes.

Ipswich has withstood the onslaughts of the Vikings and others down through the ages. During WWI, a number of zeppelin attacks were targeted on the city. Nazi bombers inflicted heavy damage on its docks and factories again in WWII. During 1943-45, Ipswich was rimmed by no less than 65 air bases of the U.S. Eighth Air Force where the staggering 3000-plus bomber raids were launched against the Third Reich. Operation Friendship welcomes American veterans to return and revisit their old haunts. Write to the Ipswich Tourist Information Center (page 291) or to the Community Relations Advisor, c/o RAF Commander, RAF Bentwaters, Suffolk, England, for details. Many of the air bases have been returned to agricultural land, but others are still operational airports for the U.S. Air Force or the Royal Air Force. Visitors are welcome, but they are advised to contact either of the above offices prior to a visit. When writing, ask for the Operation Friendship pamphlet. It lists all the original bases and their highlights.

IPSWICH—*CHARTERED IN A.D. 1200*

A Day Excursion From London

DEPART FROM LIVERPOOL STREET STATION*	ARRIVE IN IPSWICH†	NOTES
0830	0947	(1) (2)
0930	1041	(2) (3)
1130	1241	(1) (2)

DEPART FROM IPSWICH	ARRIVE IN LIVERPOOL STREET STATION	
1630	1745	(1) (2)
1825	1939	(1) (2)
1830	1950	(4)
1944	2101	(1)

Distance:	63 miles/101 km
References:	British Rail Table 11
	Thomas Cook Table 590

* See Appendix, page 296, for London station plan
† Travellers-Fare catering facility
(1) Daily, except Sundays and holidays
(2) Food service available
(3) Daily, but arrives at 1054 on Sundays
(4) Sundays and holidays only

Train Information
Ipswich Train Station: 0473-57373
Inter-City Services: 01-283-7171

Talking Timetable
Ipswich-London: 0473-216571

The tourist information center is easy to reach. It is situated at the end of Princes Street at Cornhill, for centuries the focal point and principal meeting place of Ipswich townspeople. Princes Street begins (or ends, as the case may be) at the Ipswich train station. If the weather is inclement, you can board a "City Center" bus or hail a taxi immediately in front of the station. The information center is located within the town hall, across the street from the post office. "You can't miss it," as the locals would say. Obtain a map at the information center before going off to explore the endless streets and enticing alleyways leading off Ipswich's Cornhill. Office hours are Monday-Thursday, 0900-1700; Friday, 0900-1630; Saturday, 0930-1230; closed Sunday.

The city's department of recreation has devised an excellent "Tourist Town Trail" brochure. The trail is signposted by black and white signs that are numbered to correspond with the descriptions in the brochure. No doubt, the trail was laid out for British walkers, for it is much too ambitious a course for the average Yank to complete within the prescribed period of one hour—at least it was for us! The route is circular so you can join (or leave) at any point on the trail.

Places along the "Tourist Town Trail" that we feel you'll be interested in seeing include the Butter Market, St. Stephen's Lane and Dial Lane. If you enter the Ancient House on St. Stephen's Lane, you'll be reminded of its age (500 years), for its windows represent the known world during its time—and Australia is missing because it had not yet been discovered! As you stand at Cornhill, it may be sobering to consider that only 400 years ago seven people were burned at the stake on this hill for heresy. However, before becoming too sober, we suggest you visit one of the bars in the Great White Horse Hotel. Distinguished visitors of the past include Charles Dickens, King George II, Louis XVIII, and Lord Nelson. A toast to these gentlemen would only seem proper.

Thatched roofs of Shanklin, on the Isle of Wight, line visitor-crowded thoroughfares of this resort town where poet John Keats once resided.

Hovercraft skims between mainland and Isle of Wight, augmenting regular ferry service for residents and holiday makers on England's vacation isle.

142

From London...

A DAY EXCURSION TO THE ISLE OF WIGHT

DISTANCE BY TRAIN: 88 miles (142 km)
AVERAGE TRAIN TIME: 2 hours, 40 min.

"Britain's miniature" is a term often employed to describe the Isle of Wight. Shaped like a diamond, the island is a veritable jewel of every feature of the mainland condensed into a mere 147 square miles. It is dotted with historic spots, sandy beaches, thatched villages, rolling countryside—discotheques, too, if that's your pleasure. There is fun for everyone on the Isle of Wight and getting there can be fun, too!

The majority of trains departing Waterloo Station in London for Portsmouth Harbor are Inter-City trains. As they glide through the scenery of southern England to the sea, you'll be treated to a delightful kaleidoscope of England's landscape from the wide-vision train windows. Stay aboard when the train halts briefly in the Portsmouth and Southsea Station. Your destination is the Portsmouth Harbor Station, five minutes further on.

Board the Portsmouth-Ryde passenger ferry at the end of the harbor station. Your BritRail Pass is good for the passage. The crossing time is 25–30 minutes, ample enough time for a relaxing voyage and a visit to the licensed buffet aboard for a libation, if you are so inclined.

Docking at the Ryde pier head, you have three options of sightseeing on the island by train. The trains, by the way, run right onto the pier and look every bit like those of the Bakerloo Underground Line in London. All the coaches are one class, but try to select one with ventilators at the top of the windows. It can get a bit stuffy aboard the train in summer. The three options? They are Ryde, Sandown, or Shanklin. All three lie along the nine miles of track extending from the Ryde pier head to the terminal in Shanklin. Turn the page now for a closer look at the three options.

ISLE OF WIGHT—*THE HOLIDAY ISLAND*

A Day Excursion From London*

DEPART FROM WATERLOO STATION†	ARRIVE IN SHANKLIN	NOTES
0748	1028	(1)
0848	1128	(1)
0948	1228	(1)

DEPART FROM SHANKLIN	ARRIVE IN WATERLOO STATION	
1535	1825	(1)
1641	1925	(2)
1841	2125	(1)

Distance:	88 miles/142 km
References:	British Rail Table 167
	Thomas Cook Table 521

* Via ferry service between Portsmouth-Ryde to Shanklin on the Isle of Wight. One-class service between Portsmouth Harbor and Shanklin. Buffet and bar service is available enroute.
† See Appendix, page 296, for London station plan.
(1) Monday through Friday only, except holidays
(2) Daily, including holidays
Hovercraft service between Portsmouth/Southsea and Ryde runs frequently throughout the day, crossing in 7 minutes.

Hovertravel, Ryde
65241

Ryde is the Isle of Wight's gateway. Set picturesquely on a hillside, it becomes a wonderful grandstand from which to watch the great ships of the world sailing by. Leave the pier train at its first stop, Ryde Esplanade, where you will find a tourist information kiosk ready to assist you during summer season. Ryde has six miles of sandy beach backed by pleasant wooded gardens.

Sandown is the rail stop following the Brading Station. It has all the facilities for a summer holiday, including a new pier complex. The sheltered Sandown Bay has more than five miles of attractive sandy beaches where you may find such diversions as mini golf and a canoe lake. Motor launch trips are popular in Sandown. Check at the city pier for details.

Shanklin frequently holds the British annual sunshine record. It is built on a cliff with a sheltered mile-long beach lying below. It is the end of the line for rail travel. However, it is easy to transfer to the buses operated by the island's bus company, Southern Vectis, for further points such as Ventnor, Newport and Cowes. Check with the bus station on Carter Avenue, two blocks distant from Shanklin's train station.

Our personal selection of the Isle's options would be Shanklin. It is certainly one of the prettiest towns in Britain. Shanklin's Old Village on Ventnor Road is world-famous for its quiet beauty. From there, you may descend to Shanklin's beach esplanade via a walk through Shanklin's Chine, a cleft in the town's cliff with overhanging trees, plants, ferns, and a cascading stream. Passage through the Chine costs 45 pence for adults; children, 15 pence. Check first with the town's information center at 67 High Street for all details.

Vary your return to the mainland via Hovercraft. They depart Ryde Esplanade for a 7-minute ride costing £1.60 per passenger. Docking at Southsea, take bus No. 5 to the Portsmouth train station to continue your day excursion back to London with fond memories of Britain in miniature.

Checker-work front of the 15th century Hall of the Trinity Guild, the town hall of King's Lynn, was constructed in the early part of the 15th century. It is the largest and oldest example of a medieval Merchant Guild in Great Britain. The town's tourist information office is housed in the structure along with the municipal offices. The building was used as a theater during the 18th century.

From London...

A DAY EXCURSION TO KING'S LYNN

DISTANCE BY TRAIN: 97 miles (156 km)
AVERAGE TRAIN TIME: 1 hour, 10 min.

King's Lynn, once "Bishop's Lynn" and renamed when Henry VIII took over the bishop's manor, is one of the most historic towns in England. The old section of town still seems medieval, complete with narrow streets, guildhall, and riverside quays, where the gulls reel and scream overhead. The town's former prosperity has left it with a rich heritage of architecture. Set along the east bank of the wide and muddy Ouse River, King's Lynn is the northern terminal of the London-Cambridge-Ely main line.

Streets and alleyways in King's Lynn twist and wind about on a grand scale, so a town map will be an invaluable aid. We suggest you immediately make your way from the train station to the town hall, where you will find the city information center. To do so, walk directly away from the front of the train station (which faces the west) down Waterloo Street. The street undergoes a name change at every intersection— Market, Paradise, New Conduit, Purfleet—but if one continues walking toward the west, one will come to King Street. Turn left onto King Street, which immediately becomes Queen Street. However, one should not despair, for the town hall is at the next intersection on the near left-hand corner. You will be tempted to wander about in Queen Street. It's crammed with lovely merchants' houses, each with a character all its own. Permit yourself a brief peek through the archway of No. 21 Queen Street at the Tudor warehouse with exposed beams, but further dalliance should be avoided. Proceed to the information center straight away and there equip yourself with a copy of the *King's Lynn Town Trail* booklet. With it, you'll know precisely where you are and exactly what you are looking at during your King's Lynn visit.

KING'S LYNN—*RICH IN ARCHITECTURE*

A Day Excursion From London

DEPART FROM LIVERPOOL STREET STATION*	ARRIVE IN KING'S LYNN‡	NOTES
0836	1044	(1) (2)
0936†	1210	(3)
1036	1244	(1) (2)
1236	1442	(1) (2)

DEPART FROM KING'S LYNN	ARRIVE IN LIVERPOOL STREET STATION	
1600	1805	(1) (2)
1730	1935	(1) (2)
1820	2042	(3)

Distance: 97 miles/156 km
References: British Rail Table 22
                Thomas Cook Table 589

* See Appendix, page 296, for London station plan
† Change at Cambridge
‡ Travellers-Fare catering facility
(1) Daily, except Sundays and holidays
(2) Food service available
(3) Sundays and holidays only

Train Information
King's Lynn Train Station: 0553-2021
Inter-City Services: 01-283-7171

The information center's hours are Monday-Thursday, 0900-1300 and 1400-1700; Friday, 0900-1300 and 1400-1630; Saturday, 0900-1200; and closed Sunday. Walking from the train station to the town hall takes about 10 minutes.

The previously mentioned town trail booklet is a masterpiece of simplicity. It is packed with facts about the town and its buildings. The trail follows a circular route, so you may start and finish wherever it's most convenient for you. We suggest starting at the town hall, which was rebuilt in 1421 after a fire. Ask permission to view its Treasury. There you will see the magnificent King John Cup and the Red Register, purported to be one of the oldest paper books in the world.

A focal point in King's Lynn is the Tuesday marketplace into which King Street leads. True to tradition, a country market is conducted there every Tuesday in the shadow of the Duke's Head Hotel, a most impressive Victorian structure. If you miss the Tuesday market, there's another one on Saturday at a location appropriately named the Saturday Marketplace. It is just opposite the town hall. The cattle market no longer exists in King's Lynn. It was relocated to make way for a pedestrian precinct containing a modern shopping center. You might want to wander through it enroute back to the station.

King John, who ruled England between 1199 and 1216, supposedly lost all his treasure near King's Lynn in October, 1215. One story relates that after he was wined and dined by the town's burghers, the king and his entourage headed west out of King's Lynn towards Newark. A high tide from The Wash, the bay into which the River Ouse flows, wiped out the king's baggage train on the journey. Somewhere near King's Lynn, buried who knows where under centuries of silt, lies King John's treasure. None has been recovered, since no one knows where to look for it. If you have any ideas, perhaps the burghers would be interested.

Magnificent Lincoln Cathedral has withstood fire, earthquake—even Cromwell's artillery! Each of its three towers had a lofty spire, but because one fell during a storm in 1547, the other two were removed in 1807. Its vault holds one of the four existing copies of the Magna Charta.

From London...

A DAY EXCURSION TO LINCOLN

DISTANCE BY TRAIN: 135 miles (217km)
AVERAGE TRAIN TIME: 2 hours, 10 minutes

Lincoln's landmark is its cathedral. It stands on a ridge overlooking the city. Dominating the skyline, the cathedral appears as though it might be half church, half stronghold. There are actually two Lincolns—the cathedral and castle standing politely on the hilltop and the city below girding the River Witham and buzzing with commerce. We suggest you scale the heights first and later return to the lower level by a dizzy descent down Steep Hill.

The bus station next to St. Marks rail station serves only the countryside area, not the city. So, for city bus service, walk from St. Marks Station up High Street towards the cathedral to where High Street intersects with St. Mary Street. St. Mary's Church is on the near corner. Turn right onto St. Mary Street and stay to the left of the next hotel (the Grande Hotel) to the city bus station. From there, city bus 1, 8, or 9 will take you up the hill to the cathedral where you'll find Lincoln's tourist information center at the intersection of Bailgate and Eastgate streets. As you pass between the two hotels on St. Mary Street, note the British Rail Central Station on your right. If you'd like to return to London via a different route, check out the details with the train information office there. The schedules we've given apply only to St. Marks Station.

If you abound with energy, walk straight up High Street after leaving St. Marks Station. Keep the cathedral in sight and disregard any street name changes. When you reach an area where a rope tow would be most welcome, you'll be on Steep Hill. Gain the high ground (and your breath) and you'll be at the Exchequer Gate of the cathedral. Hailing a taxi from St. Marks to the cathedral may be worth the 60-70 pence if you're not the energetic type!

LINCOLN—*HILLTOP CATHEDRAL*

A Day Excursion From London

DEPART FROM KING'S CROSS STATION*	ARRIVE IN LINCOLN ST. MARKS STATION†	NOTES
0830	1054	(1) (3)
1105	1324	(2)
1305	1510	(1)

DEPART FROM LINCOLN ST. MARKS STATION	ARRIVE IN KING'S CROSS STATION	
1435	1651	(1) (3)
1858	2142	(1) (3)
1905	2120	(2)

Distance: 135 miles/217 km
References: British Rail Table 26
Thomas Cook Table 576

* See Appendix, page 296, for London station plan
† Lincoln has two train stations—Central and St. Marks. Both serve King's Cross Station over different routes. Consult British Rail Table 29 or make inquiries with train information personnel for Lincoln Central train service.
(1) Monday through Friday only, except holidays
(2) Sundays and holidays only
(3) Food service available Monday through Friday

Train Information
St. Marks Station: 0522-27234
Inter-City Services: 01-278-2477

Earlier we mentioned the "two Lincolns." As a matter of fact, each has an information center. In lower Lincoln you will find the city information center located in the city hall. To go there, turn left after passing the general post office on High Street. The tourist center atop Lincoln's ridge is situated behind the cathedral. This office closes for lunch between 1300–1400 Monday through Friday. Otherwise, it is open from 0900–1730, except Friday when it closes one-half hour earlier at 1700. On Saturday and Sunday you'll find it operating straight through from 1000–1600. There is a wealth of information available in both offices. Both the *City of Lincoln* booklet published by the Lincoln Civic Trust and the *Official Guide, City of Lincoln* are worth their purchase prices. There is an abundance of free literature available as well.

The cathedral is the main point of interest in Lincoln. When you view its exterior and examine the spacious areas under its roof, it becomes rather difficult to comprehend that it was built by medieval craftsmen in only 20 years. Throughout the centuries Lincoln's greatest attraction has withstood earthquakes, fire, Cromwell's artillery, and Hitler's bombs. If you have but a short period of time to visit in Lincoln, the cathedral *must* take priority over all else.

Lincoln Castle was built by William the Conqueror in 1068. Today, it is a huge walled enclosure of lawns and trees. The crown courts and the old county jail are located in the castle yard. If you wish to visit the "other Lincoln," start by descending (or easing) down Steep Hill with its bow-fronted shops until you again reach High Street. You will find interest in the 12th century High Bridge. It is the oldest one in Britain to still carry a building on its structure, in this case, a 16th century timber-framed house. The route leading from the cathedral down Steep Hill to High Street and St. Marks Station is studded with interesting structures.

Trip to Jerusalem, one of Britain's oldest inns, crouches on the hillside below Nottingham Castle, so named because many crusaders stayed at the inn before setting off for the crusades. Its chimney, which runs about 60 feet through solid rock, is swept once every 30 years.

From London...

A DAY EXCURSION TO NOTTINGHAM

DISTANCE BY TRAIN: 127 miles (204 km)
AVERAGE TRAIN TIME: 2 hours, 10 min.

Nottingham is famous for many things, among them the legend of Robin Hood. Many tales have been told of Robin and his band of merry men, passed down through the ages by ballad and legend, though only scattered fragments remain of his origin. It appears that one Robert Fitzooth, reputed to be the Earl of Huntingdon, was born in 1160 during the reign of Henry II. Of noble birth, he squandered his inheritance at an early age, so either by necessity or by choice, he sought refuge in the forest. Here he was joined by men in similar circumstances, such as Little John, Will Scarlet, Friar Tuck, and—to add the love interest angle to the legend—Maid Marian.

Robin Hood reigned in the forest, defying the powers of government, protecting the poor and giving to the needy. The king's deer provided food and the king's forest provided fuel. Other necessities were obtained through barter. Taking the king's property was, of course, illegal and it drove the Sheriff of Nottingham "bananas," to the point where he offered a substantial reward for Robin's capture—dead or alive. Robin Hood eluded capture and supposedly lived to be 87 years old. Records show his death occurred on November 18, 1247. This man, who lived in an age of feudal tyranny, endeared himself to countless generations and became the legendary hero of Nottingham. A fine statue to his memory stands in the courtyard of Nottingham Castle.

Nottingham is also famous for its lace. For centuries it has been the center for lacemaking in England. The ale that Robin Hood quaffed so copiously is still a local specialty. Why not quaff some yourself in England's oldest inn, Ye Olde Trip to Jerusalem? It's been there in Nottingham since 1189 waiting for you!

NOTTINGHAM—*TALES OF ROBIN HOOD*

A Day Excursion From London

DEPART FROM ST. PANCRAS STATION*	ARRIVE IN NOTTINGHAM†	NOTES
0800	1009	(1) (2)
0854	1102	(3)
0902	1113	(1) (2)
0926	1227	(2) (5)
0953	1200	(2) (4)

DEPART FROM NOTTINGHAM	ARRIVE IN ST. PANCRAS STATION	
1510	1742	(2) (4)
1700	1909	(1)
1715	1938	(5)
1902	2102	(1) (2)
1903	2131	(2) (3)

Distance:	127 miles/204 km
References:	British Rail Table 53
	Thomas Cook Table 570

* See Appendix, page 296, for London station plan
† Travellers-Fare catering facility
(1) Monday thru Friday only, except holidays
(2) Food service available
(3) Saturdays only, except holidays
(4) Daily, except Sundays and holidays
(5) Sundays and holidays only

Train Information
Nottingham Train Station: 0602-46151
Inter-City Services: 01-387-7070

Talking Timetable
London-Nottingham: 01-388-7902
Nottingham-London: 0602-49834

The train trip from London's St. Pancras Station passes through England's Midlands enroute to Nottingham, passing St. Albans where Britain's first Christian martyr was executed and Bedford where John Bunyan wrote *Pilgrim's Progress*. For variety, you might want to return to London via Grantham, transferring there to a train for King's Cross Station. Cook's Timetables 560 and 567 will show you how, or you can consult with the train information office in Nottingham's station. It is located to your right as you exit from the trains. It's in operation weekdays from 0800-2100 and on Sunday from 0900-2100.

Nottingham Castle and Ye Olde Trip to Jerusalem pub are located within walking distance of the train station. On the other hand, Nottingham's tourist information center is located in the city's Victoria Center on Milton Street, some distance away. From the station to the center, take bus 88 and ask to be "deposited" at Victoria Center. You can locate the bus by turning right leaving the station and walking to the first traffic light (Canal Street) where a left turn and a few more steps put you in the bus queue.

Three blocks further along in the same direction on Canal Street, you will come to Castle Road running up the hill to your right. Following it a short distance brings you to Ye Olde Trip to Jerusalem pub where we suggest you rest before continuing on up Castle Road to the Nottingham Castle entrance just off of Castle Place. The pub's "grub" isn't all that bad, so you might want to arrive there about lunchtime. Books about Nottingham and the lore of Robin Hood are on sale in Nottingham Castle.

Meanwhile, back at Victoria Center, the tourist information center is open Monday-Friday from 0830-1730; Saturday, 0900-1300. It has a wide selection of literature to select from, including a walking tour of Nottingham that takes you, among other places, along one of the city's main thoroughfares, Maid Marian Way.

Tom Tower of Christ Church dominates St. Aldates Street in Oxford. The tower houses the Great Tom Bell which traditionally tolls at five minutes past nine to signify the closing of the gates to its original 101 scholars. The student body now numbers about 12,000.

From London...

A DAY EXCURSION TO OXFORD

DISTANCE BY TRAIN: 64 miles (103 km)
AVERAGE TRAIN TIME: 1 hour, 20 min.

The first glimpse of Oxford as you approach it by train from London confirms its title, "the city of spires." Towers, domes, and pinnacles soar on its skyline. It is impressive. Oxford is one of the great architectural centers of the world, with the double distinction of being not only a university city but an industrial one as well. Oxford contains examples of practically every style of architecture since the time of the Saxons. In the less than one-half square mile area comprising the city center, you may see some of the finest ancient buildings in the world. Oxford is the oldest university in Great Britain. It had its beginnings in the 12th century. Between the 13th and 15th centuries, it became an established national institution. It has a history of 800 years of continual existence. Oxford's student body has doubled in the past 30 years to about 12,000 students, of which some 9,000 are undergraduates. There is no separate university or campus. However, the majority of its buildings lie within the center of the city. Basically, the university is a federation of independent colleges. Visitors coming to Oxford during the summer miss the normal sight of students passing between classes and the student sporting activities, but the buildings alone are worth the trip.

In addition to being a seat of learning, Oxford has a strong industrial segment. Foremost in this area is car assembly for British Leyland, the inheritors of the automobile empire founded by William Morris. Printing and papermaking have become Oxford's second industry. Mixing such a wide spectrum of academic and industrial endeavors together has created problems. However, Oxford seems to have worked out a reasonable solution to all of its "town and gown" problems.

OXFORD—*ANCIENT CITY CAMPUS*

A Day Excursion From London

DEPART FROM PADDINGTON STATION*	ARRIVE IN OXFORD†	NOTES
0955	1116	(4)
1050	1150	(1) (2) (3)
1250	1351	(1) (3)
1500	1604	(1) (3)

DEPART FROM OXFORD	ARRIVE IN PADDINGTON STATION	
1715	1822	(2) (3)
1828	1940	(4)
2025	2128	(4)
2055	2205	(3)

Distance: 64 miles/103 km
References: British Rail Table 116
              Thomas Cook Table 536

* See Appendix, page 296, for London station plan
† Travellers-Fare catering facility
(1) Monday thru Friday only, except holidays
(2) Food service available
(3) Daily, except Sundays and holidays
(4) Sundays and holidays only

Train Information
Oxford Train Station: 0865-722333
Inter-City Services: 01-262-6767

Talking Timetable
London-Oxford: 01-402-3131
Oxford-London: 0865-49055/6

THE TRAVEL GUIDE COMPANY
Readers' Information Card

Gentlemen:
Please send additional FREE information regarding rail passes
and low cost transatlantic air fares:

Name _____

Address _____

City _____

State _____ Zip _____

☐ Europe By Eurail   ☐ Britain By BritRail

Like many other cities, Oxford's major problem since World War II has been its traffic. Daily, thousands of automobiles pour into the city, clogging the streets and spoiling the view of its many fine buildings. Admittedly, transitions are rather abrupt when you step from a bustling byway into the tranquility of a college quadrangle, but this typifies Oxford. The city fathers are urging everyone to return to the traditional Oxford method of propulsion—the bicycle. By the way, you're doing your share of solving the problem by arriving in Oxford by train!

The Oxford tourist information center is found on St. Aldate's Street, opposite the town hall and within a stone's throw of the most lavish of the Oxford colleges, Christ Church. The center is open year-round, Monday–Saturday from 0900 to 1730; Sundays, June through August, from 1030–1300 and 1330–1600. A 15-minute walk from the station up Park End—New Road—Queen Street (the street never changes, only its names) brings you to St. Aldate's. Or, you can take any bus marked "City Center" from the bus shelter at the train station. This mode will get you to the information center vicinity in slightly less than 10 minutes, traffic permitting!

Beginning with Easter and throughout the summer, the information center conducts guided tours every day that it is open. These tours that explore the heart of ancient Oxford leave the center at 1045 and 1415. The tour's duration is 2 hours for 50 pence. A daily coach tour from late May through September leaves the information center at 1430. The 1¾-hour trip costs £1.25 for adults and 75 pence for children. The center also has a pamphlet available for 10 pence that details a walking tour of Oxford's historic buildings, gardens, and rivers. The walking tour takes about 2 hours. With the apparent differences in the length of stride between the British and their cousins from the "Colonies," Americans should allow at least another half-hour to complete the course! (Time out for a libation should also be taken into consideration.)

Penzance pirate is portrayed on the roof of the Admiral Benbow Inn on Chapel Street in Penzance. The interior of this 400-year-old tavern is decorated with genuine ship figureheads. Its nautical theme and low-beamed ceilings add to the inn's charm.

AN "OUT & BACK" EXCURSION TO PENZANCE

DISTANCE BY TRAIN: 303 miles (488 km)
AVERAGE TRAIN TIME: 5 hours, 25 min.

Penzance lends itself more to an "out-and-back" excursion rather than a "day excursion"—although with Brit-Rail's new Inter-City 125 trains, it is now possible to visit England's most western town in the course of a day and still be back in London that evening. An excellent way to visit Penzance is to board the sleeper that departs from London's Paddington Station at 1 minute before midnight. You can go aboard about one hour prior to departure time, have the attendant make you a nightcap, and be well into dreamland by the time the train rolls out of London's suburbs. At 0758 you arrive in Penzance Station after being aroused by the attendant with your morning tea or coffee and biscuits. Following a full day's sightseeing in Penzance, you can again board the sleeper for your return to London, or board the Inter-City 125 at 1625 and return to London a shade before 2200 that evening.

Penzance also offers a diversion. When you feel it's time to move on from London to the north and Edinburgh, check out of your London accommodations and take the sleeper to Penzance. Sightsee in Penzance, then arrive back in London as described above at 2159 and leisurely transfer to King's Cross Station to board the night Scotsman at 2355. You'll arrive in Edinburgh the next morning at 0657.

Sleeper reservations should be made well in advance—don't wait until the last minute or you may be disappointed, especially during holidays and peak summer travel periods. Don't forget to check the second class sleeper availability if first class is filled up. Sometimes if you show up on the departure platform approximately 30 minutes before the train leaves, you can pick up a berth cancellation, but don't count on it.

PENZANCE— *WESTERN END OF THE LINE*

A Day Excursion From London

DEPART FROM PADDINGTON STATION*	ARRIVE IN PENZANCE‡	NOTES
0725	1242	(1) (2) (3)
1725	2231	(1) (2) (3) (5)
2359†	0758 + 1	(4)

DEPART FROM PENZANCE	ARRIVE IN PADDINGTON STATION	
1201	1720	(1) (2) (3)
1625	2159	(1) (2) (3)
2135†	0555 + 1	(6)

General Note: Alternate destinations beyond Plymouth include such points as Falmouth, Newquay and St. Ives. Consult British Rail Table 36 or make inquiries with train information personnel.

Distance:	303 miles/488 km
References:	British Rail Table 135
	Thomas Cook Table 530

* See Appendix, page 296, for London station plan
† Sleeping cars and coaches
‡ Travellers-Fare catering facility
(1) Daily, except Sundays and holidays
(2) Food service available
(3) High-speed train
(4) Daily, including holidays
(5) Reservations obligatory
(6) Daily, except Saturdays

Train Information
Penzance Train Station: 0736-5831
Inter-City Services: 01-262-6767

When you arrive in Penzance, you are literally at "the end of the line" insofar as rail travel is concerned. It would be difficult to find a grander coastline. This is Land's End Peninsula, and the sightseeing opportunities are endless. The tourist information center in Penzance is on Alverton Street. When you check with the Travel Center at the top of the exit in the station for train information, the clerk will be glad to show you the first of a series of directional signs leading to the information center.

The street leading uphill from the station is Market Jew Street. Stay on it until you reach the marketplace, a building in the middle of the street. The same street now changes names to Alverton and you'll see a sign at the market guiding you to "Land's End Information Bureau"—that's it!

Two publications available in the information center are extremely helpful to you as a visitor to Penzance. The first, *Penzance Town Trail,* will guide you on a grand tour of the town and its seacoast. It is available for 15 pence. Another smaller one, *A Day in Chapel Street and Quay Penzance,* does exactly what you might think it would—hold you captive on these two streets for hours and hours. Since the latter publication lists numerous commercial enterprises (such as the Admiral Benbow Inn where you will find "good food and drink at the sign"), it is provided free of charge. You need not confine yourself to the limits of Penzance, although you'll find it almost impossible to get away from its magnetic attractions. Local bus service can take you to Land's End and, as we have indicated on the schedule, rail connections to other equally interesting points on the peninsula can be made, such as Falmouth, New Quay, and St. Ives.

The Land's End Information Bureau can give you the background on these interesting places, and you can ask the Travel Center in the train station to work out the needed schedules for you.

Sir Francis Drake statue gazes seaward from atop Plymouth's Hoe, claimed to be the finest natural promenade in Europe. It was from this spot that Drake spied the Spanish Armada and decided to continue his game of bowls—later defeating the Spanish in running naval engagements.

From London...

A DAY EXCURSION TO PLYMOUTH

DISTANCE BY TRAIN: 224 miles (361 km)
AVERAGE TRAIN TIME: 3 hours, 40 min.

Plymouth has one of the finest natural harbors in Europe. From Plymouth Hoe (a Saxon word meaning "high place") there are magnificent views over Plymouth Sound and the harbor. Stand on this huge brow of a hill, which is claimed to be one of the world's finest natural promenades, and you stand in the midst of history. It was here that Sir Francis Drake continued his game of bowls before setting out to deal with the Spanish Armada in 1588. Earlier, in 1577, he set sail from the same harbor in the *Golden Hind* on a three-year voyage around the world. Here, too, in 1620 the Pilgrims embarked on the *Mayflower* for the New World. Too few remember that the first airplane to successfully cross the Atlantic Ocean, the U.S. Navy seaplane *NC4,* touched down in Plymouth Sound. This spot is steeped in historical heritage. Stand here proudly!

The Plymouth of today is a city of two distinct parts —the original Elizabethan section called the "Barbican," and the modern city center that has risen from the devastation and debris of the last world war. Should your time in Plymouth be limited, we suggest you concentrate on visiting the Barbican area of the city. Check with the Plymouth tourist information office in Plymouth's new Civic Center. You can reach it on foot from the train station in about 10 minutes. However, most of the walk is via underground passages where there is little to see—except other visitors who appear to be lost, too! We suggest you take a bus. Board any bus stopping at the shelter to the right of the station entrance. Pay a 9-pence fare and ask to be "deposited" at the Civic Center. Folks who are in a real hurry can hail a taxi for the trip, paying about 90 pence—call it one pound (if you're big tippers like we are).

PLYMOUTH—*PILGRIM'S PROGRESS PORT*

A Day Excursion From London

DEPART FROM PADDINGTON STATION*	ARRIVE IN PLYMOUTH†	NOTES
0725	1049	(1) (2) (3)
0825	1202	(1) (2) (3)
0925	1236	(1) (2) (3)
1025	1354	(1) (2) (3)

DEPART FROM PLYMOUTH	ARRIVE IN PADDINGTON STATION	
1525	1846	(1) (2) (3)
1645	2020	(3) (4)
1725	2036	(1) (2) (3)
1825	2159	(1) (2) (3)
1840	2240	(2) (5)

Distance: 224 miles/361 km
References: British Rail Table 135
              Thomas Cook Table 530

* See Appendix, page 296, for London station plan
† Travellers-Fare catering facility
(1) Daily, except Sundays and holidays
(2) Food service available
(3) High-speed train
(4) Daily, including holidays
(5) Sundays and holidays only

Train Information
Plymouth Train Station: 0752-21300
Inter-City Services: 01-262-6767

The Plymouth tourist information center is located in the main entrance hall of the 14-story Civic Center. It is open Monday-Thursday from 0830 to 1700; Friday, 0830-1630; Saturday, 0900-1600; and closed on Sundays. Train information is best obtained in the station Travel Center. It is on the extreme right as you pass the ticket barrier. The Travel Center is open Monday-Saturday, 0830-2000; Sunday, 0900-1800. It provides train information only.

There is a wealth of printed material available in the tourist center. A sheet describing a short walk around the interesting parts of Plymouth will suffice to catch the highlights of the Hoe and the Barbican. However, you should not overlook the expanded facts presented in the two booklets, *Welcome to Plymouth* and *Plymouth Sound.* The Mini Guide for the city (5 pence) provides more detail, particularly an overview of the countryside surrounding Plymouth. A tastefully done folder, "Plymouth's Historic Houses," contains more facts in its pages than most complete volumes. If you like houses (and who doesn't?), pick up a copy.

If you have ever sung a chorus or two of "The Eddystone Light," you are a likely customer for the engrossing book, *The Four Eddystone Lighthouses,* by Robert Sanderson. Additional information on the lighthouses may also be found in the booklet, *Smeaton's Tower and the Plymouth Breakwater.* The first Eddystone lighthouse was blown down in a storm. The second lighthouse withstood the elements but was destroyed by fire. Smeaton's Tower stood on the Eddystone Reef from 1759 to 1877 and subsequently was re-erected on Plymouth Hoe where it stands today.

If your urge "to go down to the sea in ships" overwhelms you, we suggest a boat trip on Plymouth Sound. The information center has the details, including how to view the nearby Royal Naval Base at Devonport. If your call to the sea is more limited, browsing in the Barbican area will suffice with an occasional glance seaward to impress the locals.

H.M.S Victory, Lord Nelson's flagship at Trafalgar in 1805, has been described as "the proudest sight in Britain." She lies in the Portsmouth Naval Base meticulously preserved. One of the ship's cannon partially shields the *Victory*'s starboard sheet anchor.

From London...

A DAY EXCURSION TO PORTSMOUTH

DISTANCE BY TRAIN: 74 miles (119 km)
AVERAGE TRAIN TIME: 1 hour, 35 min.

A visit to Portsmouth requires priorities—priorities involving the choice of what to see there. The city abounds in vast quantities of history, architecture, amusements, and literature. Portsmouth has variety, contrasts and veneration. Here are a few choices.

If the sea is "your thing," Portsmouth is flanked by natural harbors, east and west. It is the home of one of the world's greatest naval bases, and its resort area, Southsea, offers the largest amusement complex on England's south coast plus four miles of beaches, promenades, and gardens.

Old Portsmouth is for those who relish fine buildings. Lombard Street boasts a host of splendid 17th and 18th century houses, many with distinctive Dutch gables. On adjoining High Street, the motif is primarily 18th century, but this gives way as you approach the ultra modern "new" Portsmouth with its traffic-free shopping precinct on Arundel and Commerce Streets.

The literary greats of Portsmouth—Charles Dickens, H.G. Wells, Conan Doyle, Rudyard Kipling, Neville Shute, to name a few—have left their mark on the city in birthplaces, residences, and museums. Resting in the world's oldest dry dock in Portsmouth naval yard is Lord Horatio Nelson's flagship *H.M.S. Victory*. Alongside the ship stands the *Victory* Museum with relics of England's naval hero, ship models, and an outstanding collection of marine paintings. For priority, our first selection is *H.M.S. Victory*. It has been described as "the proudest sight in Britain," and well it is! Meticulously preserved, it stirs the imagination as you relive the events of the Battle of Trafalgar that "made all England weep." *H.M.S. Victory* is actually a tradition. Going aboard, you step back into history.

PORTSMOUTH—*BRITAIN'S NAVAL PORT*

A Day Excursion From London

DEPART FROM WATERLOO STATION*	ARRIVE IN PORTSMOUTH HARBOR†	NOTES
0748	0919	(1) (2)
0848	1019	(1) (2)
0850	1024	(3)
0948	1119	(1) (2)

DEPART FROM PORTSMOUTH HARBOR	ARRIVE IN WATERLOO STATION	
1653	1825	(1) (2)
1750	1926	(2) (3)
1753	1925	(1) (2)
1853	2025	(1) (2)

Distance: 74 miles/119 km
References: British Rail Table 167
Thomas Cook Table 521

* See Appendix, page 296, for London station plan
† Portsmouth has two train stations—Portsmouth Harbor and Portsmouth & Southsea. Portsmouth Harbor should be used for departures to the Isle of Wight as well as visits to Portsmouth Royal Navy Base. Consult British Rail Table 166 or make inquiries with train information personnel for Portsmouth & Southsea train service. Travellers-Fare catering facility.
(1) Daily, except Sundays and holidays
(2) Food service available
(3) Sundays and holidays only

Train Information
Portsmouth Harbor Station: 0705-25771
Inter-City Services: 01-928-5100

Portsmouth operates three tourist information centers, a national office at the Continental Ferry Terminal, a regional one in the Southsea Castle area, and a local center for city information in the city civic office on Guildhall Square. The information center is a brief walk from the Portsmouth & Southsea train station. Follow the signs or inquire from the Travel Center (train information) in the station. If you plan to visit *H.M.S. Victory,* stay aboard the train from London until it terminates at the Portsmouth Harbor Station. Instead of moving straight ahead to the ferry dock, exit the station on the right-hand side of the platform. From the main street (The Hard) in front of the station, you will be able to see the gate of the naval base on the left. There are no tourist information services available in this area. However, the guards at the naval base gate will be glad to assist you.

The city information office can be reached in 10 minutes' walking time from the naval base gate by proceeding up the main street to the left until you arrive at Guildhall Square. In typical fashion, the main street, High Street, will change its name to Cambridge and then again to Guildhall before you reach your destination.

Some vital statistics in history regarding *H.M.S. Victory* may be beneficial while you are waiting to go aboard. The ship was launched on May 7, 1765. (Lord Nelson was a mere child of 6 on that date.) She is a vessel of 3,500 tons with an overall length of 226-1/2 feet. All totaled, *Victory* carried 104 guns and a complement of 850 officers and men. In 1801, the ship was extensively rebuilt and given the appearance she has today. Recommissioned in April, 1803, she became Nelson's flagship. On October 21, 1805, the English fleet under Nelson's command vanquished the combined fleets of France and Spain off Cape Trafalgar. Lord Nelson was killed aboard the *Victory* in the final moments of what has been termed "the most decisive battle ever fought at sea."

Foy Boat Inn stands behind cannon where a watch house stood in 18th century Ramsgate. In the days of sails, foy-boats took provisions to ships anchored off Ramsgate. The original inn was destroyed in World War II.

From London...

A DAY EXCURSION TO RAMSGATE

DISTANCE BY TRAIN: 79 miles (127 km)
AVERAGE TRAIN TIME: 1 hour, 35 min.

This day excursion to Ramsgate encompasses the northeast tip of England's Kent County called the Isle of Thanet. Although the sea inlets have all been drained, it still bears the semblance of an island with clusters of seaside towns, each with its own character. Londoners were attracted to Thanet early in the 19th century, and it has been a thriving resort area ever since.

Ramsgate has been selected as the primary point for the day excursion, for it is the terminal stop for trains departing London's Victoria Station on the North Kent line. Enroute stops at other Isle of Thanet towns are made on this rail line at Margate and Broadstairs. More comments about them follow. It should be noted that it is possible to return to Victoria Station via another rail route from Ramsgate through Ashford, or yet another route calling at Dover and Folkestone. With so many possibilities, you should consult the timetables posted in all three of the previously mentioned Thanet towns for possible variations of your own itinerary. The train schedule shown on the following page gives details for the London Victoria-Faversham-Margate-Ramsgate-North Kent rail line only.

This frequent train service usually departs from platform 6 in the first bay of London's Victoria Station. *A word of caution:* the first cars (usually four) closest to the ticket barrier will go to Dover. The balance of the cars (usually eight) at the head of the train, will terminate in Ramsgate. The train "splits" at Faversham. You will be reminded of this again by a train announcement when the train stops briefly in the Bromley South Station after leaving Victoria Station and crossing the Thames. Stay alert and board one of the proper cars.

RAMSGATE—*SEASIDE RESORT*

A Day Excursion From London

DEPART FROM VICTORIA STATION*	ARRIVE IN RAMSGATE†	NOTES
0809	1001	(1)
0839	1026	(1)
0939	1126	(1)
1039	1226	(1)

Additional trains depart at 10 and 40 minutes past the
hour on Saturday and Sunday through 2240

DEPART FROM RAMSGATE	ARRIVE IN VICTORIA STATION	
1713	1906	(2)
1813	2006	(1)
1913	2106	(1)
2138	2336	(1)

Additional trains depart at 13 and 38 minutes past the
hour on Saturday and Sunday through 2138

Distance: 79 miles/127 km
References: British Rail Table 212
              Thomas Cook Table 514

* See Appendix, page 296, for London station plan
† See page 302 for Ramsgate station plan. Travellers-
   Fare catering facility.
(1) Daily, including Sundays and holidays
(2) Monday through Friday only, except holidays

Train Information
Ramsgate Train Station: 0843-52341

There are tourist information centers in all three Thanet towns touched by rail service—Margate, Broadstairs, and Ramsgate. The Margate information center is on Marine Terrace east of the train station near the Dreamland amusement center. In Broadstairs, its center is relatively near the train station in Pierrmont Hall. A left turn on High Street out of the train station will bring you to Pierrmont Circle and the information center. Ramsgate's information center is in the city council offices on Queen Street, some distance from the train station, which lies west of the town's center. Bus 52 from the station will take you there for 9 pence; taxi fares average around 70 pence. All three centers operate on approximately the same schedule: Monday–Thursday, 0845–1730, closing at 1700 on Friday. During summer periods, they're open on Saturday, 1000–1300 and 1400–1600; Sunday, 1000–1300. Ramsgate also operates an international information center for visitors coming from the Continent at the Hoverport on Pegwell Bay, a short distance south of Ramsgate.

Margate is the Thanet town that has been conjuring up visions of holidays for years. Its biggest drawing card is the famous Dreamland Pleasure Park set on a 20-acre complex. The municipality of Margate owns 9 miles of seafront with promenades running practically the full distance.

Broadstairs has a Victorian atmosphere about it, becoming a fashionable "watering hole" during the regency of King George IV. Victorians favored holidays in Broadstairs, one of the most eminent being Charles Dickens. A 10-pence leaflet from the information center will permit you to follow in his footsteps and see many other interesting points within the town as well.

Ramsgate, being strong on regency flavor, centers its activities around its royal harbor and marina. The harbor is a source of constant interest, as is the model village at West Cliff, a charming miniature of England's Tudor countryside.

15th century clock tower standing in St. Albans' French Row was originally a curfew tower, the bell dating back to 1335. To the left of the tower stands the Fleur-de-Lys Inn on a site where King John of France was held prisoner after the Battle of Poitiers in 1356.

From London...

A DAY EXCURSION TO ST. ALBANS

DISTANCE BY TRAIN: 20 miles (32 km)
AVERAGE TRAIN TIME: 25 min.

St. Albans takes its name from Britain's first Christian martyr, a Romano-British citizen who was beheaded for his faith on a hilltop outside Verulamium, one of the most important towns at that time in the Western Roman Empire. A magnificent 15th century Norman cathedral now stands on the hilltop and Verulamium has become a parkland on the western side of the city.

St. Albans has much to offer its visitors. Tucked away in various corners of the city are old coach inns, many with a fascinating history. The White Hart Inn, first built in the 15th century, was most recently restored in 1930. The Fleur-de-Lys Inn on French Row was erected between 1420–1440 on the site where King John of France was held prisoner following the Battle of Poitiers. Another inn, the Fighting Cocks, claims to be the oldest licensed house in England. All three of these ancient "watering holes" are open to the public during licensed hours.

French Row in St. Albans, a narrow street of medieval appearance, is fronted by a clock tower built between 1402 and 1411, using flint and rubble from Verulamium. Its original curfew bell was cast in 1335. Across from the bell tower stands the Weigh House Gate, where once candles and tapers were made and sold to pilgrims visiting the shrine of St. Albans. The path through the gate is still the shortest route for pedestrians enroute to the cathedral, proving that the ancients had a sharp eye for customer traffic flow! The St. Albans cathedral contains traces of an 8th century Saxon church. It is, of course, the most important single building in the city. It has one of the largest Gothic naves in Europe. The cathedral tower was built largely of stone from Verulamium.

ST. ALBANS—*BRITISH MARTYR SITE*

A Day Excursion From London

DEPART FROM ST. PANCRAS STATION*	ARRIVE IN ST. ALBANS	NOTES
0810	0832	(1)
1004	1022	(1)
1026	1050	(2)
1204	1222	(1)

DEPART FROM ST. ALBANS	ARRIVE IN ST. PANCRAS STATION	
1619	1652	(1)
1814	1845	(2)
1819	1842	(1) (3)
1929	1953	(3) (4)

Distance: 20 miles/32 km
References: British Rail Table 53
Thomas Cook Table 510

* See Appendix, page 296, for London station plan
(1) Daily, except Sundays and holidays
(2) Sundays and holidays only
(3) Food service available
(4) Monday thru Friday only, except holidays

Train Information
St. Albans Train Station: 56-55352

Arriving in St. Albans, leave the train station by walking uphill towards the city center on Victoria Street. At the second traffic signal, the directional sign for the tourist information center can be seen to the left on Chequers Street. The center is located just beyond the town hall. Office hours are Monday–Friday, 1000–1700; Saturday, 1000–1300 and 1400–1600; closed Sunday. The uphill walk will consume about 15 minutes. The alternative is city bus transportation that departs from a bus shelter in the station area. You can ride to the town hall for 9 pence. The bus stop for returning to the station is at the top of Victoria Street.

Many of the points of interest in St. Albans must be reached on foot. The information center has a pamphlet describing two town walks, both of which include the cathedral and the abbey church. The tour length (2-1/2 miles) may prove to be a bit too ambitious for the less experienced, less conditioned walker but both lead past one or more of the previously described inns where a libation will probably instill a desire to press on—or stay at the inn until "time" is called!

Helpful publications to take on the trails are *A Historical Map* of St. Albans and a *City Guide*. The center has them available at 10 and 25 pence, respectively. The information center is close to the marketplace. Markets are held in St. Albans every Wednesday and Saturday. If you are in town on these days, be sure to "go to market" and enjoy the opportunity of watching the locals barter back and forth with the tradesmen. Everything from apples to zinnias, including the weather and current prices, will become subjects of discussion.

The Roman city of Verulamium is engrossing. You can spend an entire day at the site, visiting its grounds, museum, hypocaust, and theater. If you go, the *Official Guide* of Verulamium will prove to be an invaluable adjunct to your visit there. It is available at the information center for 25 pence.

Tight squeeze for tour bus negotiating the High Street Gate in Salisbury. The gate marks the boundary between the two distinct areas of Salisbury—the close around the cathedral and the city's marketplace. Traditionally, the gate is closed and locked every night.

A DAY EXCURSION TO SALISBURY

DISTANCE BY TRAIN: 84 miles (135 km)
AVERAGE TRAIN TIME: 1 hour, 40 min.

Salisbury holds the distinction of being one of the few English cities *not* originally founded by the Romans. The old town, Old Sarum, had already been in existence since the Iron Age by the time the legions from Rome arrived. The Romans fortified it and the Saxons later developed it into an industrial town. All went well in Old Sarum until arguments between the occupants of the church and the castle caused a new church to be built in the valley below the original town site. This new location proved to be more popular than the old. New Sarum is now officially called Salisbury.

The center of Salisbury has traditionally been divided into two distinct areas, the cathedral and the marketplace. This tradition still exists and the gates leading to the cathedral and the buildings in the close surrounding it are locked every night. Beautiful houses of medieval and Georgian architecture overlook the green.

The marketplace has a history all its own. In the original Charter of 1227, the town was authorized to hold a Tuesday market. This got out of hand and grew into almost a daily market until protests from nearby towns resulted in a reduction of market days in Salisbury to Tuesdays and Saturdays only. Today, Salisbury maintains its traditional market days.

Salisbury boasts a brace of historic inns which have given rest and refreshment to travelers down through the centuries. The fireplaces in the King's Arms Inn have the same stone as that used in the construction of the cathedral. The Haunch of Venison, an old English chop house, was built about 1320. The Red Lion Hotel, dating back to the same era, was the starting point for the *Salisbury Flying Machine,* the nightly horse-drawn coach to London.

SALISBURY—*ANCIENT PAGAN CENTER*

A Day Excursion From London

DEPART FROM WATERLOO STATION*	ARRIVE IN SALISBURY†	NOTES
0910	1034	(2) (3)
1010	1153	(4)
1110	1236	(2) (3)
1310	1434	(3) (4)

DEPART FROM SALISBURY	ARRIVE IN WATERLOO STATION	
1620	1748	(3) (4)
1730	1911	(4)
1804	1930	(1)
1820	1947	(3) (4)

Distance: 84 miles/135 km
References: British Rail Table 142
              Thomas Cook Table 523

* See Appendix, page 296, for London station plan
† Travellers-Fare catering facility
(1) Sundays and holidays only
(2) Daily, including holidays
(3) Food service available
(4) Daily, except Sundays and holidays

Train Information
Salisbury Train Station: 0722-27591

There are two tourist information centers in Salisbury. The national center at 10 Endless Street has information regarding all of England, as well as for Salisbury. The city information center specializes in Salisbury and the area immediately surrounding it. The city office is located on Fisherton Street in the Salisbury City Hall. Fisherton Street runs from the train station to the center of the city. The city hall is on the left side of the street, about 5 minutes' walking time from the station. Business hours are Monday–Friday, 0900–1700; Saturday, 0900–1300; closed Sunday. We suggest you go first to the city information center where you can obtain a city map which should be helpful in locating the other center on Endless Street. Endless Street, by the way, *ends* at Bellevue Row at its northern extremity and *changes* to Queen Street reaching the market square to its south. You can see how easy it could be for one to become endlessly confused!

During the summer you can join a guided walking tour of Salisbury every Wednesday at 1430. The same tour is available on Tuesdays and Saturdays during May and daily from June through late September, with evening hours during that period at 1830. The starting point is from the Guild Hall facing Queen Street. The tour price for adults is 50p; children, 30p; special family rates available. Check either information center for details.

The cathedral has a unity of design that no doubt is attributable to the fact that unlike most other cathedrals, which took centuries to complete, the Salisbury Cathedral was constructed in only 38 years. In other words, it wasn't affected by several different periods of architecture. Its foundation stones were laid in 1220, during the heyday of Gothic design. One of its greatest treasures is its ancient clock mechanism which dates from 1386, one of the oldest pieces of operating machinery in the world. It originally stood in a detached belfry.

Sheffield's Town Hall on the left and its modern extension (right) aptly depict the changing attitudes of the city. The original building was opened by Queen Victoria in 1897; the latter in 1977. Both buildings were constructed from stone taken from the same quarry in an attempt to blend the two contrasting architectural styles. Another extension to the Town Hall (not visible) was opened by the Prince of Wales in 1923. It bears a strong resemblence to a French chateau.

A DAY EXCURSION TO SHEFFIELD

DISTANCE BY TRAIN: 165 miles (265 km)
AVERAGE TRAIN TIME: 2 hours, 55 min.

The name of England's cutlery city, Sheffield, is synonymous with quality. Sheffield also has the connotation of being a typical industrial center, dotted with smoke-belching chimneys and all the atmospheric nightmares that go with that sort of environment. *Not so.* Visitors to Sheffield will be surprised to find the city is quite different from its reputation. Today, though the city is proud to be one of the world's largest industrial complexes, Sheffield's environment has changed entirely—only the "Made in Sheffield, England" quality remains. Initiated in 1972, the city's clean air programs have paid magnificent dividends. Sheffield now is virtually smokeless and is probably the cleanest industrial city in Europe.

Charles Dickens probably would never recognize the town he visited to gather material for his novel *Hard Times.* He found Sheffield's fog thick enough to compare with thick soup. Nor when the fog cleared would he recognize Sheffield's skyline. Slums have been swept away and some of the boldest architecture in Britain has emerged since the city's ambitious building programs and town planning took shape at the end of World War II. A striking example is the award-winning Castle Square in the city center that blends a vehicular round-about (traffic circle) with a pedestrian underpass and a shopping center.

For a quick look at "new" Sheffield, hop aboard the "city clipper," which is a minibus that swings a circular swath through the center of Sheffield. Serving the railway station, as well as other central points, the city clipper service runs on weekdays from 0930 until 1730. Drop the exact fare of 2 pence into the fare box alongside the driver, then lean back and enjoy Sheffield's scenery.

SHEFFIELD—*TRADEMARK OF QUALITY*

A Day Excursion From London

DEPART FROM ST. PANCRAS STATION*	ARRIVE IN SHEFFIELD†	NOTES
0750	1045	(1) (2)
0848	1144	(2) (3)
0906	1209	(2) (4)
0926	1345	(2) (5)

DEPART FROM SHEFFIELD	ARRIVE IN ST. PANCRAS STATION	
1602	1851	(2) (3)
1710	2007	(1) (2)
1732	2032	(2) (5)
1903	2207	(3)

Distance: 165 miles/265 km
References: British Rail Table 53
              Thomas Cook Table 570

* See Appendix, page 296, for London station plan
† Travellers-Fare catering facility/British Transport Hotel
(1) Daily, except Sundays and holidays
(2) Food service available
(3) Monday through Friday only, except holidays
(4) Saturdays only, except holidays
(5) Sundays and holidays only

Train Information
Sheffield Train Station: 0742-26411
Inter-City Services: 01-387-7070

Talking Timetable
London-Sheffield: 01-388-7902
Sheffield-London: 0742-738555

British Transport Hotel
Royal Victoria: 0742-78822

The Civic Information Center of Sheffield invites visitors to use its many services during their stay. The office is open Monday–Friday from 0900–1730. Saturday hours are 0900–1630. The office is located in the city's central library, accessible on foot from the train station. Use the pedestrian subway (underpass) directly in front of the station and walk until you reach the far end. Exit the subway by using the stairs leading off to the right. Back at ground level, walk straight ahead, following the central library and Civic Center directional signs. A set of stairs on your right leads to the library entrance.

Should you need more explicit directions, you may inquire at the Travel Center (train information) in the station. It is located on the far left of the station hall as you exit from the trains. Hours of operation are daily from 0800 to 2000. There is a direct line telephone to the Civic Information Center, located alongside the station's magazine stand. Taxi fare from the station to the center is about 50 pence. Ask to be taken to the public library.

The free city map that you may obtain from the information center in Sheffield is nicely augmented by a *Walk About* booklet. The center sells it for 20 pence. The aim of the publication is to act as a guide to visitors for a walking tour of central Sheffield. Paced for just over 1 hour to complete, the walk is designed to show some of Sheffield's yesteryear as well as the improvements that have taken place more recently. The tour begins in front of the town hall, a short distance from the central library building. The town hall was officially opened by Queen Victoria on May 21, 1897.

For an expanded overview of Sheffield and its environs, ask for a copy of the color brochure, "Sheffield Visitor." It is packed with photos and facts that touch on the city's history, entertainment, sports, shopping, and a number of places to visit. Churches, parks, and homes also are included in this very descriptive publication.

Southampton's Bargate, one of four medieval gates in the wall surrounding the original city, has not lost its character despite numerous alterations. Constructed in the 12th century, it now houses a museum which previously was a guildhall. Its most recent alteration included a new roof and heating system.

From London ...

A DAY EXCURSION TO SOUTHAMPTON

DISTANCE BY TRAIN: 79 miles (127 km)
AVERAGE TRAIN TIME: 1 hour, 10 min.

In the minds of many, Southampton conjures visions of the great transatlantic liners, for it is Britain's prime ocean passenger port and home of many of the world's greatest passenger ships. However, many visitors know little about Southampton's span of centuries which has given it a rich heritage in the history of England and of Europe. Southampton's museums, classic buildings and ancient ruins help reveal this rich and interesting heritage.

Southampton is best seen on foot, with the possible assist from a city bus now and then. From the train station you can board any "city center" bound bus and ask the driver to "deposit" you at the Above Bar Shopping Precinct where you will find the city tourist information center, one of two information services available to Southampton's visitors. The national tourist information center is located adjacent to Dock Gate 3, some distance from the rail station. Bus 709 takes you there for 16p.

To reach the city information center on foot, turn right leaving the train station onto Blechynden Terrace and head for the Civic Center that looms ahead. Enroute, you will pass the Spitfire Museum, a tribute to R.J. Mitchell, the inventor of the famous plane that led the "Battle of Britain." A Spitfire aircraft is on display in the museum and a stop enroute is well worth the time for a visit.

Further in the same direction, you come to Above Bar Street where a right turn will bring you to the previously mentioned shopping precinct and the city information center. Purchase of the official *Southampton Handbook* for 50 pence is recommended. It contains suggestions for sightseeing and also has an engrossing history of Southampton and the area surrounding it.

SOUTHAMPTON—*AN IMPOSING HERITAGE*

A Day Excursion From London

DEPART FROM WATERLOO STATION*	ARRIVE IN SOUTHAMPTON†	NOTES
0835	0942	(1) (2)
0845	1010	(2) (3)
1035	1142	(1) (2)
1135	1242	(1) (2)

Additional trains depart weekdays at 35 minutes past the hour until 1635

DEPART FROM SOUTHAMPTON	ARRIVE IN WATERLOO STATION	
1410	1518	(1) (2)

Additional trains depart weekdays at 10 minutes past the hour until 2110

1710	1818	(3)

Additional trains depart Sundays at 10 minutes past the hour until 1910

Distance:	79 miles/127 km
References:	British Rail Table 158
	Thomas Cook Table 522

* See Appendix, page 296, for London station plan
† Travellers-Fare catering facility
(1) Daily, except Sundays and holidays
(2) Food service available
(3) Daily, including holidays

Train Information
0703-29393

As mentioned in the official handbook, there are four museums within easy walking distance of the city information center. A visit to these museums will gradually unfold a picture of Southampton's past. The closest, at the end of Above Bar Street, is the Bargate Museum which features a local history exhibition, including the Southampton D-Day tapestry. Next in line is the Tudor House Museum where the costumes, paintings and furniture of centuries past are displayed against the oak beams and stone carvings of Tudor House itself. Don't miss the tunnel entrance to the remains of a 12th century merchant's home. The kids will love it!

Third on the agenda is Wool House, once a medieval warehouse and now a showplace for the city's involvement with the sea. If you are not fortunate enough to see the *Queen Elizabeth II* during your Southampton visit, Wool House will make up for it with its history of the *Queens*, complete with models and highlighted by a scale model of the *Queen Mary* from the boardroom of the Cunard Shipping Company. If you never expected to see a marine museum in a wool house, you'll be equally surprised to find an archaeological collection in a museum building that started out as a gunnery store and bears the name of "God's House Tower." Currently, it houses the most extensive collection of post-Roman European pottery to be found in Europe.

The route between the museums, by the way, is dotted with historic buildings, such as the Duke of Wellington Pub and the Red Lion Pub. Pausing for a pint may provide a pleasant period for pondering Southampton's past.

Free guided walks through medieval Southampton depart from the Bargate at 1030 and 1430 daily during August (1030 Wednesdays only) and in other summer months, on Wednesdays, Saturdays, and Sundays. Special "discovery tours" are run Thursday evenings in July and August at 1930. Check the details with either tourist information center.

Unique wonder of the world, Stonehenge is viewed annually by more than 750,000 visitors! The monument stands on a bed of solid chalk. Because it has been constantly robbed of stone and defaced throughout centuries, visitors are no longer permitted to enter the stone circle. Time is taking its toll.

From London ...

A DAY EXCURSION TO STONEHENGE

DISTANCE BY TRAIN: 84 miles (135 km)
AVERAGE TRAIN TIME: 1 hour, 45 min.

Stonehenge is unmatched—truly one of the wonders of the world! There are many opinions regarding the use and purpose of the monument. Whatever the reason for its existence, Stonehenge remains an awe-inspiring reminder of the past.

The landscape for a few miles around the Stonehenge monument reportedly contains more prehistoric remains than any other area of the same size in Britain. There are earthworks, burial sites, erected stones, and hill carvings. Because they belong to the prehistoric period, long before any written records were made, there are many questions about them that we shall never be able to answer. Through his technology, modern man has been able to tell *how* they were made, and in some cases, to say *when* and *by whom*. The unanswered question is *why*.

Stonehenge sits on the Salisbury plain, an almost treeless, windswept plateau. Dating from 2700 B.C. to about 1400 B.C., Stonehenge comprises a circular group of stones roughly 110 feet in diameter that stand in an area surrounded by a low earthen rampart and ditch approximately 200 feet in diameter. The stones are accurately placed to record the position of the sun on the four main dates of the seasons, possibly for an agricultural or a religious purpose. The monument stands on 300 feet of solid chalk, of which only 12 inches have eroded in the past 4000 years. Unfortunately, Stonehenge has been constantly robbed of its stone throughout the centuries. Deodorus Ciculus, historian to Julius Caesar, described Stonehenge as a temple to the sun god Apollo. Modern Britons have marked the area with small clumps of trees to commemorate the Battle of Trafalgar in 1805. The Salisbury Museum contains many Stonehenge objects.

STONEHENGE—*MYSTERIOUS PAGAN SHRINE*

A Day Excursion From London

DEPART FROM WATERLOO STATION*	ARRIVE IN SALISBURY†	NOTES
0910	1034	(2)
1010	1153	(4)
1110	1235	(2) (3)
1145	1321	(4)

DEPART FROM SALISBURY	ARRIVE IN WATERLOO STATION	
1620	1753	(2) (3)
1804	1930	(1)
1820	1947	(3) (4)
2020	2148	(4)

Distance: 84 miles/135 km
References: British Rail Table 142
             Thomas Cook Table 523

* See Appendix, page 296, for London station plan
† Travellers-Fare catering facility in Salisbury train station. Food service is also available at Stonehenge site.
(1) Sundays and holidays only
(2) Daily, including holidays
(3) Food service available
(4) Daily, except Sundays and holidays

Train Information
Salisbury Train Station: 0722-27591

The 0910 train from Waterloo Station in London is met by a special Stonehenge excursion bus at Salisbury Station. The bus is the traditional British red double-decker and easy to spot. It stands in front of the station slightly to the left of the main entrance. You should board it immediately since the premium seats on the upper deck fill up fast. The round-trip fare to Stonehenge and return is £1.25. It's a travel bargain that you won't regret. Admission to the Stonehenge site is included in the fare. The Stonehenge excursion bus leaves the Salisbury Station about 1050 for a short run to the city bus terminal in Salisbury. If there are standees, (the double-decker bus seats 70), they are transferred to another bus at the terminal. Departure for Stonehenge 11 miles away will be approximately on the hour. Enroute time is about 30 minutes. With one hour allotted at the site to view the monument, you can estimate your return to Salisbury at approximately 1300-1315.

We recommend that you use the special excursion bus. Otherwise, you would be obliged to use the regular bus service between Salisbury and Amesbury, then walk or take a taxi for 2 miles to the Stonehenge site. Another excursion bus meets the train arriving in Salisbury from London at 1235 and provides the same service to the Stonehenge site.

If you're not on the excursion bus, you will have to pay 30 pence (15 for children) for admission to Stonehenge. The site opens daily throughout the year at 0930, except for Christmas Eve, Christmas Day, Boxing Day (the first weekday after Christmas), and New Year's Day. May through September, the site closes at 1900; in October at 1730; and November through February, it closes at 1600. Snack bar service and a book shop are available at the entrance to the site.

A sad note. Because of damage to the monument, visitors are no longer permitted to enter the stone circle, but can view it only from a distance. "Time," as the announcement observes, is "taking its toll."

Royal Shakespeare Theatre, built in 1932 to replace original theater destroyed by fire in 1926, employs both decorative and structural brickwork.

Anne Hathaway's Cottage, two miles from the center of Stratford, attracts tens of thousands of visitors annually during visits to Shakespeare country.

From London ...

A DAY EXCURSION TO STRATFORD-UPON-AVON

DISTANCE BY TRAIN: 121 miles (195 km)
AVERAGE TRAIN TIME: 2 hours, 30 min.

Visitors—"pilgrims" as many term themselves—began trickling into Stratford-upon-Avon soon after the first folio of Shakespeare's plays was published in 1623. That "trickle" increased over the centuries. Today, it is a torrent! Swept up in the bardolatry, admirers of William Shakespeare make the pilgrimage to Stratford-upon-Avon regardless of the consequences. It is said that one-half million visitors pass through the narrow corridors and down the twisting staircases of his birthplace every year. Sometimes, it seems like they are all there at the same time you are! Stratford-upon-Avon is crowded, totally commercialized, stereotyped, and yet inevitable. Despite any caution to the contrary, we know you'll go there.

BritRail Pass holders may travel without additional payment from Paddington Station in London to Stratford-upon-Avon via Leamington Spa, where it is necessary to change trains on *all services*. Another route is available between London's Euston Station to Coventry, where you connect with a special motor coach service to and from Stratford-upon-Avon. BritRail Pass holders may use this service by paying the supplementary charge on the coach for the road journey. The traditional Paddington–Leamington Spa–Stratford train service has two drawbacks: Service on Sundays is limited to summer months only (usually May to September), and weekday schedules on this route do not permit attendance at the evening theater performances in Stratford with a return to London the same evening. BritRail's new link through Coventry makes it possible to attend an evening performance and return to London afterwards, except on Sunday. Check British Rail's brochure "The Shakespeare Connection" for complete details.

STRATFORD-UPON-AVON
—SHAKESPEARE COUNTRY

A Day Excursion From London

DEPART FROM PADDINGTON STATION*	ARRIVE IN STRATFORD-UPON-AVON‡	NOTES
0830†	1119	(1)
1150†	1417	(1)
1350†	1633	(2)

DEPART FROM STRATFORD-UPON-AVON	ARRIVE IN PADDINGTON STATION	
1528†	1811	(1) (3)
1705†	1947	(4)
1824†	2055	(1)
2028†	2329	(1)

Distance:　　121 miles/195 km
References:　British Rail Table 116
　　　　　　　Thomas Cook Table 527

* See Appendix, page 296, for London station plan
† Transfer at Leamington Spa for all trains to and from Stratford-upon-Avon
‡ British Transport Hotel
(1) Daily, except Sundays and holidays
(2) Monday thru Friday only, except holidays
(3) Food service available
(4) Sundays and holidays only

Train Information
Leamington Spa Station: 0926-22302

British Transport Hotel
Welcombe Hotel: 0789-295252

Trains arriving in Leamington Spa from Paddington Station stop on platform 2, which adjoins platform 1. From platform 1, you board the single-class train for Stratford-upon-Avon. Returning to Leamington Spa, the train halts at platform 4, where you connect immediately with trains returning to Paddington Station from platform 3. Remember, there is no through train service on this route. You *must* change trains at Leamington Spa, going and returning.

Passengers arriving in Coventry from Euston Station should look for the special motor coach connections to Stratford-upon-Avon in the bus lanes on the right-hand side of the station. The 0840 train from London arrives in Coventry at 0947, connecting with the coach which departs at 1000, arriving in Stratford-upon-Avon at 1030. To assure coach-train connections returning to London, take either the 1730 or the 2340 coach. Check the Travel Centers (train information) in the stations for full details.

The quickest way to see the town and visit Anne Hathaway's Cottage is by open-top double-decker bus. It takes 1¼ hours at £1.50 per person. For a detailed description of the Shakespeare story, sign up for the Shakespearean guided tour, which is 2½ hours and costs £3.00 per person. Both tours depart from the Guide Friday offices at 32 Henley Street opposite Shakespeare's birthplace.

A visit to the Royal Shakespeare Theatre is a must. It is advisable to book theater seats as far in advance as possible. Telephone 0789 69191 for 24-hour information on program and seat availability. To book seats, telephone the theater box office direct at 0789 292271. The theater has three food facilities, the Terrace for lunch and dinner (around £4.00), Bank Side Square for lunch or dinner (about £1.60), and the River Room, a self-service cafeteria. All three are open to non-theater patrons.

Stratford's information center is in Judith Shakespeare's House at 1 High Street. It's open 0900-1900 Monday-Saturday; Sunday, 1400-1630.

Royal Guard stands at castle hill entrance to Windsor Castle grounds. Changing of the guard ceremony takes place daily at 1025 hours.

Royal Oak Restaurant on Datchet Road immediately opposite the Windsor Riverside train station is a delightful rally point following a castle tour.

From London ...

A DAY EXCURSION TO WINDSOR

DISTANCE BY TRAIN: 25 miles (41 km)
AVERAGE TRAIN TIME: 50 minutes

Historic Windsor Castle is the official home of English royalty. William the Conqueror built the first structure on this site, a wooden fort that doubled as a royal hunting lodge. Other English kings added to the castle during their reigns, but despite the multiplicity of royalty and architects, the castle has managed to retain a unity of style all its own. It's the largest inhabited castle in the world.

The present Queen, Elizabeth II, uses the castle far more than any of her predecessors. For this reason, it is wise to inquire if the Queen is in official residence before going to Windsor. When she is, which is usually during the month of April and for periods during March, May, June, and December, the state apartments will be closed to the public. There will still be many areas of Windsor Castle open to the public; however, you will miss seeing the splendor of the various rooms contained within the state apartments. Chances of seeing Her Majesty, should she be in residence, will be rather slim. Nevertheless, during that time you may find Prince Philip watching his polo team in Great Windsor Park. Again, it may be difficult to find the Prince, for although the castle itself occupies a mere 13 acres, the Great Park stretches over 1800 acres below the battlements of the castle. For the full appreciation of Windsor, we definitely recommend a guided tour. It takes 2 hours, costs £2.00, and it's well worth every pence of it! The tour cost includes 80p for admission to St George's Chapel and another 60p for the state apartments. The tours start daily, Saturdays and Sundays included, at 1000 and 1450 from the Windsor tourist information center. The guides are required to pass a demanding examination set by the information center. Ask at the center for details.

WINDSOR—*THE ROYAL CASTLE*

A Day Excursion From London*

DEPART FROM WATERLOO STATION†	ARRIVE IN WINDSOR RIVERSIDE‡	NOTES
0811	0859	(1)
0841	0929	(1)

Additional trains depart at 11 and 41 minutes past the hour until 1641

Sunday service departs at 20 and 50 minutes past the hour. Consult British Rail Table 148 or make inquiries with train information personnel.

DEPART FROM WINDSOR RIVERSIDE	ARRIVE IN WATERLOO STATION	
1414	1503	(1)
1444	1533	(1)

Additional trains depart at 14 and 44 minutes past the hour until 2244

Sunday service departs at 30 and 55 minutes past the hour. Consult British Rail Table 148 or make inquiries with train information personnel.

Distance: 25 miles/41 km
References: British Rail Table 148
                     Thomas Cook Table 523a

*   Second class service only
†   See Appendix, page 296, for London station plan
‡   Travellers-Fare catering facility
   Note: Train service between Paddington Station in London and the Windsor & Eton Central Station also available. Consult British Rail Table 119.

(1) Monday thru Saturday only.

Train Information
Windsor Riverside Station: 0735-61244

You have a choice of two rail routes from London to Windsor. For the schedule given here, we have selected the route departing Waterloo Station in London, arriving at Windsor Riverside Station. This line does not require changing trains enroute. The alternate route which departs Paddington Station in London requires a change at Slough to a shuttle train before arriving at Windsor Central Station. If you take the Paddington-Slough line, the shuttle train arrives and departs in Slough from track 1. Either route gives you a magnificent view approaching Windsor Castle. On either train, sit on the left-hand side (outbound) to take full advantage of the scenery.

The tourist information center is in the Windsor Central Station. Signs with the traditional "i" will lead the way from either arrival point. The grounds of Windsor Castle are immediately across the street from the information center. The center operates on a daily schedule year-round from 1000-1700. For certain, purchase an illustrated guidebook on Windsor Castle even though you plan to take the guided tour. It will become a fond reminder of your visit.

From the battlements of Windsor Castle, you may look down and across the stately Thames River onto the playing fields of Eton College where "how the game is played" has always been more important than the final score. The schoolyard and cloisters are open from 1400 to 1700 from October through March. In summer, closing is extended to 1800. Inquiries should be made at the Windsor information center where brochures and guides are available.

If you have not been introduced to the British public house, there is no better time than now! The Royal Oak, directly across the street from Windsor Riverside Station, is highly recommended. No more prim a pub can you find in all of England. Its impeccable oaken interior matches the high quality of its food and service. The inn was constructed as an alehouse in 1736 and restored in 1937.

York Minster, largest Gothic church in Britain, stands on a site previously occupied by a Roman military headquarters and a former Norman cathedral. The earlier remains are still visible. Construction of the Minster, begun in 1220, required approximately 250 years to finish.

From London ...

A DAY EXCURSION TO YORK

DISTANCE BY TRAIN: 188 miles (302 km)
AVERAGE TRAIN TIME: 2 hours, 10 min.

"The history of York," according to King George IV, "is the history of England." The Romans took it from a Celtic tribe, the Brigantes, in A.D. 71. According to legend, King Arthur captured the city sometime between 406 when the Roman legions retreated and the 7th century when the Saxons took charge. The Danes ran the Saxons off the property in 867, only to get their comeuppance from the Anglo-Saxons when Edmund tamed them in 944. In 1066, York saw the fastest turnaround ever when King Harold of England defeated the King of Norway at Stamford Ridge, 6 miles from York. Nineteen days later, York's management (and all of England, as a matter of fact) passed to the Normans when Harold was killed in the Battle of Hastings.

William the Conqueror, following his victory at Hastings, came north to quell a rebellion which he did by his version of urban renewal, known in those days as the "scorched-earth" policy. However, the ruins and rubble of the Romans, the Saxons, the Vikings, and the Anglo-Saxons never was thoroughly cleaned out. Much of it has layered up and is now being unearthed for you to view upon arrival in the city of York. Charles I, fleeing the fermenting civil war, left London in 1639 to take residence in York. Cromwell's troops finally took York in July, 1644. A condition of surrender was that there would be no pillaging, thus, the fine medieval stained glass of York Minster was saved. It is estimated that the Minster contains more than one-half of all the medieval stained glass in England.

York, along with Chester, has completely retained its ancient city walls. You will see a part of them as you exit the York train station. York is a city of all ages.

YORK—*FINE MEDIEVAL CITY*

A Day Excursion From London

DEPART FROM KING'S CROSS STATION*	ARRIVE IN YORK‡	NOTES
0725†	0940	(1) (2) (3)
0800†	1018	(1) (2) (3)
0900	1114	(1) (2) (3)
0935	1143	(1) (2) (3)
1000	1223	(2) (3) (4)

DEPART FROM YORK	ARRIVE IN KING'S CROSS STATION	
1605	1820	(1) (2) (3)
1702	1926	(1) (2) (3)
1802	2012	(2) (3) (4)
1805†	2012	(1) (2) (3)

Distance: 188 miles/302 km
References: British Rail Table 26
               Thomas Cook Table 575

* See Appendix, page 296, for London station plan
† Limited accommodations, all seats reservable
‡ Travellers-Fare catering facility

(1) Daily, except Sundays and holidays
(2) Food service available
(3) High-speed train
(4) Sundays and holidays only

Train Information
York Train Station: 0904-25671
Inter-City Services: 01-278-2477

Talking Timetable
London-York: 01-278-9326
York-London: 0904-34561

British Transport Hotel
Royal Station Hotel: 0904-53681

Following a relaxing ride aboard an Inter-City 125 train from King's Cross Station in London, we suggest that you check in with the York tourist information center. Although it is a 10-15 minute walk from the train station, you will see a lot of history enroute. Turn left and walk along the city wall toward York Minster. After crossing the River Ouse, you will arrive at the intersection of Duncombe Place and St. Leonard's Place just before the Minster. Turn left on St. Leonard's. The information center is just beyond the Theatre Royale on the right side of the street.

The center is open June–September, Monday–Saturday, 0900–2000; Sunday, 1400–1700. From October through May, the center is closed on Sunday and operates Monday through Saturday 0900–1700. City tours leave from the fountain opposite the center. Summer tour hours are 1015, 1415, and 1915 daily. The announcement describing the availability of the tours states: "The tour, which is on foot, will help you to discover the wealth of interest the city offers to its visitors and learn something of its history. There is no charge—our reward is your appreciation of this ancient and historic city." A warmer, more sincere welcome would be hard to find! York is a compact city, easy to stroll around in. Among its points of interest, York Minster draws first choice. We suggest you also visit the National Railway Museum, situated on Leeman Street not too far from the York train station. It will stand comparison with any railway museum in the world. Another is the Castle Museum, one of the most interesting folk museums in the world. It has a water mill that operates all through the summer. A walk on at least a portion of the city's walls is a must. While on the subject of walking, no doubt you will find the narrow winding streets of York the most fascinating of all the city's attractions. One of these streets, The Shambles, is reputed to be one of the best preserved medieval streets in Europe. Originally the street was crammed with butcher shops, but its overhanging, half-timbered buildings now house an assortment of stores and bookshops.

George Square, Glasgow's "most picturesque breathing space," is named after King George III, who was a bit obtrusive to colonists but generally well liked by the Scots. Beyond the Prince Albert equestrian statue stands Glasgow's tourist information office and its Queen Street Train Station.

Glasgow, like Pennsylvania's Pittsburgh and England's Sheffield, is shedding its industrial shroud of former years. Originally termed "one of the finest cities in the world to get out of," Glasgow's emergence from a soot-laden atmosphere into clean air and a freshly scrubbed facade has been no easy task, but it is well on its way.

Edinburgh was selected as a "base city" site for Scotland, since it is unquestionably the country's most beautiful city. Glasgow, on the other hand, is probably as conveniently located for access to the Scottish day excursion selections as is Edinburgh. For this reason, we are introducing the "Glasgow Connection," wherein the choice of base cities—Edinburgh or Glasgow—becomes a matter of individual selection. The excellent train service between the two cities permits visitors to move with ease between them.

Glasgow is Scotland's largest metropolis, with a population well over 1 million. It is the gateway to Loch Lomond and the western highlands. Glasgow's River Clyde flows into the Firth of Clyde, thus opening its western waterways to a myriad of islands and the Irish Sea. Glasgow abounds with sights to see, ranging from its great shipyards on the River Clyde to a variety of museums and universities. It is said that Glasgow has more parks than any other European city of its size. One in particular, George Square, opposite the Queen Street train station, projects a panorama of Scottish and British history in its statuary of those individuals who forged the British Commonwealth through their science, leadership, and literature.

George Square is fronted by the City Chambers and the North British Hotel, a member of British Transport Hotels (BTH), which also adjoins the Queen Street Station. The tourist information center is located within the square alongside the Prince Albert statue.

GLASGOW'S TRAIN STATIONS

Glasgow has two main train stations. Trains arriving from southwestern Scotland and England terminate in the Glasgow Central Station. For train travel north out of Glasgow and east to Edinburgh, the Glasgow Queen Street Station becomes the departure point. A convenient city bus service links the two train stations. However, the 15-minute walk between the two stations runs along some of the city's finer shopping areas, thereby offering the opportunity of walking off a few British "pounds."

On foot from the Queen Street Station, walk past George Square to St. Vincent Street. Turn right for one block to Buchanan Street, then turn left. Buchanan is a pedestrian shopping precinct. Halfway down Buchanan, you will intersect with a short section of Gordon Street, reserved for pedestrians (and shops). A right turn at this point, then continuing along Gordon Street, brings you to the Glasgow Central Station on your left in two blocks. From the Central Station to the Queen Street Station, merely reverse the line of march. Those wishing to avoid running the shopper's gauntlet on Buchanan Street may proceed between the two stations by traversing Queen and Argyle streets. Any policeman will be glad to provide directions.

The rail link bus service is strictly for transferring passengers between the two rail stations with no stops in between. The buses run Monday-Friday from 0700-2300; Saturday, 0800-2300; and the Sunday schedule runs from 1400-2300. Departures are about every 5 minutes during peak hours, every 10 minutes at other times. Fares are 10 pence for adults; 8 pence for children. You pay on the bus. BritRail Passes are *not* accepted for the bus transfer. The time enroute varies between 5-10 minutes, depending upon traffic conditions. The vehicles are brightly colored minibuses.

The Glasgow Central Station is a huge, sprawling complex that caters to every need of the train traveler, ranging from restrooms with bathing facilities to a grand Victorian hostelry—the BTH Central Hotel, with its internationally known Malmaison Restaurant.

MONEY EXCHANGE is only available within the station during non-banking hours. An office of the Royal Bank of Scotland is situated directly across from the main entrance of the station. After banking hours, ticket window No. 9 in the Central Station will exchange foreign currency and cash traveler's checks up to a $50 limit. The American Express office is to the left of the station entrance at 115 Hope Street. The Thomas Cook office is just one block to the right of the station entrance at 15-17 Gordon Street.

HOTEL BOOKINGS may be arranged at the tourist information center on George Square, immediately in front of the Queen Street Station. Bookings for the British Transport Hotels (BTH) system can be made in the lobby of the Central Hotel. The station entrance to the hotel is located on the far left-hand side of the station's main hall as you exit from the trains.

TOURIST INFORMATION is available in Glasgow's information center on George Square. (See Queen Street listing for hours of operation.)

TRAIN INFORMATION is displayed in the Central Station by means of a huge, overhead, manually operated train information board to your left as you exit from the trains. For expanded train information, visit the Inquiries & Reservations Office (Travel Center) on the right side of the main hall at the end of platforms 1, 2, and 3.

TRAIN RESERVATIONS may be arranged in the Travel Center. For sleeping car reservations, you will be directed to the Inter-City Sleeper Center at the entrance to platform 1.

Taxi queues are located at the main entrances of the Central Station, just beyond the Caledonia Restaurant. Other food facilities include the Arran Lounge, Royal Scot Bar, and a Rail Bar.

Tolbooth Steeple, erected in 1626, is all that remains at the intersection of High Street and Trongate in Glasgow of a once sprawling complex including the Town Hall and jail. Other interesting landmarks in this vicinity include the Tron Steeple (1637) and the Mercat Cross (replica-1979).

Glasgow's Queen Street Station is the terminal for trains serving northern Scotland and Edinburgh.

MONEY EXCHANGE: Inquiries should be made at the tourist information center on George Square across the street from the station entrance. After banking hours, ticket window No. 9 in the Central Station can provide limited banking services.

HOTEL BOOKINGS for Glasgow, and for all of Scotland through the "Book-A-Bed-Ahead" plan, may be arranged in the tourist information center on George Square. The BTH North British Hotels sits to the left of the station's main exit facing George Square. A British Transport Hotel (BTH) reservation service is available in the hotel lobby.

TOURIST INFORMATION is available at the information center on George Square. Hours of operation: (June through September) Monday–Saturday, 0900–2100; Sunday, 1400–2100; (October–May) Monday–Saturday, 0900–1700; closed Sunday. The center has a wealth of Glasgow information on hand, including an interesting pamphlet describing the 12 statues surrounding the center in George Square and a description of the various buildings fronting the square. Also available is a descriptive folder entitled, "Glasgow—50 Things to See and Do." A copy will keep you busy and a simple map on the back cover of the folder should suffice for most directions within the city center. For a complete run-down on practically every facility and service offered in and around Glasgow, ask for a copy of the green brochure, "Seeing Glasgow."

TRAIN INFORMATION is available in the Travel Center office situated on the left-hand side of the station as you face the train platforms.

TRAIN RESERVATIONS can be made in the Travel Center. For sleeping car reservations, use the "Inter-City Sleeper Center" in the Central Station.

GLASGOW GAZETTE

The city's subway system has resumed operation following an extensive modernization program. Basically, the service is a circular line with trains running in either direction beneath the city center. It provides a 3-minute service from each of its 15 stations, achieving a circular journey in about 22 minutes. A separate subway, the Argyle Line, links the British Rail suburban networks. The main interface with British Rail services, however, is the subway station at Buchanan Street linked with the Queen Street Station by a moving pedestrian platform.

For readers going on a day excursion to Loch Lomond, the route is served by an electric train service that departs from subterranean platform 10 in the Queen Street Station. To reach it after entering the main hall of the station, turn left and exit the station via the side entrance, where you turn right to follow the well-marked "Platform 10" signs.

In the Queen Street Station's Travel Center, you may obtain full information and tickets for cruising on the Clyde River aboard the Caledonia MacBrayne vessel, *Glen Sannox*. Connecting rail services to the ship's pier originate in the Queen Street Station. The third Clyde steamship to bear the *Glen Sannox* name, the vessel offers a number of interesting cruises on the Clyde River and the Firth of Clyde. On Saturdays during the summer, a special upriver cruise is conducted. Advance bookings are recommended.

If you are in Glasgow on a Tuesday evening during July or August, join the free tour of George Square and its surrounding streets which departs from the information center at 2100. If you miss that tour, you can try for another one at 1045 on Wednesdays. Train buffs in particular will not want to miss Glasgow's Museum of Transport. Reached by electric train service from Glasgow Central Station to Pollokshields East Station, the museum is situated in Albert Drive. An operating model railway is one of the museum's highlights.

THE "GLASGOW CONNECTION"

All day excursions described in Chapter 12 departing from Edinburgh also may be taken from Glasgow. In fact, three of the day excursions—Ayr, Loch Lomond, and Stranraer—require passing through Glasgow. For these excursions, readers residing in Glasgow need only refer to the appropriate day excursion schedule in Chapter 12 for the "Glasgow Connection."

Two of the day excursions—Dunbar and Dunfermline —can only be reached conveniently through Edinburgh. Consequently, readers need only refer to the Glasgow-Edinburgh shuttle service schedule to determine the "Glasgow Connection" for these day excursions.

Four day excursions—Aberdeen, Dundee, Montrose, and St. Andrews—are so situated on Scotland's rail lines that they may be reached either by direct connection from the Queen Street Station in Glasgow or through Edinburgh. A condensation of the "Glasgow Connections" for direct service appears on page 218.

Four day excursions—Inverness, Kyle of Lochalsh, Perth, and Stirling—are most conveniently reached from Glasgow by direct train service from the Queen Street Station, rather than through Edinburgh. For a condensation of the "Glasgow Connections," you are referred again to page 218 for details.

The "Glasgow Connection" for express trains to London is given on page 219 of this chapter. All services shown are subject to alteration. Readers are advised to consult with the schedules posted in the train stations or with the British Rail Travel Centers for train information before commencing each journey. The publishers cannot be held responsible for changes or inaccuracies in the schedules.

Regardless of which city you select as your "base," don't forget that the frequent train service between Glasgow and Edinburgh enables you to make a "day excursion" to the one you didn't select as your base. For what to see and do in Edinburgh, consult the following chapter on Scotland's capital for details.

"GLASGOW CONNECTIONS"

Excursion Destination	Depart Glasgow	Destination Arrive	Destination Depart	Return Glasgow	Notes
Aberdeen	0735	1037	1535	1837	weekdays
	0935	1234	1750	2051	"
	1135	1434	1950	2253	"
	1020	1411	1830	2157	Sundays
Dundee	0735	0909	1507	1645	weekdays
	0935	1108	1701	1837	"
	1135	1308	2115	2253	"
	1020	1220	1910	2026	Sundays
Inverness	0740	1152	0815	1212	weekdays
	1004	1413	1505	1913	"
	2330	0449	2350	0546	sleepers
Montrose	0735	0948	1621	1837	weekdays
	0935	1143	2036	2253	"
	0855	1115	1916	2157	Sundays
Perth	0735	0838	1533	1645	weekdays
	0935	1039	1727	1837	"
	1135	1239	1942	2051	"
	0855	1009	1912	2036	Sundays
Stirling	0935	1006	1801	1837	weekdays
	1135	1206	2216	2253	"
	0855	0928	2110	2152	Sundays

St. Andrews Train from Glasgow Queen Street Station to Dundee. Transfer to St. Andrews bus, departing every hour on the half-hour.

GLASGOW—EDINBURGH SHUTTLE SERVICE

Express Service (weekdays only) departs Glasgow Queen Street Station for Edinburgh: 0930 & hourly to 1630; also 0910, 1830, 1930, 2030 & 2130 (45 minutes). Returns to Glasgow from Edinburgh (weekdays only): 0900 & hourly to 1500; also 1900, 2000, 2100 & 2200 (45 minutes).

Intermediate Service (weekdays) departs Glasgow Queen Street Station for Edinburgh: 0730, 0800, 0830, 0900 & hourly to 1600; also 1650, 1710, 1732, 1800, 1900, 2000, 2100 & 2200 (47 minutes). Returns to Glasgow from Edinburgh (weekdays): 0700, 0805, 0830, & hourly to 1530; also 1600, 1630, 1700, 1730, 1800, 1830, 1930, 2030, 2130 & 2300 (47 minutes).

Sunday Service departs Glasgow Queen Street Station for Edinburgh at 0800 & hourly until 2300 (55 minutes); returns to Glasgow from Edinburgh at 0730 & hourly until 2230, also 2305 (55 minutes).

GLASGOW-LONDON TRAIN SERVICE
(First & second class accommodations for all services listed.)

DEPART FROM GLASGOW CENTRAL STATION	ARRIVE IN EUSTON STATION*			
	Weekdays	Saturdays	Sundays	NOTES
0710	1240	1240	N/S	(1)
0830	N/S	N/S	1736	(1)
0910	1438	1438	N/S	
1010	1528	1528	N/S	(1)
1040	N/S	N/S	1853	(1)
1205	1743	1743	N/S	
1423	1936	1936	N/S	(1)
1600	N/S	N/S	2122	(1)
1603	2116	2116	N/S	(1)
1730	2248	2248	N/S	(1)
2150	0559	0744(3)	0559	(2)
2310	0533(3)	N/S	0533(3)	(2)

Distance: 402 miles/647 km
References: British Rail Table 65
             Thomas Cook Table 565

*See Appendix, page 296, for London station plan. Travellers-Fare catering facility and British Transport Hotels available.
N/S—No Service

(1) Food service available
(2) Sleeping cars only
(3) Passengers may remain aboard until 0730

USEFUL PHONE NUMBERS
Tourist Information
British Tourist Authority: 01-499-9325
London Tourist Board: 01-730-0791

Train Information
Glasgow Information: 041-221-3223
London Transport: 01-222-1234

British Transport Hotels
Scotland (Glasgow): 041-221-3945
Central Reservations Service (London): 01-278-4211

One o'clock gun at Edinburgh Castle is fired every day except Sunday to provide an unusual time check for the city. Visiting shoppers on Princes Street (visible at the lower level in the background), unaware of the firing may be seen taking cover promptly at 1:00 p.m.

220

"This profusion of eccentricities, this dream in masonry and living rock," wrote Robert Louis Stevenson of Edinburgh, "is not a drop-scene in a theater, but a city in a world of everyday reality!" There is an understandable feeling of rock-like perpetuity enveloping Edinburgh. Formed by volcanic heat, scoured and shaped by ice-age glaciers in a valley punctuating its skyline with upward thrusting crags, Scotland's capital city of Edinburgh is nothing short of dramatic in its setting.

Edinburgh's exact origins are lost in antiquity. Yet from its earliest days, its stern, almost aloof countenance has retained and fostered those enduring qualities that have inspired great men to great achievements. Edinburgh is actually two cities. The Old Town, built on a rocky ledge running from Edinburgh Castle to the Royal Palace of Holyroodhouse, is steeped in ancient history. It huddled on high ground in typical medieval fear of attack. The New Town, which took form on the lower side of North Loch, a lake created from a swamp and eventually drained in 1816, spread serenely in a succession of streets and avenues reflecting the optimism of the latter centuries.

Its contrasts of two cities within a city are further reflected by Edinburgh's reserved exterior on the one hand, and on the other hand, by its capability of expressing great warmth and, upon occasion, a high degree of gaiety. Edinburgh has been termed one of the most attractive capital cities in the world. We take no issue with that statement. As Oliver Wendell Holmes aptly put it, "Edinburgh is a city of incomparable loveliness."

From the beauty of its setting, enhanced by its architecture, with the turbulence of its history and the quality of its citizens—Edinburgh is a city of inexhaustible delight and interest. Edinburgh Castle, Holyroodhouse, the Royal Mile, and Princes Street await your visit. Welcome to Scotland's capital city!

DAY EXCURSIONS

A "baker's dozen," 13 exciting day excursions have been selected for our readers. All were selected so that those who prefer staying in Glasgow rather than in Edinburgh can equally enjoy their day excursions. (See "Glasgow Connections" in Chapter 11.)

Scotland is known as "the land that likes to be visited." To ensure that your opportunity to see this marvelous country by rail includes as many of its features as possible, we have divided the selected day excursions into Scotland's four geographic areas: the eastern coast, central region, western coast, and the highlands.

Along the eastern coast of Scotland, starting at the North Sea fishing port of Dunbar near the English border, we then swing north from Edinburgh through the tri-cities of Dundee, Montrose, and Aberdeen—not overlooking a stop enroute at the golfing capital of the world, St. Andrews. In the central part of the country, we have selected excursions to two of Scotland's most historic cities—Perth and Stirling—plus a visit to Andrew Carnegie's birthplace, Dunfermline, and a cruise on one of the world's most famous lakes, Loch Lomond. For our forays to the western coast, we delve deep into the heart of Robert Burns' country by a visit to Ayr, the poet's favorite town. Further west on the Firth of Clyde, we call at Stranraer, the gateway to the Irish Sea and the "Emerald Isle" of Ireland.

North in the highlands, Inverness serves as the gateway to explorations of Loch Ness with its legendary monster "Nessie" and as a "base city" for a dash to the west by train to the Kyle of Lochalsh and the Isle of Skye.

Scotland has often been compared to an iceberg, not in the sense of temperature, but in the respect that there is much more to the country than first meets the eye. Come to Scotland with an open mind, a keen eye, and a sense of adventure.

ARRIVING AND DEPARTING

By Air: Prestwick, Scotland's international airport located 29 miles southwest of Glasgow, is a convenient port of entry for overseas visitors arriving in Great Britain. It is the most fog-free airport on the British Isles. Many international air carriers have service to Prestwick, thus providing an unusual opportunity for BritRail travelers to take advantage of "open-jaw" airline ticketing by arriving or departing on one leg of the transatlantic flight in Scotland, rather than both in the London complex of Gatwick and Heathrow. Direct rail service connecting with Glasgow is available from the train station in the town of Prestwick. The most convenient mode of transport between the train station and the airport is by taxi (average fare, 70 pence). There is a taxi queue at the airport arrival hall exit, and if a taxi is not standing at the Prestwick train station when you arrive, you may ask the stationmaster to summon one for you. Train time between Prestwick and Glasgow is 1 hour, departing every half-hour on weekdays, hourly on Sundays. Trains arrive in Glasgow Central Station, where you must transfer to the Queen Street Station for train connections to Edinburgh (see page 218). Airport buses run from Prestwick to Edinburgh daily at 0740 and 0930; from Edinburgh to Prestwick, daily at 0910 and 1140. The fare is £4.90. The bus fare from Prestwick to Glasgow is £2.00—all flights are met by this bus service to Glasgow.

By Train: There is only one major train station in Edinburgh—Waverley Station. Some Inter-City trains from London go on to Aberdeen after a brief station stop in Edinburgh. If you are aboard one of these trains, be prepared to "set down" in the Waverley Station as quickly as possible following your arrival. Edinburgh does have a suburban station—Haymarket—where all trains halt enroute to Glasgow or Aberdeen. Trains arriving from England via Newcastle and York bypass the Haymarket Station.

Floral clock attracts Edinburgh's citizens and visitors alike. Built in 1903 in the city's West Princes Gardens, it is the oldest floral clock in the world. A cuckoo pops out to herald every quarter hour, and the flowers are frequently changed for important events.

EDINBURGH'S TRAIN STATION: *WAVERLEY*

The train terminal in Edinburgh appears to be completely immersed in an open ravine. The area was once a swamp that was converted into a lake as a northern defense for Edinburgh Castle during the reign of King James II (1437–1460). The lake was drained in 1816 to become the site of the Princes Street Gardens separating the Old Town and New Town in Edinburgh. In 1847, rail lines were laid through the middle of the gardens to the east end where Waverley Station was constructed. The tracks are now all but concealed by landscaping. Today's Waverley Station complex is the second largest in Britain.

Waverley Station is equipped with 21 tracks strewn about in a labyrinth of steps and passageways that could easily drive a laboratory white rat "bananas." However, a plentitude of signs and the helpful presence of Edinburghers (who appear to be specially trained to assist visitors) will help you put it all together. Basically, there are three accesses to Waverley Station. The first is a set of rather steep steps connecting the north side of the station (the trackage runs east and west) with Princes Street, the city's main artery. The second and third approaches are ramps leading from the main floor of the station to the Waverley Bridge running between the Old Town and New Town. Both ramps have pedestrian walkways. The northern ramp serves incoming vehicles; the one to the south is for outgoing vehicles.

Many of the facilities sought by incoming passengers, such as banking, city information, and hotel accommodations, are located nearby in the combined offices of the Scottish Tourist Board and Edinburgh City Information Center located on the south end of Waverley Bridge. To reach the center, utilize the pedestrian/vehicle ramp on the south side of the station, turning left as you reach the Waverley Bridge level. There are several "Tourist Information" signs to help guide the way.

Tracks 12 to 18 form the backbone, or center, of the Waverley Station. Situated at the entrance to these tracks is a digital display bulletin board for train arrivals, departures, and special announcements. If your train is departing from tracks other than 12 to 18, ask the railroad personnel at the ticket barriers for directions; otherwise, you may end up in some dark corner like a white rat!

Pay special attention to multiple train departures from the same track. In other words, a line of coaches on a single train track can actually be two trains departing for two separate destinations. They are announced with red-bannered "Front Train" or "Rear Train" signs. However, it pays to ask questions—one advantage you have over the rat!

The Travel Center (train information) is located in the waiting room area of the station. Covered by a huge glass dome, the waiting area also contains digital arrival/departure information and a series of facilities, including restrooms, a magazine kiosk, and the Talisman Bar and the Talisman Buffet. The principal entrance to this area is located across the main station concourse from the stub ends of tracks 16 and 17.

The North British Hotel, topped by a mammoth 200-foot Gothic clock tower, is located between Waverley Station and Princes Street. A member of the British Transport Hotels (BTH) system, the hotel is commended as an excellent accommodation in Edinburgh and a "must" place to visit. Erected during the Age of Steam, the hotel's spacious foyer and well-appointed lounges must be seen to be appreciated.

Guests of the North British Hotel may utilize the lift (elevator) services between the hotel's lobby on Princes Street and the station level. The lift entrance in the station is under a lighted "Hotel" sign opposite the end of track 17, next to the station's waiting area entrance. Use the lift to a service passageway where signs will lead you to the regular hotel elevators.

MONEY EXCHANGE: A Bureau de Change operated by the Clydesdale Bank, is located in the Edinburgh information center. Hours of operation: (July to September 9) Monday–Saturday, 0830–2030; Sunday, 1100–1500. (May–June and September 10–30): Monday–Saturday, 0830–1930; Sunday, 1100–1500. (October–April) Monday–Friday, 0900–1730; Saturday, 0900–1230; closed Sunday.

HOTEL ACCOMMODATIONS: A service is provided by the Edinburgh Tourist Information Center. Hours of opening are: (October–April) Monday–Friday, 0900–1800; Saturday, 0900–1300; closed on Sunday. (May–June and September 9–30) Monday–Saturday, 0830–2000; Sunday 1100–2000. (July–September 8) Monday–Saturday, 0830–2100; Sunday, 1100–2100. The accommodation booking fee is 25 pence per booking.

TOURIST INFORMATION: There are two information centers within Edinburgh's information center, operating at the same hours as the accommodations section mentioned above. The first section has information on all of Scotland and is located to your left as you enter the center. The other section specializes in information regarding the city of Edinburgh. You will find it on your right as you enter, along with a self-service area for purchasing Scottish books, maps, and posters. For bus tours of Edinburgh, you will be referred to the Regional Transportation Organization, whose offices are located on the opposite end of Waverley Bridge. A half-day tour is conducted from April to November at 0930 and 1330 daily. Adult fare: £4.00, including entry fees; children £2.00.

TRAIN INFORMATION: Visit the Travel Center in the waiting room area of Waverley Station. City information is *not* available in this office. Operating hours are from 0830–2100 daily.

TRAIN RESERVATIONS may be made in the Travel Center at any one of the counters operating during the time of your visit.

Greyfriar's Bobby, a true legend of a small Skye terrier's devotion to his master in both life and death, is commemorated in Glasgow by a fountain with his statue on it. A film by Walt Disney has made Bobby world famous. The Bobby Bar may be seen in the background.

GREYFRIAR'S BOBBY

On Candlemaker Row, a short distance from Edinburgh's Royal Mile, stands a statue in tribute to a small dog's affection and fidelity to his master. In 1858, a wee Skye terrier followed the remains of his master, Auld Jock, to Greyfriar's churchyard, where the dog lingered and slept on his master's grave for 14 years until his death in 1872.

People tried to take Bobby away. They even found a home for him in the country. Still, Bobby returned to the churchyard where friends began bringing food to sustain him during his vigil. The story of Greyfriar's Bobby spread throughout Edinburgh, and soon Bobby's tale of devotion reached Queen Victoria in London, who sent a special envoy, Lady Burdett-Coutts, to investigate this unusual story.

Bobby, in the meantime, had made friends with a number of children in a nearby orphanage. The terrier brought joy and love to the children, particularly to Tammy, a crippled boy with whom Bobby would play by the hour. However, Bobby lived his own life and returned nightly to his master's grave—at first secretly, for the presence of a dog in a churchyard was unthinkable in those times. But as Bobby won hearts, he gained privileges, too. He even won the heart of the Lord Provost of Edinburgh who had a collar made for the dog in 1867 and paid Bobby's licensing fee! (The collar can be seen today in the Huntley House Museum on Canongate Street.)

Bobby never went to London to see the Queen, but royal annals reflect that the Queen actually was planning to pay *him* a visit at Greyfriar's. However, Bobby died before that honor became a reality.

A fountain with Bobby's statue on it stands close to the iron gates of Greyfriar's churchyard, where Auld Jock and his faithful dog are interred. The story of Greyfriar's Bobby was filmed by Walt Disney. We think it's worth your while to visit Greyfriar's, just as we do each time we return to Edinburgh.

ENTICING EDINBURGH

Amid the contrasting charms of its Old Town and New Town, Edinburgh takes its place among an elite group of European cities conspicuous for its romance and physical attributes. There are many aspects of Edinburgh to see on conducted tours, but the real beauty of the city is best seen by exploring it on foot and at your own pace.

Walk the Royal Mile in Old Town from Edinburgh Castle to the Palace of Holyroodhouse, passing through a fantastic assembly of picturesque old buildings, such as John Knox's House and the Canongate Tolbooth. Although the Palace of Holyroodhouse originated as a guest house for the Abbey of Holyrood, most of the palace we see today was built for Charles II in 1671. However, the most famous historical figure associated with the palace was Mary Queen of Scots, who spent six years of her tragic reign there.

As more and more enclosures were built during the post-medieval period, the term "close" came into existence in old Edinburgh to describe the narrow passageways giving access or right-of-way to the buildings in the rear of others. There are well over 100 closes in Old Town, many of which have brass tablets at their entrances to explain their historical significance.

The Royal Mile was for many centuries the center of Edinburgh life. Its citizens lived and conducted their affairs on this busy, crowded street. During your walk on the Royal Mile, you might even imagine Auld Jock plodding his weary way to his garret, with his wee dog Bobby following close at his heels.

Cross from Old Town to New Town on the Waverley Bridge, or "the mound," to enter "the most exciting Georgian city in Britain." A stroll on Princes Street will verify what many other travelers have probably told you by now—the shops are superb and the scene overlooking Princes Gardens against the backdrop of Edinburgh Castle cannot be equaled.

EDINBURGH-LONDON TRAIN SERVICE

(First & second class accommodations for all services listed.)

DEPART FROM WAVERLEY STATION	ARRIVE IN KING'S CROSS STATION*			
	Weekdays	Saturdays	Sundays	NOTES
0815	1314	1314	N/S	(1)
0915	1420	1420	N/S	(1)
1000	N/S	N/S	1605	(1)
1015	1459	1459	N/S	(1)
1115	1620	1620	1659	(1)
1215	1709	1709	1748	(1)
1315	1820	1820	1836	(1)
1415	1926	1926	1939	(1)
1515	2012	2012	2037	(1) (2)
1615	2120	2120	2124	(1) (2)
1715	2223	2254	2218	(1)
2215	N/S	0633(5)	N/S	(3)
2315	0611	N/S	0856	(3)
2330	N/S	0918	N/S	(3)
0007	0714	N/S	0715	(4)

Distance: 393 miles/632 km

References: British Rail Table 26
            Thomas Cook Table 575

*See Appendix, page 296, for London station plan.
Travellers-Fare catering facility and British Transport Hotels available.

N/S—No Service

(1) High-speed train, food service available
(2) Limited accommodations, all seats reservable
(3) Sleeping cars only
(4) Sleeping cars and regular coaches
(5) Passengers may remain aboard until 0800

USEFUL PHONE NUMBERS

Tourist Information

British Tourist Authority: 01-499-9325
London Tourist Board: 01-730-0791

Train Information

Edinburgh Information: 031-556-2451
London Transport: 01-222-1234

British Transport Hotels

Scotland (Glasgow): 041-221-3945
Central Reservations Service (London): 01-278-4211

Aberdeen's many faces are depicted in its harbor and academic countenances. Its harbor bustles with commercial fishing craft, outlying island ferries and vessels resupplying offshore oil rigs. Kings College (below) provides tranquility with its 17th century crown tower.

From Edinburgh ...

A DAY EXCURSION TO ABERDEEN

DISTANCE BY TRAIN: 131 miles (211 km)
AVERAGE TRAIN TIME: 2 hours, 50 min.

The development of North Sea oil plus the gathering strength of northeast Scotland's agriculture, fishing and manufacturing industries have combined to give Aberdeen the highest growth rate of any city in Great Britain. Therefore, you will find Aberdeen a city of many moods. It is steeped in history. It is an ancient university town and a thriving seaport as well. It has grown very cosmopolitan, yet it remains old in grace. Above all else, the Aberdonians always have time—time to help, time to be interested, time to talk.

Aberdeen lies between the Rivers Dee and Don with 2 miles of golden sand connecting them. But don't think of Aberdeen merely as a large city with a beach. Union Street bisects the city and provides a mile-long shopping center lined with excellent shops. If you can make it out of bed and down to the docks no later than 0700, you'll see the city's biggest attraction, the fish market, in full operation. Aberdeen's two colleges, Kings College and Marischal College, comprise its university complex. Both are architecturally attractive, yet totally different. Marischal College is one of the largest granite buildings in the world; Kings College is ivy covered and beautiful.

The port of Aberdeen is the jumping-off place for adventurers bound for the Orkney and Shetland Islands to the north. Don't be surprised if you see a cruise ship or two lying off Aberdeen's harbor. Aberdeen has attracted the cruise ships by constructing a new passenger landing stage in its Victoria Dock area. It would appear that everyone wants to visit Europe's offshore capital, Aberdeen. Enjoy your visit. You are certain to find your "mood" in Aberdeen.

ABERDEEN—*THE GRANITE CITY*

A Day Excursion From Edinburgh

DEPART FROM EDINBURGH	ARRIVE IN ABERDEEN*	NOTES
0725	1024	(1) (2)
0900	1208	(2) (3)
1015	1302	(1) (2)
1234	1526	(1) (5)
1658	1926	(1) (2) (4)

DEPART FROM ABERDEEN	ARRIVE IN EDINBURGH	
1440	1727	(1) (2)
1630	1923	(1)
1650	1948	(2) (3)
1823	2112	(5)

Distance: 131 miles/211 km
References: British Rail Table 241
           Thomas Cook Table 606

* Travellers-Fare catering facility/British Transport Hotel
(1) Daily, except Sundays and holidays
(2) Food service available
(3) Sundays and holidays only
(4) High-speed train
(5) Monday through Friday only, except holidays

Train Information
Aberdeen Train Station: 0224-54222
Inter-City Services: 01-278-2477

British Transport Hotel
Station Hotel: 0224-27214

Standing like a sentinel, the gleaming white Girdleness Lighthouse guarding Aberdeen's harbor will be the first welcome sign you'll see to Scotland's third largest city. It becomes visible on the right as the train curves away to the left from Nigg Bay to cross the River Dee, then glides to a halt in Aberdeen's rail station. If you look further out to sea, you will be able to spot one of the North Sea oil platforms just before the lighthouse comes into view.

Aberdeen is one of the few cities in Britain that presently maintain tourist information facilities within their train stations. (For our readers, we hope this trend is expanding to other cities, and we congratulate Aberdeen's city fathers for their thoughtfulness.) It is only a service counter and operates on a limited schedule. However, it is convenient for train travelers to orient themselves in Aberdeen and receive directions (plus a map) leading the way to the central information center in the town. Watch for the sign, "City of Aberdeen Tourist Information," pointing to the right inside the main station area.

The main tourist information center is located in St. Nicholas House on Broad Street. On foot, turn right leaving the station onto Guild Street and walk until you arrive at Market Street where the docks come into view. A left turn to Market Street, followed by a right turn onto Union Street will keep you on course (mind the shops!) until you spy Aberdeen's town hall at the head of Broad Street leading to your left. The center is a short distance up Broad Street on the left-hand side.

The center operates on seasonal hours: June and September, Monday-Saturday, 0900-1700; July and August, Monday-Saturday, 0900-2000; October-May, Monday-Friday, 0900-1700 and Saturday, 0900–1300. The center is divided into three operating sections: inquiries, accommodations, and tickets. Walking tour and bus tour information is available here, along with several interesting publications describing the highlights of Aberdeen.

Tam o'Shanter Museum on High Street in Ayr is loaded with lore of Scotland's bard, Robert Burns. The city of Ayr is a principal point for starting out on the Burns Heritage Trail, developed by the Scottish Tourist Board. The trail tours places linked to the history of Scotland's greatest poet.

From Edinburgh …

A DAY EXCURSION TO AYR

DISTANCE BY TRAIN: 88 miles (142 km)
AVERAGE TRAIN TIME: 2 hours, 30 min.

What William Shakespeare was to England, Robert Burns was to Scotland. Ayr is the acknowledged center of the celebrated "Burns Country." The town is rich in the history of Scotland's bard. Many famous landmarks remain in Ayr today to tell the Burnsian stories. The Tam o'Shanter Inn on High Street, where Tam began his celebrated ride, is now a Burns museum. The Auld Brig (Old Bridge) that for 500 years was the only bridge in town still offers a delightful passage across the River Ayr. In a conspicuous location outside the Ayr train station, a statue of Robert Burns waits to greet travelers. Burns cottage, where the poet was born, attracts more than 100,000 visitors annually.

Ayr is also an industrial town, a market center, and a fishing port—for good measure! With all these assets, Ayr is assured of retaining its prosperous, bustling atmosphere even after the summer visitors have gone. Every Tuesday and Thursday the farmers bring their cattle to market in Ayr. Year-round, the town's harbor provides the locale for those who enjoy watching the fishermen bringing in their catch. With over 2 miles of golden sandy beach, Ayr gets more than its fair share of the summer Scottish sun. Golf, bowling, and tennis are among the sports which can be enjoyed there. Ayr's delightful parks, gardens, and tree-lined avenues have all contributed to its coveted titles "Britain's floral town" (1972) and "Scotland's floral town" (1973, 1974, 1976). If you delight in old houses, Ayr has one that was built in 1470, before Columbus discovered America!

Following your visit to Ayr, you probably will be in accord with "Robbie" Burns when he wrote:

"Auld Ayr, wham ne'er a town surpasses
For honest men and bonnie lasses."

AYR—*BURNS' TAM O'SHANTER INN*

A Day Excursion From Edinburgh

DEPART FROM EDINBURGH	ARRIVE IN GLASGOW QUEEN ST.	NOTES
0805	0852	(1)

Transfer to Glasgow Central Station
(See Chapter 11)

DEPART FROM GLASGOW CENTRAL	ARRIVE IN AYR	
0935 or 1000	1049 or 1105	(1) (2)

DEPART FROM AYR	ARRIVE IN GLASGOW CENTRAL	
1615 or 1815	1728 or 1928	(1) (2)

Transfer to Glasgow Queen Street Station
(See Chapter 11)

DEPART FROM GLASGOW CENTRAL	ARRIVE IN EDINBURGH	
1830 or 1900	1912 or 1945	(1)

Additional trains depart Glasgow Central Station for Ayr on weekdays at 0730, 0835, and 0900; return to Glasgow at 1615, 1645, 1715, 1745, 1845, and 1915.

Distance: 88 miles/142 km
References: British Rail Table 228
              Thomas Cook Tables 600, 603

(1) Daily, except Sundays and holidays
(2) Second-class coaches only

Train Information
Ayr Train Station: 0292-67135

Arriving in Ayr, head for the town's tourist in formation center at 30 Miller Road. After admiring Burns's statue in front of the train station, cross the main street to the head of Miller Road and follow it until you come to the information center on the right-hand side. It is not more than a 5-minute walk—unless you stop to admire the flowers along the way. From Easter through the end of September, the office is open Monday-Friday, 0845–1930; Saturday-Sunday, 1000–1930. At other times of the year, weekday hours are 0945 to 1645 and on Saturday and Sunday from 1000 to 1800.

Literature on Ayr, the district surrounding it, and Scotland's famous poet, Robert Burns, abounds by the pound in the information center. You will want to collect such informative booklets as the one published by the district that's crammed with facts and photos. In addition, ask for a copy of the historical guide, *Ayr, Prestwick and District*. It is the best authority for a tour of Ayr on foot that we have found. City maps, area maps, and a plenitude of Burnsian publications can round out your selection.

Not available in the information center, for it is an exclusive publication of the Tam o'Shanter Museum, is its *Catalogue*, available at the information desk in the museum for 20 pence. It will lead you through the nine rooms of the inn and does exactly what its title says, catalogs by description every item in every room. An amazing document!

You will hear mention of the Burns Heritage Trail during your visit in Ayr. If you are interested in taking it or a bus to "Burns Country," you should gather all the details from the information center. The Burns Heritage Trail has been developed by the Scottish Tourist Board. It is a tour of the places linked with Scotland's poet. On the trail, you can see many places which have been developed to tell the story of Burns and his lifetime. To become more acquainted, ask for the "Heritage Trail" brochure at the information center.

RNLB Margaret, a Royal Navy Life Boat, stands ready for rescue duty in Dunbar's Victoria Harbor. The ruins of Dunbar Castle mark the narrow passageway leading from the harbor into the North Sea. The old lifeboat house on the harbor's quay is now a museum.

From Edinburgh ...

A DAY EXCURSION TO DUNBAR

DISTANCE BY TRAIN: 29 miles (46 km)
AVERAGE TRAIN TIME: 30 minutes

Put on your walking shoes. We're going to Dunbar! The town offers two wonderful walking opportunities: one through the historic center of old Dunbar to appreciate the great and varied wealth of its traditional Scottish buildings; the other along the cliffs brooding over the North Sea in the John Muir Country Park. Non-walkers and those slower of pace can take solace in Dunbar's harbor area where one may watch fishermen and their customers on the quayside buying and selling freshly caught fish as their colorful fishing boats bob about on the tide. Further assurance of a pleasant outing for all is the presence of several public houses in the harbor area. Among them, the Volunteer Arms housing the Volunteer Bar and the Haven Lounge, where one can either seek haven or volunteer, according to one's inclination.

Dunbar is situated amid some of the most beautiful countryside and coastline in Scotland. There are few places in Scotland like it where it is possible to witness the full range of history of a Scottish east coast fishing port and market center. Dunbar has always played an important part in Scotland's history. Due to its strategic location, the town has been a stronghold down through centuries. Dunbar (Gaelic), "the fort on the point," had a castle fortress at least as early as 856. The remains of the castle stand on the promontory overlooking Dunbar's Victoria Harbor. There are two harbors, the old harbor extended by Oliver Cromwell and Victoria Harbor. As part of the redevelopment, the harbor areas have had cottage-type houses built since 1951 to the special design of Sir Basil Spence, the architect of the new Coventry cathedral. Perhaps the best evidence of Dunbar's beauty is the large number of visitors walking about simply admiring the scenery.

DUNBAR—*"FORT ON THE POINT"*

A Day Excursion From Edinburgh

DEPART FROM EDINBURGH	ARRIVE IN DUNBAR	NOTES
0730	0759	(1)
0915	0939	(1) (2)
1050	1113	(2) (3) (4)
1718	1753	(1)

DEPART FROM DUNBAR	ARRIVE IN EDINBURGH	
1344	1412	(1) (2)
1726	1758	(1) (2)
1902	1929	(2) (3) (4)
2139	2207	(1) (2) (4)

Distance: 29 miles/46 km
References: British Rail Table 26
 Thomas Cook Table 575

(1) Daily, except Sundays and holidays
(2) Food service available
(3) Sundays and holidays only
(4) High speed train

Train Information
Dunbar Train Station: 0368-62753

The Dunbar information center is located in the Town House on High Street. Part of the building, incidentally, is a Tolbooth (toll gate) dating back to the 17th century when a toll road between Edinburgh and Newcastle ran through Dunbar. The center is a short walk from the train station. Station Road runs from the front of the station to where it crosses Countess Road and becomes Abbey Road. When you reach the general post office on your left, the thoroughfare does another name change to High Street and remains so until you reach the information center situated on the right-hand side.

The information center is open during summer from Monday through Saturday, 0900–1900. It's open Sundays in summer from 1100–1300. During the balance of the year, it holds to an 0900–1700 schedule on weekdays and is closed Saturday and Sunday. Note the sundial on the Tolbooth tower as you enter the information center. You can still set your watch by it— providing, of course, that the sun is shining during your visit!

For the town tour we mentioned, ask for a copy of *A Walk Around the Old Burgh of Dunbar*. A guidebook for the self-guided trail laid out along the cliffs running out of Dunbar is also available. This cliff-top trail is prominently marked on the previously mentioned street plan, as are other features of the town, including the two harbors.

An interesting part of Victoria harbor is the Dunbar RNLB (Royal Navy Life Boat) *Margaret*. Opposite its mooring is the Lifeboat Museum, which is well worth a visit. Lifeboats out of Dunbar have saved over 200 lives since beginning operation back in 1808.

There is a bowling green on the right-hand side of Station Road as you proceed toward town. We asked an old Scot, "How can such a green be so smooth and flat?" "It's easy," he explained, "plant the best of grass seed and then roll it for a few hundred years."

Unicorn figurehead of the frigate *Unicorn* glistens in the bow of Britain's oldest warship still afloat. Moored at the Victoria Dock in Dundee, the vessel is open to visitors from April to October and features an exhibition of Royal Navy development.

From Edinburgh ...

A DAY EXCURSION TO DUNDEE

DISTANCE BY TRAIN: 60 miles (96 km)
AVERAGE TRAIN TIME: 1 hour, 30 min.

As your train approaches the city of Dundee, you will be able to witness a scene of railroading history—one of disaster and yet one of triumph. Following the station stop at Leuchars, where you detrain for St. Andrews, watch as the train passes through the local station of Wormit and on to the railway bridge crossing the Firth of Tay inbound to Dundee. The bridge, a double-track structure 11,653 feet long, was opened in 1887 and was considered at that time (as it is even now) to be a triumph of railroad engineering. Look alongside the present bridge and you will see a series of old bridge piers. These remains supported a single-track bridge that was swept away during a violent storm in 1879 with the loss of a train and 75 of its passengers! Turn your gaze to the east during the crossing of the great Firth (estuary) where the Tay River empties into the North Sea and you will see a two-lane vehicular bridge 7,365 feet in length that was opened by Queen Elizabeth II in 1966. Dundee is closely related to its river, the Tay, and its rail and vehicular bridges are a vital part of its existence.

Dundee was famous for generations as the city of "jute, jam, and journalism." Its prolific writers still abound and tons of jam and preserves are still processed there, but jute is slowly sinking into the shadows of time as synthetic fibers take over in the cordage industry.

Dundee lies in the heart of Scotland where the game of golf originated. The Spalding Golf Museum in nearby Camperdown Park displays an iron club of circa 1680 among other interesting items. In Dundee and throughout the area, you also will note that the hospitality in the 19th holes throughout the region is second to none!

DUNDEE—*JAM & JOURNALISM*

A Day Excursion From Edinburgh

DEPART FROM EDINBURGH	ARRIVE IN DUNDEE*	NOTES
0725	0955	(1) (2)
0900	1025	(2) (3)
1015	1134	(1) (2)
1234	1359	(4)
1455	1614	(1) (2)

DEPART FROM DUNDEE	ARRIVE IN EDINBURGH	
1606	1727	(1) (2)
1800	1923	(1)
1819	1948	(2) (3)
1952	2112	(4)

Distance: 60 miles/96 km
References: British Rail Table 229
Thomas Cook Table 606

* Travellers-Fare catering facility
(1) Daily, except Sundays and holidays
(2) Food service available
(3) Sundays and holidays only
(4) Monday through Friday only, except holidays

Train Information
Dundee Train Station: 0382-26844
Inter-City Services: 01-278-2477

By the way, if your original day excursion plans were for St. Andrews but you failed to leave the train at Leuchars Station, you can still make it back to the golf capital by bus out of Dundee in less than 1 hour. The fare is 76 pence. However, capitalize on your error and enjoy Dundee, too.

From the train station in Dundee, the tourist information center becomes a bit difficult to locate on foot. This is due to the numerous traffic circles and pedestrian overpasses one is confronted by at the station. Take heart! Turn left leaving the station and cross over on the first available flyover (overpass) to the Club Pub. At this point, cross the street in the direction of the Tay Hotel and pass on its left-hand side to the end of the street where you again cross and walk to the left. A few yards further on you will come to a wide stairway. At its top and on the left in the city square, you will find the information center.

Office hours at the center run from 0900 to 1800 Monday through Friday; 0900-1700 Saturday; and 1400-1800 on Sunday. During the winter schedule, the center is open only between Monday and Friday from 0900-1700.

Dundee has many attractions. One which we feel will prove to be of interest to all is the frigate *Unicorn,* Britain's oldest warship still afloat. The *Unicorn* is one of the four remaining frigates in the world, the fast, lightly armed sailing ships of yesteryear now replaced by the destroyer class of naval vessel. Launched in 1824, The *Unicorn* remained in naval service until 1968 when the *Unicorn* Preservation Society was founded to preserve the ship and return it to its original condition. Ask the information center for the *Unicorn* brochure and instructions to reach its pier in the city's Victoria Dock.

Dundee's other points of interest include its old steeple, its four castles—Dudhope, Mains, Claypotts, Broughty—and the Mercat Cross, which is moved about as the population center changes.

Humble weaver's cottage in Dunfermline, birthplace of steel millionaire Andrew Carnegie, is open to the public. Carnegie's benevolence brought amenities such as a concert hall, library and sports center to the city. Old pug Engine No. 11 (below) stands in Pittencrieff Park close by the Carnegie memorial statue.

From Edinburgh ...

A DAY EXCURSION TO DUNFERMLINE

DISTANCE BY TRAIN: 17 miles (27 km)
AVERAGE TRAIN TIME: 30 minutes

Dunfermline was once the capital of Scotland and holds an important part in Scottish history. The majestic spires of the Dunfermline Abbey dominate the town's skyline. Within the abbey are the graves of seven Scottish kings, including the tomb of Robert the Bruce. The abbey was founded by Scotland's King David in the 12th century as a Benedictine monastery. In the course of time, through royal gifts and other extensive endowments, it became one of the most magnificent establishments in Scotland.

A second attraction to Dunfermline is Pittencrieff Park, a lovely area with its flower gardens, music pavilion, aviary, and museum. It was given to the town by Andrew Carnegie, the Scottish-American philanthropist who was born in a humble weaver's cottage in Dunfermline in 1835. His birthplace is open to the public, and it attracts thousands of visitors every year. A statue of the steel millionaire stands in the center of Pittencrieff. It was erected by the citizens of Dunfermline in grateful appreciation of his many gifts to his native city.

Arriving in Dunfermline by train, you can go to the center of the city either by bus or by taxi. The walk is not too distant to the abbey and the other attractions in town. However, it is a bit longer than the stationmaster's advice, "Not more than a 4-minute walk from here!" Allow 15 minutes to cover the ground between the train station and the tourist information center on Glen Bridge Street. The abbey, Pittencrieff, and Carnegie's birthplace lie in between these two points. Taxis queue at the front of the station. Sixty pence will see you to the city center. The bus stop is close to the station at an underpass on the left. The 9-pence fare will take you anywhere you may want to go within the city.

DUNFERMLINE—*ANDREW CARNEGIE BIRTHPLACE*

A Day Excursion From Edinburgh

DEPART FROM EDINBURGH	ARRIVE IN DUNFERMLINE	NOTES
0825	0855	(1)
0925	0955	(1)
1015	1045	(1)
1125	1155	(1)

And at the same minutes past each hour until 1515.
No train service on Sundays.

DEPART FROM DUNFERMLINE	ARRIVE IN EDINBURGH	
1526	1556	(1)
1628	1658	(1)
1720	1750	(1)
1828	1858	(1)

And at the same minutes past each hour until 2234.
No train service on Sundays.

Distance:	17 miles/27 km
References:	British Rail Table 241
	Thomas Cook Table 606

(1) Daily, except Sundays and holidays

Train Information
Dunfermline Train Station: 0383-26111

The tourist information center is situated at the entrance of the Glen Bridge car park. Its location again points out that Britain is still automobile oriented insofar as touring is concerned. Hopefully, more information centers will change their locale to the train stations as automobile fuel costs and availability continue to worsen. The Dunfermline center operates daily through the summer season from 1000–1800, including Sundays and holidays. Winter hours are from 1000–1700, Monday-Friday only. The printed information available at the center is heavily oriented to the abbey. However, the staff is very helpful in suggesting other things to do.

To reach the information center from the middle of town, orient yourself on Bridge Street in front of the Dunfermline City Chambers. (All city buses stop at this location.) Walk down Bridge Street toward the entrance to Pittencrieff Park to where you can turn right onto Chalmers Street. Follow Chalmers Street, staying on its right-hand side. The car park entrance is a short distance up Chalmers Street.

The triangle of interest is the Dunfermline Abbey, Pittencrieff Park, and the Andrew Carnegie birthplace. We suggest visiting the park first due to its close proximity to the information center. The second stop should be the abbey, and finally, the Carnegie cottage as you proceed back to the rail station. The abbey church is open daily from 0930-1700 from April through September. Sunday hours are 1400-1700. Between October and March, the closing hour is moved back to 1600. The abbey shop is open during the same hours as the church between April and September. At other times, sale goods are available from the church officer.

Andrew Carnegie's birthplace is open to the public Monday through Saturday 1100–1300 and 1400–1800; Sunday, 1400–1800 (May through August). From September through April, the hours are the same, except that closing time is moved to 1700.

Caledonia Canal, as viewed from Inverness Castle, leads southwest to Loch Ness, mythical lair of "Nessie," the Loch Ness monster. Known as the "capital of the Highlands," Inverness in its increasing popularity has expanded its hotels and recreational facilities to meet its visitors' needs.

From Edinburgh ...

AN "OUT-AND-BACK" EXCURSION TO INVERNESS

DISTANCE BY TRAIN: 176 miles (283 km)
AVERAGE TRAIN TIME: 4 hours, 20 min.

The position of Inverness at the eastern head of Loch Ness, Scotland's famous inland sea, earns the city its title, "Capital of the Highlands." From Inverness, you can get to more places in the Highlands than from any other location in Scotland. For this reason, we have termed the excursion to Inverness an "out-and-back" excursion, for you may want to use Inverness as a "base city" in its own right for exploring the Highlands.

If you plan to do a considerable amount of traveling throughout the Highlands, we suggest you consider purchasing the Scottish Highlands and Islands Travelpass. You will find an expanded explanation of this unique travel bargain beginning on page 284 of this edition.

Should your schedule for visiting Inverness be limited, you may want to avail yourself of the excellent British Rail sleeper services. For example, you could board a sleeper one night in Edinburgh and awaken the following morning in Inverness. You could spend an entire day sightseeing, followed by boarding another sleeper back to Edinburgh or Glasgow.

It is an ambitious program, but going in and out of Inverness by sleeper could permit you to board the 1030 train from there to the Kyle of Lochalsh (see page 257), where you arrive at 1342, then ferry to the Isle of Skye, soak in the sights, and leave Lochalsh on the 1755 to be back in Inverness by 2106 with several hours to spare before boarding the sleeper again.

But why hurry? The scenery is superb and the climate is invigorating. Take our advice and plan to spend at least several days in hospitable Inverness, exploring the Highlands at a leisurely pace.

INVERNESS—*HIGHLAND GATEWAY*

An "Out-And-Back" Excursion From Edinburgh

DEPART FROM EDINBURGH	ARRIVE IN INVERNESS‡	NOTES
0900	1508	(1) (2)
0938	1356	(2) (3)
1251	1703	(2) (3)
2255	0449*	(1)
2305	0449*	(3)

DEPART FROM INVERNESS	ARRIVE IN EDINBURGH	
0815	1234	(2) (3)
1240	1652	(2) (3)
1640	2137	(1) (2)
1642	2102	(2) (3)
2350	0652†	(4)

* Passengers may remain in sleepers until 0745 (Inverness)
† Passengers may remain in sleepers until 0730 (Edinburgh)
‡ Travellers-Fare catering facility/British Transport Hotel

Distance: 176 miles/283 km
References: British Rail Tables 229, 241
             Thomas Cook Table 611

(1) Sundays and holidays only
(2) Food service available
(3) Daily, except Sundays and holidays
(4) Daily, except Saturdays

Train Information
Inverness Train Station: 0463-32651

British Transport Hotel
Station Hotel: 0463-31926

The tourist information center in Inverness is situated on Church Street, close to where it intersects Bridge Street. The shortest route to the information center lies down Union Street which runs perpendicular to the front of the Inverness train station. Union Street ends one block further on at Chruch Street, where a left turn will bring you to the information center after a few more steps. However, there is a problem! Union Street is lined with shops loaded with Highland lore and, as a matter of fact, so is Church Street. For this reason, the tourist center probably will never be moved to the train station where it rightfully belongs. The information center is open Monday-Friday from 0900-2000. Saturday hours are 0900-1900; Sunday from 1400-1800. The office can become very crowded at times, particularly following the arrival of trains from Aberdeen, Edinburgh and Glasgow.

Here are but a few of the sightseeing possibilities in and around Inverness. Visit the castle and walk along the garden paths at the River Ness. Cruise on Loch Ness, as far away as Urquhart Castle if you like, where most of the sightings of the Loch Ness "monster" (or "beastie," as the locals call it) have occurred. Journey on the renowned railway line between Inverness and Kyle of Lochalsh over 82 miles of railroad right-of-way that involved beauty, romance, history, and endurance in its building. Forge northward to Thurso, Scotland's most northernly town, on a dramatic rail route holding 162 miles of Scotland's better scenery captive for your viewing. If you prefer the solitude that the surf breaking on a shore can bring, take a train east to Nairn, 15 miles from Inverness. And train south a mere 35 miles to Scotland's St. Moritz—where the ski boom has transformed the town of Aviemore into a continental sports village.

You may see now why we have not relegated Inverness to a standard day excursion category. There is so much to do in and around the "Capital of the Highlands" that not even a series of action-packed days could absorb all the possible activities!

Kyle of Lochalsh, a narrow channel (Kyle) connecting Loch (Lake) Alsh with the open sea through the Sound of Raasay, offers superb views to its visitors. The Lochalsh Hotel (BTH) is situated conveniently beside the ferry dock for transport to the Isle of Skye seen in the background.

A DAY EXCURSION TO KYLE OF LOCHALSH

DISTANCE BY TRAIN: 82 miles (132 km)
AVERAGE TRAIN TIME: 3 hours, 15 min.

The railway between Inverness and Kyle of Lochalsh has been accorded the distinction of being the premier scenic rail line in Britain. It is a lovely journey through the Highland towns of Dingwall, Garve, Achnasheen, and Stromeferry before terminating on the western shores of Scotland facing the Isle of Skye. The rail line passes through a region of superlative natural beauty loaded with Scottish folklore.

When the railroad opened in 1870, the western terminal was the town of Stromeferry on the salt water Loch Carron. Although the original intention was to build right through to Kyle of Lochalsh, construction money ran out and Stromeferry remained the terminus for 27 years. The remaining 26 miles of right-of-way were a formidable task of engineering. Most were forged through solid rock, requiring cuts up to 88 feet deep! Even the area of the train terminal at Kyle required blasting and removing rock. When you reach Kyle of Lochalsh, pause to appreciate the back-breaking toil that created the train station and the right-of-way leading to it.

A ferry plies between Kyle of Lochalsh and Kyleakin on the Isle of Skye. The ruins of Castle Moil stand on a promontory close to the Kyleakin ferry dock. During the time of the Vikings, the castle was the home of a Norwegian princess. History relates that the princess made quite a bundle during her stay in the castle by exacting a toll from ships passing through the narrow straits. To insure prompt payment, she had a heavy chain attached between the castle and the Kyle of Lochalsh which was drawn taut when a ship approached. The chain was probably depreciated and charged off as a business expense, for there's no evidence of its existence today.

KYLE OF LOCHALSH & THE ISLE OF SKYE

An Excursion From Edinburgh Thru Inverness

DEPART FROM INVERNESS	ARRIVE IN KYLE OF LOCHALSH*	NOTES
0634	0935	(2)
1035	1340	(1) (2)
1805	2050	(2)

Connection by ferry between Kyle of Lochalsh and Kyleakin, Isle of Skye. No train service on Sundays.

DEPART FROM KYLE OF LOCHALSH	ARRIVE IN INVERNESS	
0700	0939	(2)
1108	1351	(2)
1714	2011	(1) (2)

No train service on Sundays

Distance:	82 miles/132 km
References:	British Rail Table 239
	Thomas Cook Table 610

*British Transport Hotel

(1) Food service available June–September
(2) Daily, except Sundays and holidays

Train Information
Kyle of Lochalsh Train Station: 0599-4205

During the summer, the 1035 train from Inverness includes a special observation saloon car, for which a supplement is payable. The special car returns to Inverness in the late afternoon, departing from Kyle of Lochalsh at 1714. A guide aboard the observation car offers interesting commentary en route. If you are unable to obtain a seat in that car, ask at the railway station magazine stand for a British Rail illustrated booklet entitled *Inverness to Kyle of Lochalsh* (15 pence). It describes much of the scenery en route, along with a liberal sprinkling of Scottish folk tales.

In Kyle of Lochalsh, you'll find the tourist information center conveniently located midway between the train station and the ferry dock. It is open from Monday-Saturday, 0930-2100. On Sundays, you'll find it open from 1430-1730. To reach it, use the stairs to the overpass and then walk downhill.

Don't pass up the opportunity of visiting the Isle of Skye. The ferry fare is 15 pence per person each way, and you'll be treated to one of the finest land and seascapes in the world during the 7-minute crossing. The ferry departs every 15 minutes during peak season, but check its return schedule to Kyle of Lochalsh to assure that you are not left on the Isle when your train departs the Kyle! Holders of the special Scottish Highlands and Islands Travelpass (page 285) may start their exploration of Skye from this point. For a quick review of the village of Kyleakin and its points of interest, check the tourist information three-sided sign just outside the Castle Moil Restaurant, a short distance from the ferry dock.

It is a relatively short walk from Kyleakin to Castle Moil. For other diversions, check on both sides of the strait at the ferry dock for special excursion craft that explore the area by sea. There are daily boat cruises departing from the Kyleakin pier every 2 hours. Special cruises to the white coral beaches of Sandaig run every Sunday. Seals can often be seen basking and cavorting on the beach at Sandaig.

Superb view of the scenery surrounding one of Scotland's most famous bodies of water, Loch Lomond, is enjoyed by passengers aboard the paddle-wheel steamer *Maid of the Loch*. The vessel, launched in 1953, steams daily from its pier in Balloch throughout the season.

From Edinburgh ...

A DAY EXCURSION TO LOCH LOMOND

DISTANCE BY TRAIN: 69 miles (111 km)
AVERAGE TRAIN TIME: 1 hour, 30 min.

The enchantment of Loch Lomond is one of Scotland's most prized assets. The largest body of fresh water in Great Britain, Loch Lomond abounds with magnificent scenery best viewed from the decks of the paddle wheel steamer *Maid of the Loch*.

Maid of the Loch is not a quaking, shaking veteran of a century past. She was launched in May 1953 to replace two ailing and time-expired veterans of Loch Lomond, the *Princess May* and the *Prince Edward*. *Maid of the Loch* is the largest inland steamer in Britain and the last of paddle wheel design. The spotless engine room may be viewed from a pasenger deck where its hissing steam and the whirling crank-shafts driving the paddle wheels are sources of fascination to young and old alike.

Loch Lomond's broad southern end, 5 miles in width, is enhanced by a scattering of small islands silhouetted against a background of dark blue water and rugged mountains. As the loch gradually narrows to the north, until only a few hundred feet of water separate the shores, Loch Lomond begins to look every bit like a Norwegian fjord.

The *Maid of the Loch* evokes the nostalgia of paddle wheel steamers, along with the most modern of amenities. The well-appointed dining salon, with its sparkling white table linen, glistening silver service, and cheerful serving persons, retains a touch of bygone elegance. There is a self-service food facility aboard for those who prefer it, along with a fully licensed lounge offering a wide selection of refreshments. Every comfort has been considered for the full enjoyment of the ships' passengers. *Maid of the Loch* will be waiting at the Balloch dock for immediate departure following your arrival by train from Glasgow.

LOCH LOMOND—*BY YON BONNIE BANKS*

A Day's Cruise on Scotland's Famous Lake, Loch Lomond, from Edinburgh/Glasgow

DEPART FROM EDINBURGH	ARRIVE IN GLASGOW QUEEN ST.
0805	0852

DEPART FROM GLASGOW QUEEN ST.	ARRIVE AT BALLOCH PIER
0915	1001

DEPART BALLOCH PIER ABOARD LAKE STEAMER	RETURN TO BALLOCH PIER FOR TRAIN
1030	1400

DEPART FROM BALLOCH PIER	ARRIVE IN GLASGOW QUEEN ST.
1410	1457

DEPART FROM GLASGOW QUEEN ST.	ARRIVE IN EDINBURGH
1530	1617

Steamer cruises operate on Loch Lomond from late May to early September. Weekday departures 1030 and 1430; Sunday departures 1110 and 1410. Short evening cruises depart at 1940 weekdays through mid-August. (Check train information/tourist information offices for complete information.) Typical weekday morning cruise and connecting train schedules shown above. Lake steamer vessel: *Maid of the Loch,* built in 1953. Operated by Caledonian MacBrayne, Ltd., in association with British Rail. Full food and beverage services aboard.

References: British Rail Tables 228, 253
Thomas Cook Tables 600, 602a

Train Information
Balloch Pier Train Station: 0389-52384

Your BritRail Pass is valid for train service to Balloch Pier. However, you must purchase a day return ticket aboard the *Maid*. To the head of the loch and return to Balloch Pier (the cruise we recommend), adults pay £3.60; children (5-13) and senior citizens pay half fare, £1.80. If you plan to enjoy the three-course luncheon served in the vessel's splendid dining room, we suggest you purchase meal tickets at the same time you pay for your passage. Payment is made at the ticket office aboard the vessel.

Aside from the charming cruise up and back on Loch Lomond from Balloch Pier, several other tours are available. Tour No. 1 involves the *Maid of the Loch* to Inversnaid near the head of Loch Lomond where you debark and board a bus to Stonachlachar. There, you board the steamer *Sir Walter Scott* on Loch Katrine that takes you to Trossachs Pier, where another bus transports you to Stirling (page 277) for train service back to Edinburgh or Glasgow. Tour No. 1 conducted in reverse order out of Stirling becomes Tour No. 2.

Tour No. 3 involves the afternoon cruise of the *Maid*, as well as the one in the morning. Leaving Balloch Pier at 1030 and arriving at Inversnaid at 1215, you move overland by bus to Stonachlachar for a view of Loch Katrine. Tour No. 3 varies from the others in that you return by bus to Inversnaid where you again board the *Maid* at 1650 and sail back to Balloch, arriving at 1850. Tickets for the tour of your choice may be purchased aboard the *Maid*. Both tourist information centers in Edinburgh and Glasglow have all the details.

The two daily cruises on Loch Lomond by the *Maid of the Loch* make it possible for you to debark at any one of its enroute stops, explore the area and return to Balloch on the later afternoon cruise. Getting off at Rowardennan, for example, you could scale the 3,192-foot summit of Ben Lomond. It's a 5-hour round trip, but the magnificent view from this vantage point is nothing short of spectacular.

18th century Town Hall dominates the broad main street of Montrose, a city that has served as a fashionable Scottish spa for almost three centuries. Montrose profited from trade with the Low Countries, consequently bringing Flemish-style architecture into its own decor.

From Edinburgh ...

A DAY EXCURSION TO MONTROSE

DISTANCE BY TRAIN: 90 miles (145 km)
AVERAGE TRAIN TIME: 2 hours, 10 min.

Travelers who have visited many villages, towns, and cities throughout Europe and the British Isles can "read" the history of a place in its architecture and street names. Montrose is an outstanding example of the point we are making.

Even at first glance, Montrose does not look like a typical Scottish town. Its broad main street, High Street, has many elegant houses with the gabled ends on the street side. The town hall of Montrose is fronted by a broad piazza. From its facade, Montrose looks more like a page out of a Flemish picture book rather than a Scottish one. Its great houses are surrounded by garden walls—not ordinary ones, but remarkably high garden walls. There are oddly named streets, such as "America" and "California"—another hint that the history of Montrose is in many ways different. And so it is!

For centuries, the merchants of Montrose traded with the Low Countries. It was only natural that they would bring back to Montrose some of the things they admired on the Continent, for example, houses with gabled ends to the street side as they are constructed in Holland. The wide streets? From the promenades of Europe, no doubt. And what about the street names? Almost within living memory, ships sailed from Montrose to America carrying emigrants out and returning ladened with lumber.

Baffled by the high garden walls? Over 300 years ago the streets of Montrose ran red with blood when a band of Highlanders raided the town. Within months, the majority of walls within the town were built up to their present height to prevent intruders from coming over the walls and attacking up through the gardens. Explore for yourself these remarkable facts of history in Montrose!

MONTROSE—*SEASIDE RESORT*

A Day Excursion From Edinburgh

DEPART FROM EDINBURGH	ARRIVE IN MONTROSE	NOTES
0700	0841	(1)
0840	1043	(2) (3)
0925	1143	(1)
1015	1212	(1) (2)

DEPART FROM MONTROSE	ARRIVE IN EDINBURGH	
1526	1727	(1) (2)
1717	1923	(1) (2)
1737	1948	(2) (3)
1910	2112	(4)

Distance: 90 miles/145 km
References: British Rail Table 229
              Thomas Cook Table 606

(1) Daily, except Sundays and holidays
(2) Food service available
(3) Sundays and holidays only
(4) Monday through Friday only, except holidays

Train Information
0674-2220

When you arrive in Montrose from Edinburgh, take a moment at the train station to direct your gaze to the west, away from the town. You will see a tidal basin where thousands of wild fowl forage for food, including the pink-footed Arctic goose during the winter. Seasonally, there is a great gathering of swans in the basin, dotting the water with their white tufts of plumage like so many bread crumbs scattered on a watery lawn. From the station, turn right on Western Road until it reaches Home Street, where a quick left followed by a right turn one block away onto High Street puts you in view of the town hall and its grand piazza. Stay on the right-hand side of High Street and walk a short distance south. Just before reaching the town's public library, you will come to the information center at 212 High Street where you will find a wealth of information available regarding both Montrose and the area surrounding it. At the moment, we are not aware of the existence of any published walks through Montrose, but expect that this situation will soon be remedied. The information office has a street map on sale for 5 pence, on which many salient items of interest are listed.

In its own right, Montrose is one of Scotland's leading seaside resorts, and it can become quite crowded during the peak summer season. Four miles of magnificent sandy beaches attract many an inlander to seek the sea at a time like that! However, beaches have a way of indicating their latitudes just as places reflect their history in their names and facades. Beaches in Britain, for example, attract huge crowds in summertime, but note the distribution of the people on the beach—with exception of a hardy few, the majority of holiday makers are disposed on the sands and precious few, if any, are actually in the surf!

The city's large indoor swimming pool and two 18-hole golf courses, plus numerous other sports facilities, make up for the other-than-tepid temperature of the North Sea waters off Montrose.

The Round House of Perth, the city's water pumping station since 1832, was restored in 1973 to serve as a tourist information center. Latin motto over the main door, "Aquam Igne et Aqua Haurio" (I draw water by fire and water) is attributed to its designer, Dr. Adam Anderson.

From Edinburgh...

A DAY EXCURSION TO PERTH

DISTANCE BY TRAIN: 58 miles (93 km)
AVERAGE TRAIN TIME: 1 hour, 30 min.

"Behold a river more mighty than the Tiber!" History relates these words were uttered by a Roman commander as he caught his first glimpse of the River Tay approaching what is now the modern city of Perth. Beginning as a tiny mountain stream at Ben Laoigh, the Tay trickles down the hillsides, gaining tributaries as it flows on its 120-mile journey to the sea. Perth stands astride the Tay, her history inexorably linked with the "river more mighty than the Tiber."

Two vehicular bridges, plus a rail bridge (all with pedestrian footpaths), cross the River Tay today, but "Old Man River" Tay kept the locals quite busy in earlier years when floods swept away the first bridge in 1210 and its successor in 1621, leaving travelers no alternative but ferries for the 150 years to follow.

Another attraction in the city is its Round House, Perth's first waterworks which oddly enough now houses the city's information center. The Round House, which, externally, stands today exactly as originally constructed in 1832, was restored in 1974. It is probably the most unique (and interesting) tourist center in all of Britain! It has been described as "one of the most extraordinary architectural essays in Scotland." Seeing is believing, and see it you must. To get there, exit the train station toward King's Place and follow it to the right in a downhill direction toward the river. En route, King's Place changes names to Marshal Place, but does not change direction until it reaches the river. The Round House information center is on the near left-hand side. In addition to its distinctive design, there's an unusual water fountain at its entrance. Inside, you can view a 360-degree panoramic color slide and hear a stereophonic sound presentation. Here's one building you surely shouldn't miss!

PERTH—*FIRST CAPITAL OF SCOTLAND*

A Day Excursion From Edinburgh

DEPART FROM EDINBURGH	ARRIVE IN PERTH*	NOTES
0938	1103	(2) (3)
1000	1238	(1)
1217	1409	(3)

DEPART FROM PERTH	ARRIVE IN EDINBURGH	
1514	1652	(2) (3)
1924	2102	(2) (3)
1945	2122	(1) (2)

References: British Rail Table 229
Thomas Cook Tables 609, 611

Distance: 58 miles/93 km

* Travellers-Fare catering facility/British Transport Hotel

(1) Sundays and holidays only
(2) Food service available
(3) Daily, except Sundays and holidays

Train Information
Perth Train Station: 0738-23366
Inter-City Services: 01-278-2477

British Transport Hotel
Station Hotel: 0738-24141

The information center hours from June through September are Monday–Saturday, 0900–2000; Sunday, 1700–2000. Its winter schedule from October through May is Monday–Friday, 0900–1300 and 1415–1715; Saturday, 0930–1230; closed Sunday. Closing hours during July and August are extended until 2200.

Publications available for sale at the information center which we can recommend are the "Round House" (5p), and "Walks in Perth" (10p). A street plan and index is available for 5p. However, for most visitors, the city map appearing in the free booklet, *What's On? Where? —In and Around Perth*, should suffice. Other publications such as *Georgian Perth, Perth, A Town Survey*, and *A History of St. John's Kirk* (church) will provide an extended inspection of Perth's historic buildings.

Scone Palace, one mile north of Perth, stands close to the historic spot where Scottish kings were crowned through 1651. The palace is open to the public, and there is an admission charge. You can reach it by bus No. 60 from the Leonard Street bus station. Check with the information center for details if you plan to go. By the way, don't plan to heist the stone of Scone. It's safely back in Westminster Abbey!

Tay Street fronts the river on the city side. Without straying too far from the river, it is possible to enjoy the riverside and visit enroute places of interest in Perth such as St. John's Kirk, the Perth Art Gallery and Museum, and the Fair Maid's House as described in Sir Walter Scott's famous novel *The Fair Maid of Perth*. Turn left off Tay Street at Queen's Bridge and proceed 2 blocks to sight St. John's to your right. Returning to Tay Street, continue to walk to the Perth Bridge, where you will find the art gallery and museum on George Street close to the bridge approach. In quest of the Fair Maid's House, ask directions upon leaving the museum. It is situated on North Port, a short distance away, but there are several ways to reach it.

Home of golf, St. Andrews lives golf! The clubhouse of the Old Course (above) lies almost within the city itself. Founded about 1200, St. Andrews Castle (below) stands steeped in history. Among its many attractions is the infamous 24-foot-deep bottle dungeon.

From Edinburgh...

A DAY EXCURSION TO ST. ANDREWS

DISTANCE: 57 miles (92 km)
AVERAGE TRAIN TIME: 1 hour, 20 min.

No town in the world is so completely identified with one game as St. Andrews is with golf. No matter where in the world you have played the game, there is nothing as exhilarating as a round on the Old Course at St. Andrews. Anyone can play at St. Andrews. You do not need to belong to a club and you do not need an introduction. The links belong to the townspeople and, as such, are open to all.

Current greens fees for the Old Course, probably the most famous in the world, run £5.50 on weekdays and £6.50 on Saturdays. The course is closed on Sundays. Club rentals cost £3.25 for 5 hours, £3.75 for all day. Caddy fees on the Old Course (no carts, please) are £5.00 plus £1.00 tip. To obtain full details and reservations, we suggest you telephone the St. Andrews links secretary at (0334) 75757 or the district information center at (0334) 72021 at least one day in advance of your intended visit. Including the Old Course, the town of St. Andrews has four golf courses. In total, the area surrounding St. Andrews lists 15 courses to choose from.

St. Andrews and history go together hand-in-hand. Such stellar sights as the St. Andrews Castle with its bottle dungeon and secret passage vie for your attention along with the ruins of St. Andrews Cathedral, once the largest in Scotland. Mary Queen of Scots had a house in St. Andrews which you can still see. The town is the home of Scotland's oldest university (1412). Long before Columbus discovered America or Cooke discovered Australia, students were attending St. Andrews University. Another institution of higher learning in St. Andrews is St. Mary's College, with its unique quadrangle, founded in 1537. To visit St. Andrews is to establish a tangible link with the past.

ST. ANDREWS—*WORLD'S GOLF CAPITAL*

A Day Excursion From Edinburgh

DEPART FROM EDINBURGH	ARRIVE IN LEUCHARS*	NOTES
0625	0742	(1) (2)
0725	0835	(1) (3)
0825	0942	(1) (2)
0925	1040	(1) (2)
1005	1122	(2) (4)

DEPART FROM LEUCHARS	ARRIVE IN EDINBURGH	
1634	1750	(1) (2)
1800	1923	(1)
1820	1958	(1) (2)
1833	1948	(3) (4)

Bus service from Leuchars Station to St. Andrews and v.v. runs hourly, operated by W. Alexander & Sons, Ltd., telephone Kirkcaldy 6146116. Trip takes 20 minutes. Board bus at platform 2 in St. Andrews bus station.

Distance: Train, 51 miles/82 km
              Bus, 6 miles/10 km

References: British Rail Table 241
              Thomas Cook Table 606

*British Transport Hotel in St. Andrews

(1) Daily, except Sundays and holidays
(2) Second class coaches only
(3) Food service available
(4) Sundays and holidays only

Train Information
Leuchars Train Station: 0334-206

British Transport Hotel
Old Course Hotel: 4371-74371

Leuchars is the rail station serving St. Andrews. This becomes rather obvious when you arrive, for there are signs at both ends of the station announcing "Leuchars Alight for St. Andrews." Buses meet all the express trains arriving from Edinburgh and Glasgow. The bus fare to St. Andrews is 47 pence.

From the bus station in St. Andrews, walk to your right on City Road, which changes its name to Alfred Place, before reaching South Street. Turn left on South Street and walk on the right side to Queens Gardens and the information center located directly across South Street from the St. Andrews Church and the *Citizen* newspaper office. The center is open during July and August, Monday–Saturday from 1000 to 1300 and 1400 to 1900; closed on Sunday.

St. Andrews Castle may be reached by proceeding again along South Street (with no name changes, by the way) until reaching Castle Street where you turn left for 2 blocks to the castle. Continuing one block further on South Street would have put you in front of the cathedral ruins.

Golfer or not, you must see the Royal and Ancient Clubhouse of St. Andrews during your stay. The Royal and Ancient Golf Club was founded by 22 citizens in 1754. The present clubhouse was built in 1854. The club is the ruling authority of the game. From the castle ruins, walk along The Scores until you come to Gillespie Terrace. From this point, the clubhouse and the 18th hole of the Old Course come into view.

Of all the places and views in St. Andrews, we give our nod to St. Andrews Castle overlooking St. Andrews Bay. Initially constructed in 1200, it was destroyed and rebuilt during the Scotland/England war only to be demolished again during the Reformation. The savagery of those times may be noted on a stone outside the castle gate where George Wishart was burned at the stake. The castle has lain in ruins since the 17th century when much of its stone was removed for repairing the harbor.

Stirling Castle, astride its great 250-foot rock promontory, has dominated much of Scotland's history. Showplace of Stirling City, the castle and its surrounding buildings house a variety of exhibitions including a new multi-vision sight and sound show plus shops and a tea garden for relaxing.

From Edinburgh...

A DAY EXCURSION TO STIRLING

DISTANCE BY TRAIN: 37 miles (59 km)
AVERAGE TRAIN TIME: 50 minutes

Stirling Castle cannot be ignored. It stands on a 250-foot rock overlooking the River Forth Valley from which you can see one of the finest panoramic views in Scotland. The area surrounding the crag on which the castle sits has given up relics of early man's presence from the Stone Age down through the Bronze Age. Oddly enough, there is no evidence that the Romans occupied the area, but it is almost incredible to believe they didn't "take the high ground."

The castle, as seen today, began to develop around 1370 with the accession of the Stewart kings. It served as a royal residence from then until Mary Queen of Scots' son, James VI of Scotland, departed for London in 1603 to become James I of England. Scotland's tragic queen spent the first 5 years of her life in and around Stirling. Stirling Castle is perhaps the finest example of renaissance architecture in Scotland, most of its buildings dating to the 15th and 16th centuries.

Between the castle and the old town of Stirling stands Landmark, a new concept in an old building. Landmark combines a multi-screen theater and exhibition with a bookshop and a craftshop. According to its innovators, it is the first building in Europe to be designed specifically to bring alive the history of a town. Ten projectors and stereophonic sound create an audiovisual presentation not unlike Cinerama. The theme is Stirling Castle through seven centuries. All is bustle and noise as ships from France and Holland offload their cargoes and farmers drive their cattle to market. Stirling's market, now the city's Broad Street, is shown lined with shops selling everything from swords to spices. Meanwhile, "back at the castle," a roistering banquet is being held in the great hall packed with honored guests.

STIRLING—*AND STIRLING CASTLE*

A Day Excursion From Edinburgh*

DEPART FROM EDINBURGH	ARRIVE IN STIRLING†	NOTES
0917	1014	(1)
1000	1135	(2)
1017	1108	(1)

DEPART FROM STIRLING	ARRIVE IN EDINBURGH	
1605	1659	(1)
1912	1949	(2)
2005	2059	(1)

Distance: 37 miles/59 km
References: British Rail Tables 228, 229
               Thomas Cook Table 609

*Second-class coaches only
†Travellers-Fare catering facility

(1) Daily, except Sundays and holidays
(2) Sundays and holidays only

Train Information
Stirling Train Station: 0786-3812

All of the information you might need for an enjoyable day excursion in Stirling is available in the Stirling tourist information center on Dumbarton Road. To get there from the train station, make a left turn onto Murray Place, a short distance in front of the station. Walk to the first traffic light and turn right onto Dumbarton, immediately opposite the city wall. The center's hours of operation during July and August are Monday–Saturday, from 0900-2000. On Sunday, the center is open between 1200-1700. It operates on more restricted hours during winter.

By purchasing Stirling's *Official Guide*, you will have a document which contains a walking tour, "Around the Top of the Town," a very thorough examination of the castle and the old town below it. The guide is packed with other interesting facts, including the development of Stirling's rich heritage from the Stone Age into the 20th century. The guide is profusely illustrated and will certainly be among those items you'll take home with you.

Other publications describing similar walks around Stirling are available in the center. One of particular interest should be *Stirling Old Town*, published by the Stirling District Council. It covers a course of 1¼ miles and starts at a brass plaque set in the town wall opposite the information center.

Throughout Stirling during the summer months, the presence of flowers is always evident. You will notice this first in the train station and it continues all around town. Possibly, Stirling developed its love for flowers from the King's Knot, an octagonal stepped mound that was laid out as the royal gardens in 1627-1628 beneath the walls of Stirling Castle by an Englishman brought from London to supervise the project, William Watts. The raised central portion of the Knot is thought to have originated as a Bronze Age burial mound. It was probably used as an outdoor royal court for tournaments before being incorporated into the formal gardens by Mr. Watts.

Gateway to Ireland, Stranraer's importance is primarily as the terminal of ferry service to Larne in Northern Ireland. In keeping with this functional motif, the city tourist information office is located at the ferry pier entrance to assist travelers arriving in or departing from Scotland.

From Edinburgh...

A DAY EXCURSION TO STRANRAER

DISTANCE BY TRAIN: 147 miles (237 km)
AVERAGE TRAIN TIME: 4 hours, 45 min.

Stranraer is primarily the terminal for passenger and car ferry service to Larne in Northern Ireland. Rail connections from Larne to Belfast take about 45 minutes, so it's possible for rail travelers to go to Northern Ireland via this route. However, we wish to emphasize that BritRail Pass is not accepted for travel on trains operated in Northern Ireland by the Northern Ireland Railways. Travelers wanting to cross from Stranraer to Larne and then on to Belfast are advised to purchase regular rail tickets. Such tickets, including those for the ferry crossing, are sold in all main British Rail stations.

We suggest that all arrangements for visiting Northern Ireland be attended to prior to departing on the journey, rather than enroute. One important requirement is a control ticket each passenger *must* have prior to boarding the Larne-Stranraer ferry. These tickets are issued free of charge. Any train information office can give you the details.

The crossing between Stranraer and Larne usually takes 2¼ hours, and trains are waiting at the terminals to take travelers on to the final destinations. In both ports, the train terminal is directly alongside the ferry dock. Porter service is available for those who are heavily laden.

Stranraer has direct express train connections with London, including overnight sleepers. Frequent train service connecting with the ferries to and from Larne is also available out of Glasgow. Edinburgh passengers should use the Edinburgh-Glasgow train service for the fastest connections to Stranraer. Holders of the Scottish Highlands and Islands Travelpass should note that the Travelpass cannot be used for travel from Edinburgh or Glasgow to Stranraer.

STRANRAER—*GATEWAY TO NORTH IRELAND*

A Day Excursion From Edinburgh or Glasgow

DEPART FROM EDINBURGH	ARRIVE IN GLASGOW QUEEN ST.	NOTES
0700	0747	(1) (2)
0930	1017	(1) (2)

Transfer to Glasgow Central Station
(See Chapter 11)

DEPART FROM GLASGOW CENTRAL	ARRIVE IN STRANRAER‡	
0835	1130†	(1) (2)
1135	1413*	(1) (2)

DEPART FROM STRANRAER	ARRIVE IN GLASGOW CENTRAL	
1836†	2123	(1) (2)

Transfer to Glasgow Queen Street Station
(See Chapter 11)

DEPART FROM GLASGOW QUEEN ST.	ARRIVE IN EDINBURGH	
1732	1819	(1) (2)
2200	2247	(1) (2)

Distance: 147 miles/237 km
References: British Rail Tables 221, 228
               Thomas Cook Tables 600, 603

*   Connects with steamer service to Belfast, via Larne
†   Connects with steamer service from Belfast, via Larne. Consult train information offices for train/steamer schedules for Sundays and holidays.
‡   Food service available at entrance to Stanraer Pier, across the street from the city tourist information office.
(1) Daily, except Sundays and holidays
(2) Second-class coaches only

Train Information
Stranraer Train Station: 0776-2262

As we have indicated in the picture caption on page 280, the Stranraer information center operates from a strategic position at the entrance to the ferry port. This office is primarily equipped to assist motorists using the ferry service. Rail passengers must walk back along the quay from the train terminal to the information center. The walk can be made in about 5 minutes, but we do not recommend making it if you plan to board the ferry. Ferry vessels have been known to depart as much as 15 minutes ahead of schedule. Sealink's Stranraer ferry terminal is situated directly across the street from the information center. Ticketing and reservations are available in the facility, along with a rather comfortable passenger lounge with restrooms and refreshments. If you have a long train trip ahead of you, stocking up on provisions in the terminal is suggested.

The old section of Stranraer clusters around its port area, Port Rodie. There are interesting streets and small alleyways with a variety of sights. The Stranraer Castle, a relic of the 16th century, adds a certain attraction to the area. The information center can provide you with a map of Stranraer and suggest various sights to see on a walking tour. The area is renowned for its golf, fishing, and swimming activities and becomes heavily populated with vacationing persons during the summer.

There is an interesting hotel in Stranraer, one which you might mistake as the town's castle when you first see it. Its name is the North West Castle (Hotel), and it's complete with a castle tower which cleverly conceals two well-stocked bars! Again, if you are anticipating a long train trip, you may want to bolster your spirits here in the tower. In the lower bar, there are some fossilated wooden beams, while topside in the Explorers Lounge you are treated to a fine view of the harbor. The hotel was originally the home of Sir John Ross, the famous Arctic explorer. A brochure at the hotel desk gives the full history.

Isle of Skye, one of Scotland's major attractions, stands starkly against the skyline as visitors approach aboard the ferry from Kyle of Lochalsh to Kyleakin. From Kyleakin, bus service via Broadford and Sligachan serves Portree, the island capital.

For those with a roving spirit, Scottish Highlands and Islands Travelpass is a wonderful way of seeing the far north and west of Scotland. With only one ticket, the Travelpass gives you access to a holiday of unlimited travel over virtually the whole of the Highlands and islands of Scotland by train, bus, and ferry. Rail routes take you through some of the most beautiful scenery in the Highlands—areas often inaccessible by car. Buses take you to remote villages, and ferries take you to all the major islands clustered along the northern and western coastline of Scotland, some of which are a real sea journey away.

The Travelpass is for the serious visitor and a true bargain in that it allows considerable savings over normal fares. It provides a convenient and low cost way of seeing some of Scotland's most beautiful country-side, such as Kintyre, the Isle of Mull, the Outer Hebrides, Northwest Sutherland, Orkney, and the Spey Valley.

The Travelpass is valid for use from March through October. It is issued for a 10-day period, during which time you may travel over any route marked in the free public transport map provided to you when your Travelpass is validated. You may follow *Britain by BritRail's* "base city—day excursion" satellite system of establishing yourself in a favorite city, town, or village and use it as a center to choose a different excursion every day. Or, you can plan an extensive tour, moving to a different and new place either daily or as the mood moves you. There is no limitation regarding the number of times you can travel over a particular route. For example, you could travel daily from Inverness to Kyle of Lochalsh during the period your pass is valid. The Travelpass also is good for through services between the areas it covers and Glasgow or Edinburgh.

TRAVELPASS

The Scottish Highlands and Islands Travelpass may be used as follows:

By Train (2nd class)

On all regular services provided by British Rail in the Scottish Highlands north and west of Crianlarich, north of Dalwhinnie and west of Nairn, and on through-services between the area and Glasgow or Edinburgh.

By Bus

On all regular services provided within the area by Highland Omnibuses Ltd., W. Alexander & Sons (Northern) Ltd., W. Alexander & Sons (Midland) Ltd., Scottish Omnibuses, Ltd., (Eastern Scottish), Western SMT Co. Ltd., Sutherland Transport & Trading Co. Ltd., Westerbus, Morar Motors Ltd., A. MacDonald of Acharacle, D. MacLennan of Shieldaig, Arran Coaches, West Coast Motor Service Co., John Mitchell (Stornoway) Ltd., Scottish Postbus Service. Also on through-services between the area and Glasgow or Edinburgh.

By Ship

1. On all regular services of Caledonian MacBrayne Ltd. on the west coast of Scotland.
2. On the following Caledonian MacBrayne Ltd. services on the Firth of Clyde: Gourock-Dunoon; Wemyss Bay-Rothesay; Colintraive-Rhubodach; Ardrossan-Brodick; Claoniag-Lochranza; and cruises between Gourock, Dunoon, Rothesay, Brodick, and Tighnabruaich.
3. On the Scrabster-Stromness service of the P&O Ferries, Orkney and Shetland Services.

Conditions of Use

The ticket, which must be produced for validation at one of the following offices, is nontransferable and must be signed and shown upon request.

British Rail Waverley Station Edinburgh
British Rail Central Station Glasgow
British Rail Queen Street Station Glasgow
Travel Center Buchanan Street Glasgow
Travel Center Clyde Street Bus Station Edinburgh
Duncan Duffy Ltd, Travel Agents-offices in Oban, Argyll;
  Fort William, Lochaber; Inverness.

Here are but a few of the great adventure trips that the Scottish Highlands and Islands Travelpass makes possible:

• North from Inverness to Thurso, the most northernly of Scotland's towns, then through the Port of Scrabster to the village of Stromness on the Orkney Islands. Vary your return route by busing through Tongue to Lairg to rejoin the rail route to Inverness.

• Lairg serves as a departure point to the coastal villages of Durness, Kinlochbervie, and Scourie by bus; alternately, Lochinver and Elphin to the west or Bonar Bridge and Dornoch east of Lairg.

• By rail from Inverness to Garve, where bus service runs to Ullapool where the ferry departs for Lewis Islands in the Outer Hebrides. Then bus to a trio of remote towns, Ness, Barvas, and Callanish from the ferry port of Stornoway.

• From the Kyle of Lochalsh, the Isle of Skye bus transportation network moves you about the island to visit Portree, Kilmaluag, Uig, and Dunvegan, or Armadale where ferry service is available to the Inner Hebrides Islands of Canna, Eigg, Muck, and Rhum. Ferry from Armadale to Maillaig for rail service to Fort William.

• The rail head of Oban provides access to ferry boats to mountainous Colonsay or the northwest passage to the southern islands of the Outer Hebrides. From Oban, buses run through the long arm of Kintyre Peninsula to such ancient sites as Campbeltown, Machrihanish, and Southend.

To help you plan your tour, you will receive the previously mentioned illustrated public transport map, plus a comprehensive timetable, when you validate your Travelpass.

It should be noted that train travel is by second class coach and that the Travelpass cannot be used as partial payment for first class train travel. There is no reduced rate for children using the Travelpass. The 1981 price was $113.

Train departure announcements vary from the most modern digital devices to hand-operated bulletin boards, such as this one in the Glasgow Central Station. Always check in the station for departure time, destination and loading platform prior to boarding your train.

RECOMMENDED READING LIST

Country Inns & Historic Hotels: Great Britain, * by E. O'Reilly (Burt Franklin & Co, 235 E 44th St, New York NY 10017). Everything you need to know about charming hostelries, how to find them and what to do. 256 pp, $5.95.

A Literary Guide to England & Scotland. * Classic landmarks from literary history, maps, indexed. 192 pp, $6.95.

"Insider's Bargain Britain," available from British Tourist Authority (see page 290).

London Information Guide. * Source book to London services, facilities and attractions, $7.95.

Turn Left at the Pub. * Scenic walking tours through British countryside and towns, $4.95.

Fodor's Great Britain 1981. * Sightseeing, hotels, shopping, $10.95.

Egon Ronay's Lucas Guide 1981. * Rates and evaluates 3,000 hotels, restaurants and inns of Great Britain and Ireland, budget to deluxe, 860 pp, $9.95.

Europe In A Suitcase, by Muriel Scudder. What to wear, packing, tipping, passport info, $3.00 parcel post; $3.50 1st class. Write to: Muriel Scudder, Box 72, Shelter Island Heights NY 11965.

* These publications may be obtained in major bookstores or by writing to:
The Forsyth Travel Library
Box 2975-BB
Shawnee Mission, Kansas 66201

RECOMMENDED INFORMATION SOURCES

The Travel Guide Company
Box 20334
Columbus, Ohio 43220

Joyer Travel Report
8401 Connecticut Avenue, NW
Washington, D.C. 20015

1001 Sources for Free Travel Information
Travel Information Bureau
Box 105
Kings Park, New York 11754

BRITISH TOURIST AUTHORITY OFFICES IN NORTH AMERICA

New York: 680 Fifth Avenue, New York NY 10019 (212) 581-4700

Chicago: John Hancock Center, Suite 3320, 875 North Michigan Avenue, Chicago IL 60611 (312) 787-0490

Los Angeles: 612 South Flower Street, Los Angeles CA 90017 (213) 623-8196

Dallas: Mercantile Commerce Building, Suite 2115, 1712 Commerce Street, Dallas TX 75201 (214) 748-2279

Toronto: 151 Bloor Street West, Toronto, M5S 1T3 Ontario, Canada (416) 961-8124

BRITRAIL TRAVEL INTERNATIONAL OFFICES IN NORTH AMERICA

New York: 630 Third Avenue, New York NY 10017 (212) 599-5400

Chicago: 333 North Michigan Avenue, Chicago IL 60601 (312) 263-1910

Los Angeles: 510 W. Sixth Street, Los Angeles CA 90014 (213) 626-5104

Toronto: 55 Eglinton Avenue East, Toronto M4P 1G8 Ontario, Canada (416) 486-8766

Vancouver: 409 Granville Street, Vancouver V6C 1T2 British Columbia, Canada (604) 683-6896

BRITISH TOURIST INFORMATION CENTERS

Below is a partial listing of British Tourist Information Centers applicable to cities appearing in this edition of *Britain By BritRail*.

Key to Listing:

* Provides summer service only
+ Accommodation services available to personal callers
(B) 'Book-A-Bed-Ahead' accommodations
(N) National—general information on entire country in addition to regional & local
(R) Regional—regional & local information
(L) Local—detailed local information only

ENGLAND/WALES

Bath + (N)
Abbey Churchyard
(0225) 62831

Birmingham + (N)
110 Colmore Row
021-235 3411/2

Brighton + (N)
Marlborough House, 54 Old Steine
(0273) 23755

Bury St. Edmunds * + (B) (N)
Abbey Gardens, Angel Hill
(0284) 64667;
63233 (winter; tel only)

Cambridge + (N)
Wheeler Street
(0223) 358977

Canterbury + (L)
22 St. Peter's Street
(0227) 66567

Cardiff +
Castle Street
(0222) 27281

Chester + (B) (N)
Town Hall (0244) 40144
ext 2111

Coventry + (N)
36 Broadgate
(0203) 20084/51717

Dover + (B) (N)
Townwall Street
(0304) 205108

Folkestone + (B) (N)
Harbour Street
(0303) 58594

Gloucester + (L)
6 College Street
(0452) 421188

Greenwich * (L)
Cutty Sark Gardens
01-854 8888

Hastings + (B) (R)
4 Robertson Terrace
(0424) 424242

Ipswich + (B) (N)
Town Hall, Princes Street
(0473) 55851

**Isle of Wight
Shanklin** + (R)
67 High Street
(0983) 862942

King's Lynn + (R)
Town Hall, Saturday Market Place
(0553) 61241

Lincoln + (N)
90 Bailgate
(0522) 29828

London
  British Tourist Authority (N)
  64 St. James Street, SW1
  01-499 9325

  London Tourist Board + (N)
  01-730 0791
  26 Grosvenor Gardens
  Harrods, Knightsbridge
  Selfridges, Oxford St.
  Victoria Station

Margate (R)
  Marine Terrace
  Thanet (0843) 20241/2

Nottingham (N)
  18 Milton Street
  (0602) 40661

Oxford + (B) (N)
  St. Aldate's Chambers, St. Al-
  date's (0865) 48707/49811 (Mon-
  Fri); 40170 (accommodations)

Penzance + (B) (N)
  Alverton Street
  (0736) 2341/2207

Plymouth (N)
  Civic Center
  (0752) 264851/2

Portsmouth & Southsea (L)
  Civic Offices, Guildhall Square
  (0705) 834092/3

Ramsgate (R)
  Council Offices, Queen Street
  (0843) 51086

St. Albans + (N)
  37 Chequer Street
  (0727) 64511/2

Salisbury + (B) (N)
  10 Endless Street
  (0722) 4956

Sheffield (R)
  Central Library, Surrey Street
  (0742) 734760/1/4

Southampton (L)
  Above Bar Precinct
  (0703) 23855 ext 615

Stratford-upon-Avon + (B) (N)
  Judith Shakespeare's House
  1 High Street
  (0789) 293127

Windsor * + (B) (N)
  Central Station
  (07535) 52010

York + (B) (N)
  De Grey Rooms, Exhibition
  Square
  (0904) 21756/7

SCOTLAND

Aberdeen + (B) (L)
  St. Nicholas House, Broad St.
  (0224) 23456; 24890/21814

Ayr + (B) (L)
  30 Miller Road
  (0292) 68077

Dunbar (B) (R)
  Town House, High Street
  (0368) 63353

Dunfermline * + (L)
  Glen Bridge Car Park
  (0383) 20999

Edinburgh + (B) (N)
  5 Waverley Bridge
  031-332-2433

Glasgow (B) (R)
  George Square
  041-221 7371/2

Inverness + (B) (L)
  23 Church Street
  (0463) 34353

Kyle of Lochalsh * + (B) (L)
  (0599) 4276

Loch Lomond + (B) (L)
  Balloch
  0389-53533

Montrose + (L)
  212 High Street
  (0674) 2000

Perth (B) (R)
  The Round House,
  (0738) 22900/27108

St. Andrews + (L) (B)
  South Street
  (0334) 72021

Stirling + (B) (L)
  Dumbarton Road
  (0786) 5019

Stranraer + (B) (N)
  Port Rodie
  (0776) 2595

USEFUL PHONE NUMBERS—LONDON

Area Code (01)

Tourist Information

London Tourist Board—head office and bookshop at 26 Grosvenor Gardens (from 0900 to 1730) Tel: 730-0791

Teletourist Service—recorded information on London events & attractions, 24 hours daily. Tel: 246-8041

British Tourist Authority—headquarters at 64 St. James St. Tel: 499-9325

Rail Information

Inter-City Services to:

East Anglia and Essex:	283-7171
West Yorkshire, Northeast, East Coast to Scotland:	278-2477
Midlands, North Wales, Northwest, West Coast to Scotland:	387-7070
West of England, West Midlands South Wales:	262-6767
Southeast and South:	928-5100

Sleeper Reservations

Euston Station:	387-9400, ext 3901
King's Cross Station:	278-2411
Paddington Station:	723-7000, ext 2608

London Transport Underground Services: 222-1234

Scheduled Airlines

Aer Lingus (Irish)	437-8000/734-1212
Air Canada	759-2636
Braniff International Airways	491-4631
British Airways	370-5411
British Caledonian Airways	668-4222
Delta Air Lines	668-0935
Icelandair	499-9971
Laker Airways	668-9363
Pan American World Airways	734-7292
Trans World Airlines	636-4090

British Transport Hotels (BTH)

Central Reservations Service	278-4211
Charing Cross Hotel, Strand	839-7282
Great Eastern Hotel, Liverpool St.	283-4363
Great Northern Hotel, King's Cross	837-5454
Great Western Royal Hotel, Praed St.	723-8064

Victoria Student Travel Service
Need student I.D. Approx 50p charge
per accommodation booking   730-8111

Youth Hostel Association
14 Southampton Street   836-8541

American Express
6 Haymarket, Piccadilly   930-4411

24–Hour Post Office/Long Distance Telephones
Trafalgar Square Post Office at
St. Martin's Place   930-9580

River Boat Information Service   730-4812

Intercity Bus Information
For Green Line Bus   834-6563

Bike Rentals
Rent-a-Bike, Kensington Student Centre,
Kensington Church Street   937-6089
Saviles, 97 Battersea Rise   228-4279

U.S. Embassy, Grosvenor Square   499-9000

Canadian Embassy, Canada House,
Trafalgar Square   629-9492

Emergency Police or Ambulance   dial 999

Medical Help

Middlesex Hospital, Mortimer St.	636-8333
Westminster Hospital, Horseferry Rd.	828-9811
Royal Dental Hospital, 32 Leicester Sq.	930-8831

USEFUL PHONE NUMBERS—EDINBURGH

Area Code (031)

Tourist Information

City of Edinburgh Tourist Information & Accommodations,
5 Waverley Bridge. Tel: 226-6591

Scottish Tourist Board, 5 Waverley Bridge.
Tel: 332-2433

Teletourist Service—recorded information on Edinburgh
events & attractions. Tel: 246-8041

British Rail, Waverley Station	556-2451

Scheduled Airlines

Aer Lingus (Irish)	225-7392
British Airways	225-2525
British Caledonian Airways	225-5162
City Transport Information	556-5656

British Transport Hotels (BTH)

Caledonian Hotel, Princes St.	225-2433
North British Hotel, Princes St.	556-2414
Student Travel Center	668-2221
American Express, 139 Princes St.	225-7881
Emergency: Fire, Police, Ambulance	dial 999

USEFUL PHONE NUMBERS—GLASGOW

Tourist Information

Area Code (041)

Tourist Information, George Square	221-7371/2
	or 221-6136/7
British Rail, passenger inquiries	221-3223
Sleeper reservations	221-2305

Scheduled Airlines

Aer Lingus (Irish)	248-4121
Air Canada	332-9141
British Airways	332-9666
British Caledonian Airways	332-1681
Northwest Orient Airlines	226-4175

British Transport Hotels (BTH)

Central reservations office	221-3945
Central Hotel, Gordon St.	221-9680
North British Hotel, George Square	332-6711
Scottish Youth Hostels Association	332-3004
American Express, 115 Hope St.	221-4366
Emergency: Fire, Police, Ambulance	dial 999

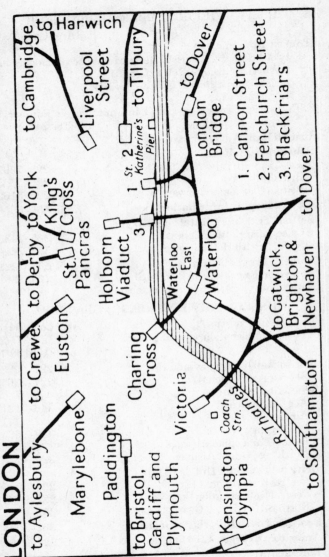

LONDON

to Aylesbury
to Crewe · to Derby · to York
to Cambridge — to Harwich

Marylebone
Euston
St. Pancras
King's Cross
Liverpool Street

Paddington
to Bristol, Cardiff and Plymouth

Charing Cross
Holborn Viaduct
to Tilbury
St. Katherine's Pier
1 2
3

to Dover
London Bridge
1. Cannon Street
2. Fenchurch Street
3. Blackfriars

Victoria
Coach Stn.
R. Thames

Kensington Olympia

Waterloo East
Waterloo

to Catwick, Brighton & Newhaven
to Dover

to Southampton

Courtesy Thomas Cook Timetable

296

Inter-terminal links
by London Underground

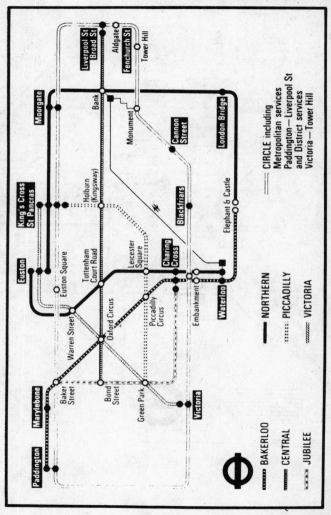

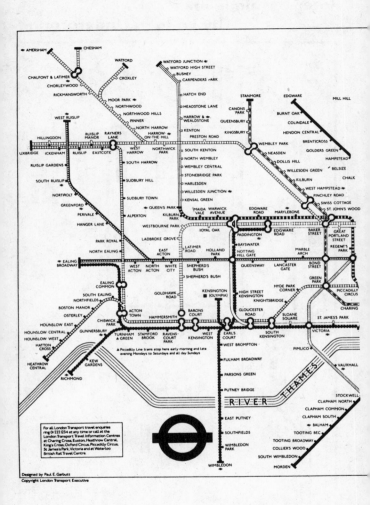

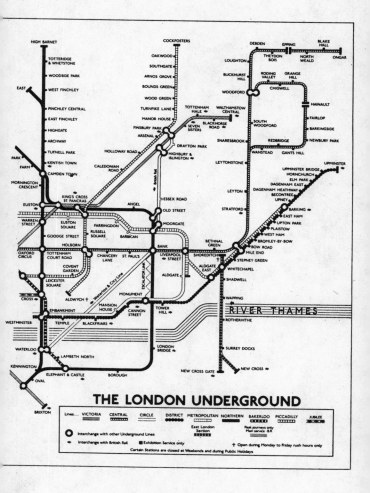

THE LONDON UNDERGROUND

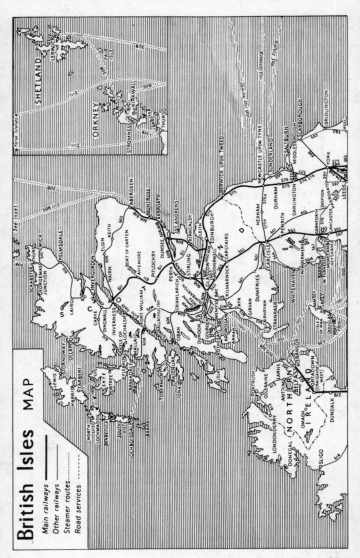

British Isles MAP

Main railways
Other railways
Steamer routes
Road services

Courtesy Thomas Cook Timetable

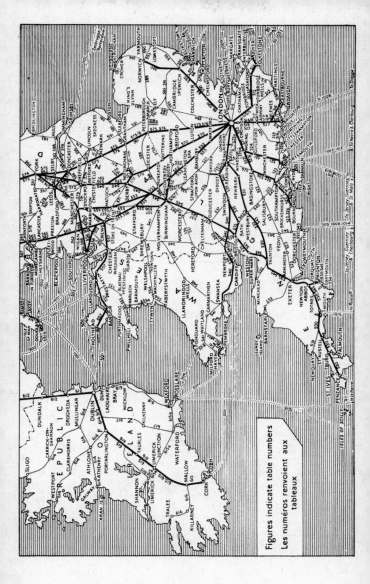

Figures indicate table numbers
Les numéros renvoient aux
tableaux

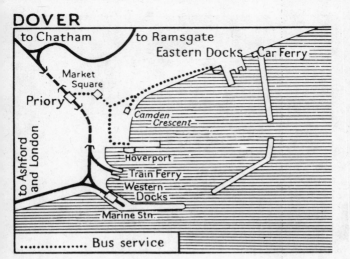

The plans shown here are provided for orientation of readers for those day excursions to points on the English Channel with cross-channel port facilities. (Ref: Dover p-119; Folkestone p-123; Ramsgate p-175)

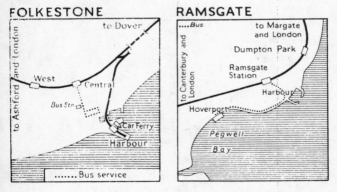

Courtesy Thomas Cook Timetable

BRITISH TRANSPORT HOTELS

For instant computerized reservations, call toll free (U.S.) 800-221-1354. New York State and Canada, call collect 212-335-3200. Or, write to BTH Hotels, Inc., P.O. Box 48, Rego Park, New York, New York 11374. Below is a partial listing of BTH Hotels in Great Britain applicable to those cities mentioned in this edition of *Britain by Britrail*.

BTH HOTELS IN ENGLAND

London:
  Charing Cross Hotel, Strand, WC2. 01-839 7282
  Great Eastern Hotel, Liverpool St. 01-283 4363
  Great Northern Hotel, King's Cross N1. 01-837- 5454
  Great Western Royal Hotel, Praed St W2. 01-723 8064
  Grosvenor Hotel, 101 Buckingham Palace Rd SW1.
    01-834 9494
Sheffield:
  Royal Victoria Hotel, Victoria Station Rd.
    (0742) 78822
Stratford-upon-Avon:
  Welcombe Hotel, Warwick Rd. (0789) 3611
York:
  Royal Station Hotel, Station Rd. (0904) 53681

BTH HOTELS IN SCOTLAND

Aberdeen: Station Hotel, 78 Guild St. (0224) 27214
Edinburgh:
  Caledonian Hotel, Princes St. 031-225 2433
  North British Hotel, Princes St. 031-556-2414
Glasgow:
  Central Hotel, Gordon St. 041-221 9680
  North British Hotel, George Square. 041-332 6711
Inverness: Station Hotel, Academy St. (0463) 31926
Kyle of Lochalsh: Lochalsh Hotel, Ferry Rd. (0599) 4202
Perth: Station Hotel, Leonard St. (0738) 24141
St. Andrews: Old Course Hotel, Tel: St. Andrews 4371

A SELECTION OF
BRITISH RAIL ONE-WAY FARES
(As of January 1, 1981)

Deciding whether or not you should purchase a BritRail Pass becomes a matter of simple arithmetic. Plan your trip to Great Britain, decide what places you want to visit, and use the fares listed below to determine if the cost of the individual rail segments has exceeded the cost of a BritRail Pass. Round-trip fares are slightly less than double the one-way charge. Children 5–13 years of age, inclusive, pay half fare. All fares are subject to change without prior notice.

From London to:	One-Way Fares First Class (U.S.$)	Economy Class (U.S.$)	From London to:	One-Way Fares First Class (U.S.$)	Economy Class (U.S.$)
Aberdeen	128	86	Nottingham	37	25
Aviemore	125	84	Oxford	19	12
Ayr	95	66	Penzance	91	61
Bath Spa	34	23	Perth	109	75
Birmingham	35	24	Plymouth	67	45
Brighton	16	11	Portsmouth	22	15
Cambridge	18	12	Salisbury	25	17
Canterbury	17	12	Sheffield	48	32
Cardiff	48	32	Southampton	24	16
Chester	55	39	Stratford-upon-Avon	31	23
Coventry	30	20	Windsor	7	5
Dover	23	15	York	65	41
Dundee	109	75			
Edinburgh	103	71	**From Glasgow to:**		
Folkestone	21	14	Aberdeen	44	29
Glasgow	97	66	Birmingham	81	53
Gloucester	31	22	Dundee (Tay Bridge)	24	16
Hastings	19	12	Inverness	51	34
Inverness	128	87	Manchester	58	39
King's Lynn	28	19	Oxford	97	65
Leamington Spa	29	20	Perth	14	9
Lincoln	41	26	Sheffield	70	47
Manchester	59	41	Stirling	5	3
			York	61	41

Thomas Cook
Continental Timetable

Each issue of the Timetable generally contains:

- 800 tables of rail timings in the 24-hour clock over every British and European main-line railway.
- Detailed, individual tables for Europe's most important trains, including the high-speed Trans-Europe-Express network and the through routes from Britain to the Continent.
- Quick-reference index maps of the routes covered, with their respective table numbers.
- Shipping services linking Britain, Ireland, Continental Europe, and Scandinavia, and throughout the Mediterranean.
- Steamer services on the Rhine, the Danube, the Göta Canal, and the Swiss and Italian lakes.
- Motorail (auto) trains in Britain and on the European Continent, with loading times and accommodations.
- Plans of railway termini for London, Belfast, Dublin, Folkestone, Dover, Harwich, Liverpool, Newcastle-upon-Tyne, Ramsgate, Manchester, Weymouth, and 47 other European cities.
- Rail links between European cities and their international airports.
- Cross-Channel hovercraft services with connections to and from London and Paris.
- Monthly temperature figures and annual rainfall for many cities and resorts.
- List of principal resorts not served by rail, with nearest railhead and means of access.
- Foreign geographical names with corresponding English-language forms.
- Passport and visa regulations for all countries in Europe.

(continued on next page)

- Comparative international times in Europe, with dates of daylight saving time where adopted.
- World list of Thomas Cook/Wagons-Lits offices.
- Tables of European currencies with notes and coin values.
- Advance details of Continental Summer services in each monthly issue from February to May.
- Editorial page with last-minute alterations and additions and a summary of recent changes.

The Thomas Cook *Continental Timetable* is published in England on the first of each month. The Timetable is available in the U.S. and Canada through the FORSYTH TRAVEL LIBRARY, sales agent for the Timetable in North America.

Single copy price, including postage, $15.95

Special offer: Timetable and the New Thomas Cook Rail Map, including postage, $20.95. Rail Map separately $5.45 + 75¢ postage.

Prices are subject to change without notice.

ORDER FORM

Forsyth Travel Library
Box 2975, Dept. ER
Shawnee Mission, KS 66201

Please send a current issue of the Thomas Cook Continental Timetable. Enclosed is my payment of:
- ☐ $15.95 for the current Timetable
- ☐ $ 6.20 for the Rail Map
- ☐ $20.95 Special – Timetable and Rail Map
- ☐ $.89 protective plastic cover for Timetable

Departure date: _____

Name: _____

Address: _____

_____ Zip Code _____

Please enclose check or money order made payable to:
Forsyth Travel Library

Note: In a hurry? Order by phone: (913) 384-0496. No collect calls. Charge to Visa or Master Card ($1.00 service charge on all phone orders). No COD.

EURAILPASS

Eurailpass is a convenient card – paid for in advance – that entitles you to **unlimited 1st class rail travel** throughout 16 countries of Europe. Eurailpass gives you **unlimited mileage** to travel the length and breadth of Europe, to explore one, two or more countries, to stop and go where you want, when you want, in total freedom. Or, if you prefer, base yourself in a city of your choice and make an unlimited number of different excursions by train each day.

EURAIL YOUTHPASS

Eurail Youthpass is a convenient card – paid for in advance – especially conceived for people under 26 years of age. It entitles you to **unlimited 2nd class rail travel** throughout 16 countries of Europe. More than 100,000 miles of rail lines to choose from. You can see as much or as little of Europe as you want, but you see it from the European's point of view.

You may buy a Europabusrider in connection with your Eurailpass or Eurail Youthpass. The supplemental charges are given below.

15 days ...........U.S. $250* Europabus, add $20	2 months ........U.S. $530* Europabus, add $40		
21 days ...........U.S. $320* Europabus, add $25	3 months ........U.S. $650* Europabus, add $50		
1 month ..........U.S. $390* Europabus, add $30	Eurail Youthpass	1 mo $270	2 mo $350

*Children under 12, pay half price, under 4, they travel free.

In view of their special character, Eurailpass and Eurail Youthpass are not refundable in case of loss, theft or once use has begun. In any other case, they must be submitted to the issuing office within one year from the date of issuance and before the first date of their validity. Any refund is subject to a 15% cancellation charge.

Prices indicated are applicable as of January 1st, 1982, and are subject to change without notice.

ORDER BLANK
for EURAILPASS & EURAIL YOUTHPASS

Please rush a: (check one)

1st class Eurailpass valid: ☐ 15 days ☐ 21 days
☐ 1 month ☐ 2 months ☐ 3 months
☐ 1-month Youthpass ☐ 2-month Youthpass
☐ Europabus supplement added

Full Name _____
(as it appears on your passport)

Street
Address _____
(permanent residence)

City _____

State_____ Zip_____

Passport Number _____

Expected Departure Date _____

Date of Birth_____
(for Eurail Youthpass & children under 12)

Date_____ Signature_____

Please mail my Eurailpass to:

_____

_____

_____

Enclose certified check or money order payable to:
THE TRAVEL GUIDE COMPANY,
Box 20334, Columbus, Ohio 43220
OR

Charge: (check one) _____ Visa _____ Master Card

Card No. _____

Expiration Date_____
TELEPHONE ORDERS
Call before 2 P.M. Eastern Time & we'll mail pass same
day. Payment only by Visa or Master Card. Have card
handy when calling.

TELEPHONE ORDER NO: (614) 889-9100

MAPS OF GREAT BRITAIN

A good map can add greatly to your pretrip planning and your total trip enjoyment. Know where you are going and how to get there. We are happy to offer a fine selection of British Maps specially imported for use by travelers.

CITY MAPS – All are fully indexed complete, current and comprehensive. Showing streets, railroads, stations, attractions, lakes, parks, etc. Folded with protective cover.

____ Aberdeen	$3.95	____ Glasgow	$4.95
____ Bath	3.49	____ Leeds	4.95
____ Belfast	3.95	____ Leicester	4.95
____ Birmingham	4.95	____ Liverpool	4.95
____ Bournemouth	4.95	____ London	5.95
____ Brighton	4.95	____ Manchester	4.95
____ Bristol	4.95	____ Newcastle-upon-Tyne	4.95
____ Bromley	3.49	____ Nottingham	4.95
____ Cambridge	3.95	____ Oxford	3.49
____ Canterbury	3.49	____ Plymouth	3.49
____ Coventry	3.95	____ Portsmouth	4.95
____ Croydon	3.49	____ Southampton	4.95
____ Dublin	5.95	____ Stratford-upon-Avon	3.95
____ Ealing	3.49	____ Weymouth	3.49
____ Edinburgh	4.95	____ Wimbledon	3.49
____ Exeter	3.49	____ Windsor/Slough	3.49

GREAT BRITAIN ROAD MAPS – By Geographers A-Z Maps/U.K. Detailed road maps showing all major highways, roads, bridges, railways, cities, towns, canals, etc. In full color, with booklet index and mileage charts. Folded with protective cover.

____ South East & Central England (Scale: 1″=5 miles) $4.95
____ South West England & South Wales (Scale: 1″=5 miles) 4.95
____ Wales & Central England (Scale: 1″=5 miles) 4.95
____ Northern England (Scale: 1″=5 miles)....................................... 4.95
____ Scotland North & South (Scale: 1″=5 miles) 5.95
____ Great Britain Road Map (Scale: 1″=11½ miles)........................ 4.95
____ SPECIAL: All 6 maps & London (a $36.65 value) .... Only $32.95

TO ORDER:

1. Indicate quantity desired in front of each title.
2. Calculate postage charge: 20¢ per map – minimum $1.00/maximum $4.00.
3. Enclose check or money order payable to – FORSYTH TRAVEL LIBRARY
4. Send complete page with payment to:
   FORSYTH TRAVEL LIBRARY
   P.O Box 2975. Dept. BF
   9154 West 57th Street
   Shawnee Mission, Kansas 66201

U.S. PASSPORT OFFICES

Boston: John F. Kennedy Federal Building, Government Center, Boston MA 02203

Chicago: 230 South Dearborn Street, Chicago IL 60604

Honolulu: Federal Building, Room C-106, New Federal B Building, 300 Ala Moana Boulevard, Honolulu HI 96813

Los Angeles: Hawthorne Federal Building, Room 2W16, 15000 Aviation Boulevard, Lawndale CA 90261

New Orleans: Federal Office Building, Room 400, International Trade Mart, 2 Canal Street, New Orleans LA 70130

New York: 630 Fifth Avenue, New York NY 10020

San Francisco: Federal Building, Room 1405, 450 Golden Gate Avenue, San Francisco CA 94102

Seattle: Federal Building, Room 906, 915 Second Avenue, Seattle, WA 98174

Washington, D.C.: Department of State, 1425 K Street, NW Washington DC 20524

Note: U.S. visitors to Great Britain do not need a visa. A valid passport is required.

TIPS & TRIVIA

Do not be surprised to see a 15% value added tax (VAT) added to your bill for items purchased or services rendered. The VAT appears on just about everything, excluding bus/rail transportation.

Tipping: for luggage, generally tip 10 pence per bag. Taxis, 15% with a 10 pence minimum tip. Service staff in hotels: generally 10-12% if service charge not included in bill.

Imports: you can import into Britain 400 cigarettes; 1 liter of liquor and 2 liters of table wine; or 2 liters of sparkling wine and 2 liters of table wine; 2 ounces of perfume and 9 ounces of cologne; photographic film for your own use.

BritRail Pass

ORDER FORM 1981

BRITRAIL PASS gives you unlimited rail travel in England, Scotland and Wales for periods ranging from one week to one month. Child, ages 5-13 inclusive.

	First Class		Economy	
	Adult	Child 5-13 years	Adult	Child 5-13 years
7 days	☐ $147	☐ $ 74	☐ $107	☐ $ 54
14 days	☐ $219	☐ $110	☐ $162	☐ $ 81
21 days	☐ $272	☐ $136	☐ $205	☐ $103
1 month	☐ $317	☐ $159	☐ $243	☐ $122

YOUTH PASS (ages 14-25 inclusive)

7 days Economy	☐ $ 93	21 days Economy	☐ $183
14 days Economy	☐ $144	1 month Economy	☐ $215

SENIOR CITIZENS (age 65 and over)

7 days First Class	☐ $107	21 days First Class	☐ $205
14 days First Class	☐ $162	1 month First Class	☐ $243

BRITRAIL SEAPASS—a surcharge on your BritRail Pass provides one or two journeys on any ship or hovercraft service to France, Belgium, Holland and Ireland. One convenient ticket valid for six months allows the connecting rail trip between London and the port of embarkation to be made outside the validity of the BritRail Pass.

ONLY SOLD IN CONJUNCTION WITH A BRITRAIL PASS.

IRELAND		CONTINENTAL Belgium-France-Holland	
One journey	☐ $37	One journey	☐ $25
Two journeys	☐ $74	Two journeys	☐ $50

LONDON TRANSPORT Go-As-You-Please ticket available—unlimited travel on all red buses and Underground trains.

LONDON TRANSPORT	Adult	Child 5-15 years inclusive
3 days "Go As You Please"	☐ $27	☐ $11
4 days "Go As You Please"	☐ $31	☐ $14
7 days "Go As You Please"	☐ $43	☐ $18
14 days "Go As You Please"	☐ $75	☐ $31

HIGHLANDS AND ISLANDS TRAVELPASS—steamer, bus and rail services throughout Highlands and Islands of Scotland. Ten days ☐ $113.

OPEN TO VIEW—one-price entrance fee to more than 400 places of interest in Britain. One month ☐ $19.00 (Nonrefundable) (Child 5-15 years inclusive) ☐ $9.50

ORDER BLANK

Full Name_____
(as it appears on your passport)

Street
Address_____
(permanent residence)

City _____

State _____ Zip _____

Expected Departure Date _____

Date of Birth_____
(senior citizen & child)

Please mail my BritRail Pass to:

_____

_____

_____

Any refund subject to 10% cancellation fee.

Enclose certified check or money order payable to:
THE TRAVEL GUIDE COMPANY,
Box 20334, Columbus, Ohio 43220
OR

Charge: (check one) _____Visa _____Master Card

Card No. _____

Expiration Date _____

Telephone orders accepted with Master Card or Visa only. Call (614) 889-9100.
Sorry, no collect calls.
Prices indicated are applicable as of April 1, 1982, and are subject to change without notice.

OTHER RAIL PASSES

In addition to the Eurailpass and Eurail Youthpass, many European railroads issue their own. Here are a few with rates available at press time and subject to change.

Austria Ticket: Unlimited rail travel in Austria, including steamers on Lake Constance and Lake Wolfgang.

	1st Class	2nd Class
9 Days	$155.00	$110.00
16 Days	$210.00	$155.00

Benelux Tourrail: Belgium, Netherlands, Luxembourg. 15 days (8 days travel) March 1–Sept. 30. 1st class $94; coach $63. On sale only in Benelux countries.

Finnrailpass: Unlimited travel on all trains of the Finnish State Railways.

	1st Class	2nd Class
8 Days	$ 90.00	$ 60.00
15 Days	$132.00	$ 88.00
22 Days	$177.00	$118.00

France Vacances: Unlimited 1st or 2nd class travel on the French rail system.

	1st Class	2nd Class
7 Days	$170.00	$115.00
15 Days	$220.00	$150.00
1 Month	$345.00	$230.00

Germanrail Tourist Card: Unlimited travel in Germany, with bonus coupon for reduced round-trip ticket to Berlin included.

	1st Class	2nd Class
9 Days	$165.00	$120.00
16 Days	$220.00	$165.00

Interrail Card: Sold to persons under 26 years of age. Unlimited 2nd class rail travel for 1 month. Sold in the major train stations of all 16 Eurailpass countries, plus Great Britain, Hungary, Yugoslavia, and Morocco. While traveling in country issuing the pass, holders must purchase 2nd class tickets at 50% discount.

Approximate cost: $170.00.

Ireland: "Rambler Pass" (rail only), 8 days $62; 15 days $88; rail & bus, 8 days $76; 15 days $110.

Italian "Go Anywhere" Ticket: Unlimited rail travel in Italy.

	1st Class	2nd Class
8 Days	$114.00	$ 72.00
15 Days	$139.00	$ 87.00
21 Days	$166.00	$102.00
30 Days	$202.00	$127.00

Portuguese Rail Tourist Ticket: Personal tickets available year-round at all major railroad stations in Portugal. (For 2nd class travel only.)

5 Days	$ 35.00
10 Days	$ 55.00
15 Days	$ 75.00

Rover Ticket (Holland): Unlimited rail travel throughout Netherlands rail network (purchase in Holland).

1 Day	1st Class: 52.5 guilders ($24)*
	2nd Class: 35 guilders ($16)*
8 Days	1st Class: 108 guilders ($49)*
	2nd Class: 72 guilders ($33)*

Scandinavian Rail Pass: Unlimited rail travel in Denmark, Finland, Norway, and Sweden for 21 days. Not valid on Stockholm's local rail system.

1st Class	2nd Class
$268.00	$179.00

Swiss Holiday Card: Unlimited rail travel in Switzerland.

	1st Class	2nd Class
4 Days	$ 82.00	$ 60.00
8 Days	$113.00	$ 79.00
15 Days	$141.00	$104.00
1 Month	$197.00	$141.00

The above listing is partial and not inclusive of all offerings of special discount tickets and passes. Due to the fluctuation of the dollar, some prices are approximate. Prices shown as of January 1, 1981, and subject to change without notice. For detailed information, write or call **THE TRAVEL GUIDE COMPANY**, Box 20334, Columbus, Ohio 43220. (614) 889-9100.

*At 1980 exchange rate.

METRIC CONVERSIONS

Approximate Conversions TO Metric

LENGTH

When You Know	Multiply By	To Find
inches	2.5	centimeters
feet	30.0	centimeters
yards	0.9	meters
miles	1.6	kilometers

VOLUME

When You Know	Multiply By	To Find
teaspoons	5.0	milliliters
tablespoons	15.0	milliliters
fluid ounces	30.0	milliliters
cups	0.24	liters
pints	0.47	liters
quarts	0.95	liters
gallons	3.8	liters

Approximate Conversions FROM Metric

LENGTH

When You Know	Multiply By	To Find
millimeters	0.04	inches
centimeters	0.4	inches
meters	3.3	feet
meters	1.1	yards
kilometers	0.6	miles

VOLUME

When You Know	Multiply By	To Find
milliliters	0.03	fluid ounces
liters	2.1	pints
liters	1.06	quarts
liters	0.26	gallons

TEMPERATURE
(exact)

Celsius: x 9 ÷ 5 + 32 = Fahrenheit
Example: 37°C x 9 = 333 ÷ 5 + 32 = 98.6°F

70°F is 21°C
Boiling point: 212°F or 100°C

Fahrenheit: -32 x 5 ÷ 9 = Celsius
Example: 98.6°F - 32 = 66.6 x 5 ÷ 9 = 37°C

In Brief: 1 liter is nearly 2 pints
1 kilo is about 2 lbs
10 grams is about 1/3 oz
1 meter is about 39 inches

GEOGRAPHIC INDEX

All places which have a main entry appear in heavy type.

BRITAIN BY BRITRAIL'S READER REPORT

The author and publisher would appreciate your candid criticisms and comments regarding this edition of *Britain By BritRail*. Please address your response to *Britain By BritRail*, c/o George W. Ferguson, Box 20334, Columbus OH 43220.

We would like to know if *Britain By BritRail* was helpful to you and what particular features you liked best. We also would like to know if you have any suggestions for improving the book.

We are interested in you—your age, your education, your occupation, your previous travels and travel plans for the future. How did you get to Britain? Did you use a BritRail Pass? A SeaPass? What other travel books did you use during your trip? What travel books and references did you use when you planned your trip? Did you use the services of a travel agency?

Did you have a good trip? Would you go again?

Let us hear from you!